The big jones Cookbook

The
big jones
Cookbook

Recipes for Savoring
the Heritage of Regional
Southern Cooking

Paul Fehribach

THE UNIVERSITY OF CHICAGO PRESS
CHICAGO AND LONDON

Paul Fehribach is the co-owner and executive chef
of Big Jones, a nationally acclaimed restaurant in Chicago's
Andersonville neighborhood.

The University of Chicago Press, Chicago 60637
The University of Chicago Press, Ltd., London
© 2015 by The University of Chicago
All rights reserved. Published 2015.
Printed in the United States of America

24 23 22 21 20 19 18 17 16 15   1 2 3 4 5

ISBN-13: 978-0-226-20572-4 (cloth)
ISBN-13: 978-0-226-20586-1 (e-book)
DOI: 10.7208/chicago/9780226205861.001.0001

Library of Congress Cataloging-in-Publication Data
Fehribach, Paul, author.
The Big Jones cookbook: recipes for savoring the heritage of
regional Southern cooking / Paul Fehribach.
     pages; cm
Summary: A cookbook of Southern cuisine as featured at Big
Jones Restaurant in Chicago, Illinois.
Includes bibliographical references and index.
ISBN 978-0-226-20572-4 (cloth: alk. paper)—ISBN 0-226-20572-X
(cloth: alk. paper)—ISBN 978-0-226-20586-1 (e-book) 1. Cooking,
American—Southern style. 2. Big Jones (Restaurant: Chicago, Ill.)
I. Title.
TX715.2.S68F44 2015
641.5975—dc23   2014040936

♾ This paper meets the requirements of ANSI/NISO Z39.48-1992
(Permanence of Paper).

Contents

Preface

I was the kid in school who read far more books than most would think wise for a young boy who had a wish to bond with his peers over such pursuits as sports, cars, or, as the years rolled on, girls. Like many households back then, ours had the complete set of *Encyclopaedia Britannica*, and I read those volumes with great relish, particularly the many details of the American story—from the earliest failed settlements to the Revolutionary War, the Indian Wars, the World Wars, and the Space Race that was still under way as I was coming of age. I'd read the assigned history textbook by the end of the second week of class, then spend my ample spare time diving deeper into history, most often in those encyclopedia entries. It was the beginning of a lifelong journey, and I've never outgrown that very basic curiosity. Many years later, it would come to define my cooking and become the creative engine of my first restaurant.

It's hard to pinpoint a moment in my life when I realized I wanted to be a chef, which to me means not only commanding a kitchen but feeding people, because it was something I wanted to do from a very young age. From the first day I could see over the counter, I wanted to be right at the heart of the kitchen, trying to figure it out, trying to learn what makes us tick: where we come from, why we do what we do, and especially how all of the delicious foods I loved came to the table.

My earliest memory of field-to-table cooking was on my family's farmstead east of Jasper, Indiana, along one of the branches of the old Buffalo Trace. My grandparents had a generations-old blackberry patch out along the edge of the tomato field. When I was four or five years old, several branches of the family gathered at the old farm, as we often did back then, and we kids were led to the blackberry patch by a few of our aunts. We spent the next couple of hours on a sunny July morning dodging barbs while picking ripe berries and occasionally getting a few into the gallon-size buckets we were charged with filling, rather than into our gluttonous mouths. By the time we had filled our buckets, our faces were covered in mottled swatches of purple.

We did eventually get some blackberries back to the house, and in what seemed like an instant the most rapturous pies emerged from the oven— thick, sweet purplish lava bubbling up between the most perfectly golden crusts, the scent of the blackberry patch wafting through the kitchen as steam fluttered through the top vents of the crusts. Talk about heaven. I didn't realize it then, but that singular experience would later compel me to return to my roots in my cooking, always thinking of and emulating the farm that raised five generations of my family.

My dad's mom died before I was old enough to remember her, but my many aunts helped maintain the farm kitchen, and I remember a few things about it, most notably the pantry, which was the size of many folks' bedrooms. From a two-acre kitchen garden, my grandmother raised a family of thirteen, putting up her harvest every year in meticulously organized rows of jars containing everything from blackberry jelly and raspberry jam to pickled beets and all manner of pickled and sweet relishes. I didn't think anything of it at the time, but in retrospect I was witnessing a dying way of eating, one that I'd eventually set out to revitalize for our world's changing demographics and economic realities.

Since I grew up in a family that cooked at home, I've come to advocate home cooking every chance I get, and my hope is that this book will inspire readers to cook at home more often, and perhaps more ambitiously. Realistically, however, for many of us the idea of cooking at home most days of the week is a fantasy, with so many households depending on two incomes, having kids in school, along with the many other pressures of everyday life. The reality for many people is that cooking has become a recreational pastime for weekends or leisure time. Many adventurous eaters make a Saturday out of a trip to the farmers' market and then putting their market ingredients to use with inspiration from cookbooks, food television shows, or family heirloom recipes. Time well spent in my opinion. Still, eating many meals out is here to stay.

Even though home cooking is a tradition that is rooted in our collective agrarian history, the everyday home-cooked meal is a thing of the past for most people. That does not, however, mean we can't enjoy that same spirit of cooking when we dine out. As restaurants become the family table of our culture, we chefs and our staffs have begun to play the roles of moms and grandmas and dads and the eager sons and daughters pitching in, and our network of farms is our homestead. What I've sought to do is create a cuisine that is rooted in the ethics of my grandparents' farm, where no food was ever served that they themselves or someone they personally knew did not raise, grow, shoot, or forage. It's a simple concept but challenging nonetheless, as our menus must change as frequently as the weather—but this is how it is when you eat close to the land, as we all did in generations past and as we all can do again. We don't have to surrender to mass-produced foods of dubious origins. We can create a new family table. This has always been my dream: to offer people food as pure and unadulterated as that which raised generations of my family on that farm with the blackberry patch.

A Growing Obsession

In retrospect, it seems like a question I should have been prepared to answer, but when we opened Big Jones, I wasn't ready for it. The question every food writer, journalist, and many of our customers asked was, "Why did you decide to do Southern food?" It took me aback at first, because to me the answer was obvious—why not cook Southern food? In fact, I hadn't thought much about it, other than questioning whether I could make a go of such a restaurant in Chicago. But of course people wanted to know why. *What was my inspiration, what makes Big Jones tick?*

At times, this question exasperated me, but a chef can't let that show. A chef has to be all smiles. The question gnawed at me, though. When I'd cooked French, Mexican street food, and Southeast Asian, it had never been asked, perhaps because people thought it was obvious why I wanted to make pad thai or crème brûlée over and over. I wondered if chefs with non-Italian surnames got asked why they wanted to cook Italian food. It was as if a non-Southern chef who loves Southern cooking was a curiosity, especially in a northern city. In Chicago, circa 2008, there was little regional Southern cooking, although there were a few good spots for soul food and a couple for Cajun/Creole. Fundamentally, this was a sign that Southern cooking had not yet achieved its deserved reputation as one of the world's great regional cuisines, but that is changing.

One of the reasons I decided to cook Southern was because it seemed no one else had done it, or at least not like I thought about it. During my years working in the front of house at both Hi Ricky Asia Noodle Shop and Schubas Tavern, I spent a lot of my time reading and plotting my eventual breakout with the restaurant I would call mine. Since a fateful post-college trip, I'd held a special affinity for the cooking of New Orleans, and my imagination had been captured from afar by Paul Prudhomme's and then Emeril Lagasse's success. During my time at Schubas Tavern, I dived a little deeper into Southern cooking to broaden our offerings there. While the format of that particular institution—still my favorite live music club anywhere—did not permit me to do too much with what I was learning about some other parts of the South, I did discover the Lowcountry through the writings of Vertamae Grosvenor and John Taylor, and I was struck by a lightning bolt. By the time I was positioned to make my move, I knew I wanted to explore Southern cooking.

Just because I was falling in love with Southern cooking didn't mean my more rational side couldn't have decided to do something else. But I stuck with Southern food because once I fell for it, I delved deeper and deeper into its many regional variations, traditions, and the rich tapestry that is its history and the foundation of its future. From New Orleans to Charleston and then into the Appalachian mountains and the Carolina Piedmont, the Delta Region and Deep South, I couldn't believe what I was discovering. During my culinary upbringing, I was taught to revere the French, idolize the Chinese, and give great respect to Italian, Continental, and eventually Mexican cooking. Yet here was our own homegrown cuisine, emerging in my mind as on par with all, yet completely unappreciated and underserved, at least in Chicago.

Eventually, when I read John Egerton's seminal *Southern Food: At Home, on the Road, in History*, I realized that Kentucky, right by my home country, was regarded as having one of the greatest cooking traditions in all the South. True, I grew up across the Mason-Dixon Line, but if you travel south or east from my part of Indiana, you'll see that the Kentucky countryside looks very much the same and the cooking is even more similar—fried chicken and abundant vegetable dishes at virtually every celebration, an obsession with cakes and pies bordering on the insane, cured and smoked pork products permeating seemingly every aspect of cooking, pantries full of pickles and relishes, and a healthy appetite for wild-caught fish and hunted game from deer to rabbit to squirrel and even possum. Our part of the country is even called Kentuckiana. So, while I may not be from the

South per se, I began to realize why I felt such a magnetic attraction to Southern cooking. At least as far as Appalachian cooking goes, it shares many currents with the food on which I was raised.

Before we opened Big Jones, there was much consideration given to the structure of the menus and how the offerings would help define our brand. The pragmatic part of me wanted to offer up the cooking of south Louisiana, the distinctive cuisines of the urban and diverse Creoles and rural, Caucasian Cajuns, because this style has been successful in restaurants all across the country. I loved the cuisines and could easily see myself cooking and eating from them every day. But the Lowcountry, Delta, and my own Kentuckiana home called me, as did the mountains of Appalachia and even the bygone swamps of Florida, my maternal grandmother's birthplace and lifelong home. There were too many stories to tell, and I wanted to tell as many of them as I could. Though it would take time for our cooking to evolve fully, our diverse Southern regional focus was born.

From grade school through high school, geography and history were my two favorite subjects—they captured my imagination in a way that other subjects did not. I reveled in the stories of different places and times not just from around the country but from all over the world. The South has such an incredibly diverse geography—from the Tidewater to the swamps and Sea Islands of the Lowcountry and Florida; the rolling hills of the Deep South to the Caribbean-esque Gulf Coast with its wildlife, world-class fishing, and those storied swamps and bayous of south Louisiana; the mind-bending flatness of the Delta; all of the nuances from the interior states of Tennessee, Kentucky, and Arkansas; and then the Appalachian Mountains, one of the most biologically diverse and majestically beautiful tracts of land on Earth.

And there is the history. Besides the dramatic geographic and economic differences one can encounter across the South, each region has a unique set of ethnic and racial influences that continue to evolve. These are the ideas that cause my mind to churn. Having been born an outsider, I can say that while I love the South's cooking for all of these reasons, I don't hold any particular regional affinity and have found much to be celebrated in every part of the South.

Anthelme Brillat-Savarin once wrote: "Tell me what you eat, and I will tell you what you are." This is the promise of Southern cooking, and through it we can go to times and places throughout the South, past and present, and experience them through the dishes they have left us; we can connect with this history and geography through the achingly powerful senses of smell and taste, the experience of consuming food.

So the question is answered: the South has one of the world's richest and most distinctive regional cuisines, and I'm here to tell you its story. Not the whole story certainly—that would require many more restaurants and many volumes beyond this one. I am here to take you to the South, to times and places we can travel together and experience through the most distinctive dishes created by southerners—whether they were slaves, housekeepers, small farmers in the mountains, fishermen from coastal communities, chefs in prestigious French Quarter restaurants, or slaves in antebellum plantation kitchens.

Miss Lewis and the Book That Changed Everything

Shortly after we opened, a young African American couple enjoying a late dinner thanked me for the experience and asked if I'd read any Edna Lewis. I hadn't, but on their fervent recommendation I looked her up. Our menus at Big Jones changed almost immediately, and my own cooking has changed forever.

Published in 1976, Edna Lewis's *The Taste of Country Cooking* tells the story of the traditional foodways with which she grew up in the early twentieth century in Freetown, Virginia—and, boy, did they eat well. What really struck me about the book was how the cooking of this African American family and community of very modest means transcended race. It very easily could have been my own family's cooking at that time. More important, the dishes translate beautifully today. The book was laid out in seasonal menus long before big city chefs held any pretension of seasonal cooking.

The *Taste of Country Cooking* started me on a search for more and even older culinary writing. In this day and age of modernist envelope-pushing and painfully long and micro-portioned tasting menus, Ms. Lewis's cooking is refreshing in that it's not trying to push any envelopes; it's not trying to win any awards or wow any media folks or trendinistas; it just is—confident in its simplicity.

I also found a deliciously subversive aspect to *The Taste of Country Cooking* that was borne out in many more cookbooks as my collection grew. Big agribusiness and the food-processing industry would have us believe that their modern hybrid and GMO crops and cheap processed foods are the only way to feed the world. Yet here was proof that a family of poor African Americans—because of their ingenuity, work ethic, and spirit—could eat better than most upper-middle-class Americans do today. Sure, it was a lot of work, but in many families throughout history, the joy of a beautiful meal has always been worth the work of getting food to the table. I argue all the time that the labors of eating well are a far more worthy use of time than most of what we do these days, whether it's watching reality TV or getting caught up in the latest Internet gossip about a celebrity scandal. Perhaps *The Taste of Country Cooking*'s most compelling quality is that each story and recipe are brimming with the dedication and love that should be part of every family's basic nutrition yet so rarely is. It inspired me to further commit to seeing that kind of devotion to the pure, true flavors that only homegrown food can produce.

My studies in old Southern cookbooks haven't found another book as influential as *The Taste of Country Cooking*, but I did learn that folks rich and poor, black, white, mixed, or other who had land and were willing to do the work themselves (or have the help do the work for them) ate mighty well. The lack of reliable refrigeration and canning technology made eating by the seasons a necessity, so diets were varied and therefore far more interesting. These old cookbooks are fascinating for their many receipts. *The Kentucky Housewife* (1839), for instance, boasts 1,300 receipts, and *Common Sense in the Household* (1879), 1,000, to name just two. Receipts were the historic predecessors of recipes—basic explanations of process and ingredients that rarely included precise measurements and ingredient lists. Thus, they required a great deal of experience and training to utilize for good results. A *receipt* was simply a paragraph of text explaining a procedure and mentioning ingredients along the way, while a *recipe* has an ingredients list with precise measurements and a separate narrative of instructions. What we know today as recipes were an innovation of the late nineteenth century, so the word *receipt* often comes up in discussions of historic cooking.

Cooking Our History and Making It New

As a big-city chef, I have always felt pressure to create new things, push boundaries, and lead the pack with the most novel, interesting dishes. Modernism is a major force in dining, and while it is undisputable fact that food is cultural and thus always evolving, the ingredients and techniques the modernist kitchen has given us—gellan gums, agar, and the whole host of hydrocolloids, transglutaminase aka "meat glue," sous-vide, and the like will probably someday become as commonplace as baking powder, which was a very new ingredient barely more than a hundred years ago. So, in many ways I have embraced modernism, but ultimately it's something best left to other chefs who want to geek out over trend-setting ingredients and cutting-edge kitchen equipment. I'm much more likely to geek out over the history of a particular dish or the story behind this heirloom oat or that heritage breed hog. So even as I am a chef in Chicago, one of the leading cities worldwide for avant-garde cuisine, I've chosen a path less traveled and, as the famous poem by Robert Frost goes, "that has made all the difference."

Much has been said over the last generation about the value of comfort food and how much people miss those cozy, simple dishes they knew from home. Trend-spotters in industry publications have repeatedly prognosticated that comfort food will be huge, the next *big thing*. The problem is that comfort food has tended to exist in restaurants in two ways. First, the processed, prefabricated, and microwaveable garbage that is hawked in chain restaurants and bad bar-and-grills and diners these days; and second, in fine-dining restaurants that typically seek to "elevate" this country cooking into something that hardly resembles the food that inspired them in the first place. I'm not faulting the chefs who want to elevate this dish or that—it's a natural instinct for us creative people, and many chefs create wonderful and compelling menus this way—but again my path is different. Comfort food isn't even a term I like, preferring to call those dishes country cooking since they are all rooted in America's agrarian past—and frankly for any dish associated with these deep-rooted traditions, integrity of both ingredients and basic cooking techniques is paramount. America's metaphorical grandma didn't take shortcuts much less pop in microwaveable dishes, so the infiltration of this cooking by processed foods is a major departure from its very spirit.

One passing conversation with my dad led me to focus even more on old cookbooks and to develop what has become our trademark historic cooking at Big Jones. When I have the chance to get home and visit the family in the woods outside Jasper, Indiana, I always grill my dad with questions about their ways of eating and drinking on the farm where our family first settled in 1836 five generations ago. We are a German Catholic farming family that was traditionally oriented. Grandma Rose and Grandpa Albert had eleven kids, bringing the household to thirteen hungry bellies. My dad told me that they almost never took more than a single, standard kitchen-size trash can a week to the dump, which astounded me. A household of thirteen! I decided right then and there to become as efficient in my own cooking as they had been, and as Edna Lewis's family had been, too. I thought the best way to learn to minimize waste was to mine old cookbooks for receipts and wisdom, and they've become the primary outside influences on my cooking.

Many of our dishes and special-event menus have a date listed next to them. This is always a reference to the inspiration of the dish or menu, always a time and place in the South with a story I want to tell. I add the dates either because I found an interesting receipt in a cookbook or was able to parse together a dish or menu by reading any manner of literature from that time. It's a way to engage guests in a conversation about how traditional Southern foods have always evolved and will continue to do so. As a bit of a history buff, I enjoy presenting many dishes not as we know them today, but as they originated, as in my Reezy-Peezy, ca. 1780, a slave-kitchen staple that is the ancestral dish of the more familiar hoppin' john, which is often made with black-eyed peas. The reezy-peezy of 1780, however, was often made with Carolina Gold rice middlins, the "shorts" or broken grains from the milling process that are separated and cooked as grits, and Sea Island red peas—the very crops we use to make the dish, giving us all a special opportunity to connect with the past.

Much of our cooking at Big Jones is, in fact, very modern. When we do a dish with modern techniques and ingredients, I always take the opportunity to remind my cooks and my staff that history leads us to the present day, and the present will be history in the future. So, while our historically focused cooking draws attention for its nineteenth-century fried steak receipts and 1930s-era étouffées, you will also find us paying homage to the changing foodways of the South with much more contemporary expressions such as the "Banh mi Po' Boy," which relates to the cuisine of the Vietnamese immigrants who have sent delicious shockwaves through south Louisiana's cooking, becoming part of the fabric that will be tomorrow's history. We also nod to the Mexicans who are leaving their own mountain communities for Appalachia, and finding that hominy and pigs and goats feed us so deliciously here as well, and into which their traditional cooking blends seamlessly.

Like our menus at Big Jones, this book is dedicated to all of the people who have done the work, cultivated the fields, foraged the forests, fished the seas and salt marshes, tilled the fields, threshed the grains, slaughtered the animals, built and tended the fires, and lived and breathed the craft that is Southern food. I am able to do what I do only because of you, and it is my dream that as our present becomes history, I have done a little something to enrich us all.

Lessons in Regional Southern Cooking

When we first opened, we called our cuisine "Contemporary Coastal Southern," even as our cooking was far more regional. Part of it was a marketing decision, hoping to evoke a link to New Orleans and Charleston, and it partly reflected a desire to create a restaurant you could theoretically drop on King Street in Charleston or Magazine Street in New Orleans that the locals would enjoy. While we emphasized local and artisan ingredients in addition to a Southern pedigree, we combined them in new and novel ways, as any modern Southern restaurant would, often deconstructing dishes and applying modernist techniques, with no real emphasis on "traditional" Southern—which I always viewed as a very malleable concept, since one person's tradition is another's heresy.

But Big Jones *isn't* located on King or Magazine Street. It's in Chicago, home to expatriated (and often homesick) southerners looking for a connection to their home, and non-southerners, most of whom have had only passing experiences with Southern food, maybe through extended family, but more likely via a vacation or business travel to New Orleans, Atlanta, or other points south. We industry folks have always known that typical tourists most often get served mass-produced facsimiles of traditional dishes; and while savvy food tourists know where to get the good stuff, there's often a disconnect between what many Yankees think of as Southern food and what it really is, which is a regionally diverse, richly varied cuisine. It's not that they don't have a good idea what great Southern food is; it's often simply a lack of exposure to its many variations. Sadly, in many cases, it's a Foodservice, Inc., facsimile of Southern food in a tourist trap.

The problem is that since we're not in the South, many folks, mostly non-southerners, take their limited knowledge of Southern cooking and apply rigid constraints to their expectations of what we should be serving. Two particular examples come to mind, and in both instances I can demonstrate why, even in the case of such a historic and traditionally based cuisine as Southern, dogma has no place.

I often think of my maternal grandmother Melba Morelos's way of frying vegetables—in lard, of course, but she always used a wheat flour dredge. She's as Southern as it gets, born and raised in Fort Myers, Florida, back when it was still a little fishing village, with family history in Stone Mountain, Georgia, and later moving on to Texas and then east Tennessee. Of course, many folks would tell you that to fry vegetables in wheat flour is a mortal sin—you must fry vegetables in cornmeal. But I still dream of her fried cauliflower, which is one of the dishes that most makes me ache for her kitchen. I once asked my grandma why she used wheat flour to fry her vegetables. Her answer? "I like it better." I'd say a southerner cooking vegetables in the South is making Southern food, and just as there's more than one way to skin a squirrel, there's more than one way to fry a vegetable.

Gumbo is another great example. Our staple gumbo, Gumbo Ya-Ya, is made with a very dark, smoky, almost charred roux, like you will almost never find in New Orleans, but will experience at locations west (mostly) and south of town, in Cajun country. Now, someone can have an excellent Creole seafood gumbo at Galatoire's or Commander's Palace, and a great chicken and andouille gumbo at any number of places downtown or in the French Quarter, and come by Big Jones looking for a "New Orleans fix." Unfortunately, gumbo like we make it is hardly to be found in New Orleans restaurants. Sometimes the gumbo is returned to the kitchen with the guest's admonition that it "tastes burnt." We've learned to take that occurrence in stride, comp the gumbo, and buy them a drink—but we're not about to change our gumbo. Our gumbo has legions of die-hard fans, and for those who don't take a liking to it right away, it's our hope that at least we've given them a little bit of exposure to something Southern they haven't experienced before. When guests are willing to engage in conversation about the topic, many are astounded to learn that many Cajuns, particularly south of I-10, don't use roux in their gumbo at all! At the end of the day, we know every dish can't please every person. There's plenty of food on the menu, and our salutations to New Orleans abound.

Southerners, on the other hand, typically take right to most of our cooking because they grew up with all the regional variety, even the door-to-door variations of things like pimiento cheese recipes in the Piedmont or gumbo in Cajun country, where everyone has their own take—just like chili in Texas or barbecue anywhere there's a fire. That said, they often find themselves at Big Jones because they miss some things they grew up with—crowder peas, vinegary greens, fried okra, good biscuits, cornbread without a peck of sugar in it, you name it. We've always felt an obligation to do what we can to make them feel at home. My interest in Southern food reached a boiling point because it reminded me of home and appealed to my natural curiosities in history and geography. It's made a comfortable home for me, one I enjoy sharing with southerners and non-southerners alike.

About This Book

Since the day we opened, guests have frequently requested recipes for everything from cornbread to gumbo to green goddess dressing and everything in between. It's always been our policy to give anyone a recipe from Big Jones's files if they just took the time to write and ask for it specifically, with a couple of notable exceptions—our fried chicken and cornbread recipes have been top secret until the publishing of this book. All the while, as our cooking became more focused and our reputation grew, the call for recipes came ever more frequently, and so it seemed time to make a recipe book available for sale. Most of these recipes, after all, were already written, leaving me only the need to scale them for home cooks and have them tested for use in your kitchen, a very different environment from our professional kitchen at the restaurant.

The Big Jones Cookbook started as an idea to put together three dozen or so of our most-requested recipes into a small, staple-bound leaflet to easily get the requested recipes into the hands of anyone who wanted them. As I started compiling recipes, it quickly became apparent that thirty-odd popular recipes left a fairly lopsided view of our cooking. I decided that the book, when fully compiled, would need to represent our kitchen as the microcosm that it is: a self-contained modern homestead kitchen, utilizing whole hogs and putting up the full seasonal rotation of pickles and preserves as creatively as we can while maintaining proper respect and deference to practices and flavor combinations that are time-tested, yet always with an eye to improvisation. It became clear that this would be a book of far greater scope, and as reality set in I had to accept that we wouldn't be able to do a fully representative volume, at least not yet, because over the course of a year we use well over four hundred recipes just for our regular menus, specials aside.

Selecting barely more than one hundred recipes for the book, in order to keep the scope of it manageable and create an affordable finished product, proved quite a challenge in itself. I wanted to fully represent our cooking style, which meant that all seasons of produce and a full rotation of bakery recipes should be available, and even glimpses of charcuterie production and the art of pickles and preserves would need to be included. Consequently, many of these recipes are not generally available at the restaurant all the time, but only in season or on special menus. Ramps, for instance, are only in season for a few weeks; pawpaws, maybe two weeks. But these are special ingredients we appreciate, and I wanted to share with you some ways to use them, if you can find them at your local market. Other recipes utilize widely available pantry ingredients and are staples at Big Jones, and I wanted to make it possible for you to reproduce our cooking in your home.

As a longtime home-cooking enthusiast myself, putting these recipes into print means much more than giving you ingredients lists and basic instructions. I've been fortunate to have ample time over the years to cook at home, and I also bring thirty years of professional cooking experience to the table. In my spare time, I often volunteer to present cooking demonstrations to regular folks at farmers' markets, festivals, or wherever I have the chance to inspire people to cook at home. My desire is not only to motivate you to put your pans to the fire, but also share as much of my knowledge as I can to enable you to cook restaurant-quality food in your home kitchen. It would be pointless to present these recipes without offering the information you need to cook them as well yourself as we do at Big Jones, so I hope that's what we've done with this book.

A lot of thought was given to how to organize the book, and it presented a unique challenge because our cooking is regionally diffuse. Cookbooks have often been organized into your basic courses of appetizers, entrées, sides, desserts, et cetera, or even by seasonal menus. But the regional nature of our cooking presented a special opportunity to do what I love doing—telling stories about the South and its unique and delicious foodways. Each region is different and has its own stories to tell. Since our ambition is to tell the South's story through food, why not organize the book by region? The notable exceptions of breads, the bar, the pantry, and the whole hog, or charcuterie, are given their own sections since these are arts in and of themselves, and they are often much more universal and hard to pin to a specific part of the South. Our whole hog program—which we call *boucherie* after the Cajun word for butchering—while modeled very much after the Cajun tradition, is offered in the back of the book since these recipes are highly ambitious for home cooks. Nonetheless, I felt compelled to offer them because they are sometimes requested by guests as well as colleagues, and it would be impossible to fully represent our cooking without including the most common recipes of our boucherie program.

Whatever your level of ambition—even if all you ever wanted to do was to be able to make our cornbread or beignets at home—my goal in this book is to give you the knowledge necessary to cook as well in your kitchen as we do in ours. I haven't held back any secrets here. My quest is to advance both home cooking and Southern cuisine, and my hope is that this book is useful to those ends and that you enjoy making the recipes I have offered. All else aside, the way we cook at Big Jones is laid bare here, so hopefully this book is illuminating in that respect alone.

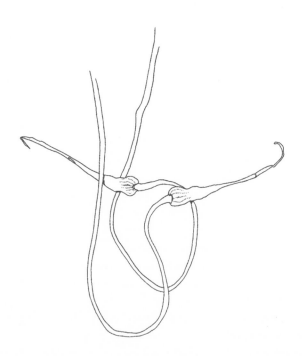

Acknowledgments

I would like to thank these folks for making this book possible:

Mark Armantrout, my partner and best friend, for his love, support, unwavering work ethic, dedication to sustainable agriculture and animal welfare, and putting up with a chef's work schedule.

Mom and Dad, Joseph and Sandra Fehribach, and my many brothers and sisters—Dean, Brett, Pam, Gavin, and Lori—for being the most supportive, loving family anyone could hope for. Every day in my cooking, I hope I can show my guests a taste of the many joys we have shared as a family.

We are all blessed here in Chicago with a wonderful network of farms and suppliers that make a difference not only in their stewardship of the land and water, but by inspiring us with their produce. Thanks to Kilgus Farmstead, Spence Farm and Stewards of the Land, Genesis Growers, Three Sisters Garden, Little Farm on the Prairie, Moore Family Farm, Green Acres, Seedling, Oriana's Oriental Orchard, Gunthorp Farm, the Slagels, LaPryor, Catalpa Grove, Mint Creek, Nick Nichols, Growing Power, Ellis Farm, Mick Klug, and, more broadly, the Green City Market.

In many ways, this could be considered "The Little Anson Mills Cookbook": thank you, Glenn Roberts, for your leadership, and Catherine Schopfer, for the best service I have ever had from a supplier, bar none. Your milled goods continue to awe me every day.

The contributions of African Americans to American cuisine, and Southern cuisine specifically, cannot be overstated and are seldom recognized. Unfortunately, history does not remember many of their names, but we can be thankful for what they have left for us all to enjoy. Thanks also to the authors who have brought so much light to my heart through their books and stories of the African Americans we do remember: Edna Lewis, Jessica B. Harris, Abby Fischer, Judith Carney, Mary Moore Bremer, Dori Sanders, Vertamae Grosvenor, Sally Ann Robinson, and many more yet to come.

I've been lucky to work with some of the best minds in public relations over the years: special thanks to Ellen Malloy of Morsel for her friendship and guidance, and Jamie Estes of Estes Public Relations.

Thank you to a few authors—John Egerton, Edna Lewis, Eugene Walter, and Matt Lee and Ted Lee—without whom I might still be a Southern cooking neophyte, without the deep understanding their words have gifted me.

Thanks also to the Southern Foodways Alliance and Director John T. Edge, for giving true meaning to our work as cooks, by finding and documenting the stories that reflect us as we are, and by setting a table where we can all celebrate our history and consider our future together as one people.

Many chefs, sous chefs, and cooks have made meaningful contributions that made this book possible, notably Corey Fuller, Andrew Swanson, Phyllis Thomas, Joshua Hutton, Carrie Bradley, Reynaldo Reyna, Velman Miranda, and Oscar Ortiz. Thanks also to Andrew Shay, brilliant illustrator of this book and able mixologist, and dining-room captain since we opened our doors.

Most of all, thanks to you, my reader, and our guests at Big Jones, for supporting our work and giving me the chance to live this dream that is still evolving, but which I hope will make a difference in the lives of everyone it touches—I hope that Big Jones enriches your life in some small way and that this cookbook is practical and inspirational.

Breads

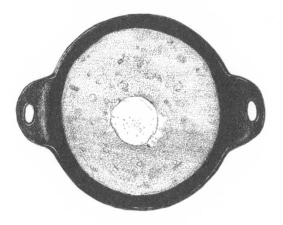

They say that smell is the sense with the most enduring memories, which is surely why I am so obsessed with home-baked breads.

My mom used to make a simple home-style white bread for Thanksgiving for which I have yearned every day of my life. While I remember the taste so vividly, that sense is inextricably linked to the aroma, and home-baked bread is one of the most indelible smells we encounter in our lives. After all my years of experience in baking, I still can't make a bread that nourishes me in the same way as that simple pan bread my mom used to make, because those sensory memories are intertwined with childhood, family, and the goodwill and innocence of the holidays.

I'm not sure exactly where I got the notion that bread tastes better in the house in which it was baked, but I have always felt strongly that Big Jones should produce every type of bread we can. That compulsion is based more upon the preservation of the aroma, texture, and taste of freshly baked breads than it is a philosophical question, but it's an interesting question nonetheless—if you could instantly transport freshly baked bread, *Star Trek*–style, anywhere else on the planet, would it still taste the same, even minutes out of the oven? Fundamentally it would, but great bread does lose something when transported—when you bake bread at home and serve it for a meal, the smell from the baking process lingers; and even as it fades to imperceptible levels, it adds a layer to the experience, echoing the aromas that waft about your palate as you chew, and breathe, and swallow, and breathe.

As a cook, the happiest moments in my life come when I arrive at the restaurant from a break or a trip, and I walk into a bustling dining room, filled with the aroma of freshly baked cornbread. It gets me every time, fills me with pride, and as the aroma takes over my consciousness, if only for a moment, lets me know I'm home.

One of my essential eccentricities that every Big Jones employee, front of house or back of house, learns during their first hours on the job is that cornbread goes straight from the oven to the table, period. How we do it involves a little choreography, but when that bread is put in front of you, I want you to know by the smell and taste that we baked it just for you. The cornbread we serve isn't your share of cornbread that we baked for hundreds of people—we baked yours just for you. When the stars align and service goes just right, there is always the smell of freshly baked cornbread in the air. Yes, the cornbread recipe I'm sharing with you is special, and we hear every day from guests that it's the best cornbread they've ever had, but I think just as often that perception is because we actually bake it to order. It's tricky, but worth it.

I've considered many ideas for other breads at Big Jones, and I'll make a little admission here. I spent a few years studying artisan baking while considering opening a bakery, so at least in theory we have a lot of options on the table. At the beginning and end of every day, though, I find myself wanting these traditional breads, baked at home.

Skillet Cornbread

We make hundreds of skillets of cornbread every week, using small 7-inch cast-iron skillets that are perfect for serving two to four people. Making your cornbread at home as good as ours is easy: one of the essential tricks is to preheat the skillet so the edges of the bread start to cook at once, giving them extra time to turn crispy before the center cooks to creamy perfection. You should feel free to make this recipe in muffin pans if you prefer—just get the heaviest muffin pans you can find. Some companies such as Cajun Cast Iron and Lodge make cast-iron muffin pans, which I highly recommend over the lightweight nonstick variety common in the kitchen section of department stores.

I got the idea for this particular style of cornbread—using a portion of hominy in place of some of the cornmeal—from the hominy bread recipes you can find in old colonial and early antebellum cookbooks. You might call it a lazy form of spoonbread, but the clever part is that it has just enough structure so you can hold it in your hands, which is a great sensation when the bread is piping hot. The masa flour provides an extra-fine texture and is also the secret behind our cornbread's down-pillow softness. Anson Mills makes an excellent true masa flour. Commercial dry masa flours make a weak substitute but do work.

Lard or bacon drippings make far and away the best cornbread, although we are known to use duck fat, goose fat, or chicken fat in a pinch, or clarified butter on request for vegetarians. If you go the vegetarian route, a warning: you must use clarified butter, because the butter solids will burn by the time the cornbread is done baking. For your convenience, instructions for making clarified butter are included in the pantry section in the back of this book.

PREP TIME: 50 minutes
EQUIPMENT NEEDED: 12-inch cast-iron skillet, 4-quart mixing bowl, small bowl, wire whisk, pot holder, wooden spoon, ladle
SERVES: 6 to 8

1 cup fresh lard, bacon fat, or unsalted butter, divided
1½ cups stone-ground white cornmeal
¾ cup fine masa flour
2 teaspoons cream of tartar
1 teaspoon baking soda
2 teaspoons kosher salt
½ teaspoon cayenne pepper
6 large eggs
3 cups lowfat buttermilk

⚜ Preheat oven to 425°F. Place ½ cup of the lard, bacon fat, or butter in a 12-inch cast-iron skillet, and then put in the oven to melt as the oven preheats while you make the batter.

⚜ Melt the remaining ½ cup of lard, bacon fat, or butter, then set aside in a warm spot. Combine cornmeal, masa flour, cream of tartar, baking soda, salt, and cayenne pepper in a 4-quart mixing bowl, and whisk to combine thoroughly. In a separate small bowl, whisk the eggs until frothy, then whisk in the buttermilk and combine thoroughly. While whisking, add the other ½ cup of the butter or lard, pouring in a thin, steady stream to incorporate thoroughly. Pour the wet mixture into the dry mixture all at once, and slowly stir them with a wooden spoon to combine until smooth and lump-free. The batter will resemble a slightly loose pancake batter.

⚜ Remove the pan with the hot butter or lard from the oven, and place on a pot holder. Carefully ladle the batter into the center of the pan, dropping each fresh ladleful onto the last, so that the butter pools around the edges.

⚜ Continue until all batter is in the pan.

⚜ Return the pan to the oven, and bake just until set in the center, about 30 minutes. It should feel springy when you tap it with your finger. Serve hot at once with lots of butter.

Sally Lunn

One of the South's storybook breads, Sally Lunn has been popular since the earliest cookbooks from the antebellum period. The delightful cake-like texture makes it perfect for slathering with butter while still hot from the pan, and it also makes spectacular French toast.

The recipe is believed to date to a thirteen-century bakery in England called Sally Lunn. Why it became so popular over many other breads is probably a story lost to the centuries, but I suspect it might have something to do with the fact that the baker is excused from the long, arduous process of kneading, which must have been a tough labor before the days of fans, air conditioners, or stand mixers.

Sally Lunn deteriorates fairly quickly after baking, becoming drier and more brittle, so if you're planning to serve it as your bread with a meal, time it to come out of the oven as close to mealtime as you can. It's best to start 3 to 4 hours before you plan to serve.

PREP TIME: 3 hours

EQUIPMENT NEEDED: 1-quart saucepan, digital food thermometer, stand mixer with flat beater or a hand mixer, sifter, rubber spatula, wooden spoon, 2-pound loaf pan, wire cooling rack

MAKES: one 2-pound loaf

½ cup whole milk
¼ cup plus 1 tablespoon granulated sugar
1 teaspoon instant baker's yeast
¼ cup (½ stick) unsalted butter, at room temperature
3 large eggs
1 tablespoon kosher salt
3 cups all-purpose flour, sifted before measuring, then resifted

❧ In a 1-quart saucepan, warm the milk and 1 tablespoon of the sugar over low heat until it is lukewarm (about 110°F on a digital food thermometer). Then stir in the yeast and set aside in a warm place until the yeast is foaming and active, about 10 minutes. The yeast will form a foamy raft atop the milk.
❧ In a stand mixer with the flat beater attachment, or in a 4-quart mixing

bowl with a hand mixer, cream the butter with the remaining ¼ cup sugar until light and fluffy. Add the eggs, one at a time, incorporating each until the mixture is smooth and foamy. It will become a little thinner with the addition of each egg. After the last egg, continue mixing for another few minutes until very light and fluffy, double the original bulk.

🌱 Add the salt, then sprinkle about one-third of the flour into the eggs and fold in with a rubber spatula. Fold in half the milk mixture, then another third of the flour, then the other half of the milk, followed by the last third of the flour. Do not knead. The dough should be soft and quite sticky. Cover with plastic wrap, and set to rise in a warm place until doubled in bulk, about 2 hours.

🌱 Preheat oven to 350°F.

🌱 Use a wooden spoon to "punch down" the dough, then place in a buttered 2-pound loaf pan, cover gently with plastic wrap, and set in a warm place to rise again to one and a half times its original size, about another hour. Once risen, remove plastic wrap and place on the center rack of the oven. Bake until the internal temperature reads 185°F on a digital food thermometer and the top is golden brown, about 45 to 55 minutes. Allow to cool for 10 minutes before turning out onto a breadboard to serve hot, or cool on a wire rack to use later.

Popovers

Popovers are far and away my favorite quick bread—as close as it gets to kitchen magic. Just a few ingredients and no added leavening—the eggs do all the lifting—and with a little savvy technique, you get a hollow roll that is at once delightfully crispy at first bite, giving way to an irresistible creamy body with a rich yet clean egg flavor that pairs well with just about anything you want to serve alongside or slather over them.

Popovers are thought to be an Americanization of the famed pudding of Yorkshire, England, and it seems fairly certain that they are derivative. The primary difference is that popovers eliminate the drippings from the roast beef pan that define a Yorkshire pudding. They appear in Mrs. Dull's *Southern Cooking* from 1928 and Edna Lewis's *The Taste of Country Cooking* among many other Southern cookbooks. I selected them for the menu at Big Jones because they are not only wonderful when properly prepared, but fairly scarce nowadays. I love finding and reviving old recipes, and this is one of the best because popovers are unique and versatile. You can easily bake them at home, and by following some simple instructions we've developed through much experience with this delicacy, you can make them as well as we do.

Our staff loves these hot out of the oven with cane or maple syrup. Personally, I'm likely to stuff them with goat cheese, a slice of bacon, and a slice of avocado, fold them over, and enjoy how the creaminess of the goat cheese and avocado dance with the chewiness and fine crispness of the bacon and popover. It's my favorite breakfast sandwich. Fortunately, it's an easy 30-minute breakfast for you at home with this recipe and some good bacon.

PREP TIME: 1 hour
EQUIPMENT NEEDED: 12-cup muffin pan, 4-quart mixing bowl, wire whisk, sifter, small ladle
MAKES: 12 popovers

¼ cup lard or clarified unsalted butter
3 large eggs
1½ cups skim milk
1½ cups all-purpose flour, sifted before measuring then resifted
1 teaspoon kosher salt
¼ teaspoon cayenne pepper

☙ Preheat the oven to 425°F. Using a muffin pan with cups that hold ½ cup, place 1 teaspoon of the butter or lard in each muffin cup. Put the muffin pan in the oven to melt the butter or lard as the oven preheats while you make the batter.

☙ In a 4-quart mixing bowl, crack the eggs and make sure to remove any bits of shell. Whisk thoroughly until frothy. Whisk in one-third of the milk, then sift one-third of the flour over the wet mixture while whisking it in. Whisk vigorously to break up any lumps until you have a smooth, thick batter. Whisk in another third of the milk, followed by a third of the flour, and repeat once more until all is incorporated and the batter is smooth. Stir in the salt and cayenne.

☙ Remove the muffin pan from the oven and place on a heat-proof surface. Carefully ladle ¼ cup of batter into the center of each cup, so that the oil pools around the sides. The batter should sizzle a bit as it's poured into the hot pan. Return the filled pan to the lower rack of the oven and bake for 20 minutes, then reduce heat to 325°F and bake for another 20 minutes. The popovers are done when massively puffed and a deep rich golden brown, about 40 to 45 minutes. Serve at once with butter and jam, or use to make Eggs New Orleans (page 85).

Farmstead Biscuits

When I started to mature as a cook and learn about American regional cooking, I was stunned to learn that biscuits were considered a Southern food (I had a similar revelation with fried chicken) because they were something I grew up with in southern Indiana, and we were some biscuit-eating folks even north of the Mason-Dixon. Of course after many years of studying culinary history and comparing its stories with what I knew about American history, I learned that the food I grew up with, while in the very far south of the old Union, was very much Southern in lineage and heritage, sharing a history and ethnic background with much of Appalachia and the Piedmont regions. Biscuits are one of those foods that helped me understand why I fell in love with Southern food so deeply—it's very much the same cooking on which I was raised.

Biscuits have an interesting history. Most folks don't realize that baking powder hasn't been around very long, only since the late nineteenth century, and baking soda not that much longer. Cooks used to have to go to all sorts of laborious lengths to get even a little rise out of their biscuits; beaten biscuits surely caused their share of carpal tunnel syndrome in the days before soda biscuits became the norm.

Today we can enjoy these as an easy quick bread. I call them farmstead biscuits because this is as close as it gets to the biscuits on my great-grandparents' old farmstead years ago—lard, flour, a little leavening, and buttermilk. Properly made, they are rich, tangy, and flaky: the perfect accompaniment to butter, jam, sorghum, eggs, or any salt pork or gravy you feel like cooking up.

PREP TIME: 1 hour
EQUIPMENT NEEDED: 10-by-18-inch sheet pan or cookie sheet, sifter, 4-quart mixing bowl, rolling pin, 2-inch biscuit cutter
MAKES: 12 biscuits

2¼ cups pastry flour, sifted before measuring (if you can't find pastry flour, you may use 1¼ cups all-purpose and 1 cup cake flour)

1½ teaspoons baking soda

¾ teaspoon cream of tartar

½ teaspoon kosher salt

¼ cup plus 3 tablespoons fresh lard, duck fat, or unsalted butter, chilled and cut into small bits

½ cup plus 2 tablespoons lowfat buttermilk

⚜ Preheat oven to 425°F.

⚜ Butter a 10-by-18-inch sheet pan and have at the ready. Sift the flour before measuring, then add the baking soda, cream of tartar, and salt to the flour, and sift again into a 4-quart mixing bowl. Add the lard to the flour mixture. Using your hands, begin flattening the lard between your fingers while working it into the dough, then begin rubbing the lard into the flour between your hands until it is evenly incorporated but the mixture still looks rough and mealy.

⚜ Add the buttermilk and mix quickly for a few seconds with your fingers. Allow to stand for 20 seconds for the flour to hydrate, then resume mixing, working to push the dough into a rough ball with as little effort as possible. Once the dough holds together, flour your hands well and knead the dough for only four turns, then turn out onto a floured work surface. Press out the dough with your hands to 1 inch thick, crimping and pressing in the edges to form a solid disk with smooth, squared edges. Use a rolling pin to roll out to ¾ inch thick. Use a biscuit cutter (2 inches is ideal) to cut out biscuits, using a straight down-and-up motion without twisting the biscuit cutter, and place on the buttered baking sheet. When all biscuits are cut, you can re-form scraps to make more biscuits—just be careful to work the dough as little as possible.

⚜ Place the biscuits on the top shelf of the oven and bake for about 25 minutes, until deep golden brown and fluffy in the center. Serve hot with gravy or butter and preserves.

Sweet Potato Biscuits

One of the most popular dishes from our early days' brunch menu was char-grilled andouille, redeye gravy, and these delicious biscuits. I learned them from my friend Wade Turnipseed, son of Arkansas, although his parents grew up in the Mississippi Delta. It doesn't get any more Southern than this. The mashed sweet potato lends these a soft texture, besides the delicious sweet potato flavor. They are slightly sweet and have a freshly baked bread aroma that's terribly addictive, boosted by the warm, comforting cinnamon spice.

These are even better with sorghum than regular biscuits—try slathering them with butter while still hot and then drizzling sorghum over the melting butter, or serve with pan-fried ham (page 120) or andouille and redeye gravy.

You can use canned sweet potato for this recipe, the results will be fine; but for truly great biscuits like we serve at Big Jones, make these in the fall or winter with new crop sweet potatoes from your local farmers' market.

PREP TIME: 1 hour for baking sweet potatoes (may be done ahead of time); 1 hour for mixing and baking
EQUIPMENT NEEDED: 10-by-18-inch sheet pan or cookie sheet, sifter, 4-quart mixing bowl, rolling pin, 2-inch biscuit cutter
MAKES: 18 biscuits

1 cup baked sweet potato pulp
2½ cups all-purpose flour, sifted before measuring
3 tablespoons granulated sugar
½ teaspoon ground cinnamon
½ teaspoon ground nutmeg
½ teaspoon freshly ground pepper
2 teaspoons baking soda
1 teaspoon cream of tartar
½ teaspoon kosher salt
½ cup fresh lard, duck fat, or unsalted butter, chilled and cut into small bits
¼ cup plus 1 tablespoon lowfat buttermilk

✤ One to three days before you plan to make your biscuits (this recipe also works well with leftover sweet potatoes), wrap two medium sweet potatoes in foil and bake until tender. Allow to cool on the countertop for an hour, and then refrigerate until you are ready to make your biscuits.

✤ Preheat oven to 375°F.

✤ Butter a 10-by-18-inch sheet pan and have at the ready. Peel baked sweet potatoes, then measure out 1 cup of the pulp and set aside. Sift the flour before measuring, then add the sugar, spices, baking soda, cream of tartar, and salt to the flour, and sift again. Add the lard to the flour. Using your hands, begin flattening the lard between your fingers while working it into the dough, then begin rubbing the lard into the flour between your hands until it is evenly incorporated.

✤ Add the sweet potato pulp and buttermilk to the flour mixture, and mix quickly for a few seconds with your fingers. Allow to stand for 20 seconds for the flour to hydrate, then resume mixing, working to push the dough into a rough ball with as little effort as possible. If the dough becomes too sticky, flour your hands. Once the dough can form a ball, knead just four turns, then turn out onto a floured work surface. Press out the dough with your hands to 1 inch thick, crimping and pressing in the edges to form a solid disk with smooth, squared edges. Use a rolling pin to roll out to ¾ inch thick. Use a biscuit cutter (2 inches is ideal) to cut out biscuits, and place on the buttered baking sheet. When all the biscuits are cut, you can re-form scraps to make more biscuits—just be careful to work the dough as little as possible.

✤ Place the biscuits on the middle shelf of the oven and bake for about 30 minutes, until deep golden brown and fluffy in the center. Serve hot with gravy or butter and preserves.

Cheddar Biscuits

The most indulgent of biscuit recipes, cheddar biscuits are as addictive as they are rich, so make sure you have company on hand when you make these, lest you wind up eating them all yourself! Interestingly, I had my first cheddar biscuit in the Mississippi Delta at a small café in the charming small town of Greenwood, surrounded by cotton and sweet potato fields. It was one of those days I felt like I learned a little bit about what it truly means to be Southern.

In my opinion, these are best enjoyed with good apple butter as a quick and simple breakfast. Of course, you can expand from there, using them to make bacon breakfast sandwiches or serving them with eggs and bacon or ham. When you're serving cheddar biscuits, always have some fresh fruit at hand to help cut the richness. Served in late summer with peaches or in fall with pickled peaches are two great alternatives to the apple butter option.

PREP TIME: 1 hour

EQUIPMENT NEEDED: sifter, 4-quart mixing bowl, box grater, rolling pin, 2-inch biscuit cutter, 10-by-18-inch sheet pan or cookie sheet

MAKES: 15 biscuits

1½ cups pastry flour (if you can't find pastry flour, you may use 1 cup all-purpose and ½ cup cake flour)

1 teaspoon cream of tartar

2 teaspoons baking soda

½ teaspoon kosher salt

6 tablespoons (¾ stick) unsalted butter, very cold

¼ pound sharp cheddar cheese, shredded on the large side of a box grater

½ cup plus 1 tablespoon buttermilk

⚜ Make sure all ingredients are very cold. Preheat oven to 425°F.

⚜ Sift the flour, cream of tartar, baking soda, and salt together into a 4-quart mixing bowl. Flour your hands and the larger side of a box grater well, and coarsely grate the butter into the flour, pulling up enough of the sifted flour mixture to prevent the butter from clumping. Add the cheddar cheese and toss, making sure the butter bits and cheese are evenly distributed throughout the flour.

⚜ Add the buttermilk to the flour mixture, and work it in quickly with your fingers, then pause for 20 seconds to allow the buttermilk to hydrate the flour before resuming mixing. Working the dough as little as possible while keeping your hands well-floured, press the dough together until it forms a single rough mass.

⚜ Knead it exactly four times, then turn out onto a floured surface. Roll out ⅔ inch thick, constantly crimping the edges to ultimately shape the dough into an even disk with smooth, squared edges. Cut with whatever size biscuit cutter you prefer (2 inches yields biscuits that are crispy on the out-side, fluffy on the inside), and transfer to an ungreased 10-by-18-inch baking sheet. Bake until puffed and a deep golden brown, about 25 minutes. Serve right away, with apple butter (page 229) or pepper jelly (page 223).

Beignets

Perhaps the most talked-about item we have ever served, our beignets have been the subject of many a love letter, tweet, blog, and Facebook post. We've also never sold a beignet, and our official policy is they never leave the restaurant, meaning we don't cater them or sell them to go. The only way to enjoy our beignets is to come in for brunch, when they are served complimentary, as bread service.

We get many, many requests to prepare beignets for carry-out. While our customer service philosophy directs us to try to find a way to say "yes" to every request, we've always answered that question with a firm "sorry, no can do." Why? I invite you to find out for yourself—make this recipe, enjoy a few straight out of the frying pot, and set a few aside in a card-board or plastic box for an hour or so, try them again, and they just aren't as good. This is one item we absolutely want everyone to enjoy straight from the fry pot, as the texture is incomparable when they are still hot, and they don't reheat well with their powdered-sugar coating.

We've provided this recipe to many folks who have asked for beignets to go for their parties and celebrations. It's one of the reasons I decided to do this book—now you can make these delicious, melt-in-your-mouth nuggets any time you need a fix.

PREP TIME: 90 minutes for mixing and rising, 30 minutes for rolling and
    frying
EQUIPMENT NEEDED: 1-quart saucepan, digital food thermometer, 4-quart
    mixing bowl, wire whisk, long-handled wooden spoon, 4-quart cast-iron
    kettle or countertop deep fryer, rolling pin, pizza cutter, digital clip-on
    candy thermometer
MAKES: 15 beignets

½ cup whole milk

2 tablespoons granulated white sugar, divided

1 teaspoon instant baking yeast

2 large eggs

¼ teaspoon ground nutmeg

¼ teaspoon ground cloves

1 teaspoon pure vanilla extract

½ teaspoon kosher salt

1½ cups all-purpose flour

¼ cup rice flour

¼ cup (½ stick) unsalted butter, melted

Vegetable oil for deep frying

Powdered sugar for dusting

⚜ In a 1-quart saucepan, heat the milk to lukewarm (about 110°F on a digital food thermometer). Remove from heat, then stir in 1 tablespoon of the sugar and the yeast. Set aside in a warm spot until the yeast is foaming and active, about 10 minutes.

⚜ In a 4-quart mixing bowl, whisk the eggs with the nutmeg, clove, vanilla, and salt until smooth. Whisk in the yeast mixture, then fold in the flours with a spatula or wooden spoon, followed by the melted butter. Cover with plastic wrap, and set in a warm spot at about 100°F to rise for an hour or until doubled in bulk.

⚜ Prepare a cast-iron kettle or countertop fryer with at least 1 inch of oil for deep frying, and preheat to 325°F using a digital clip-on candy thermometer.

⚜ Once the dough has doubled in bulk, remove the plastic wrap and punch the dough a few times until it is back to its pre-risen size, then roll out ⅜ inch thick on a well-floured work surface. Use a pizza cutter to cut into 2-by-2-inch squares. Rest for 10 minutes to relax the gluten and to let it rise a bit more before frying. Cook for 2½ minutes on the first side and 2 minutes on the second. Drain on paper towels for 1 minute before tossing in lots of powdered sugar.

Buckwheat Banana Pancakes

I may have been a strange kid, but I was always a little disappointed when we had regular batter pancakes for breakfast. Not entirely disappointed, mind you—I was still going to get syrup and butter, which is always a plus. But I was disappointed just a little bit, because I always preferred buckwheat pancakes. I liked their spicy, grassy taste with the buttery, syrupy mess I'd inevitable slather all about; white pancakes never felt like the best vehicle for this feat of childhood gluttony.

You can imagine how challenging it was to grow up into a world where no restaurants ever served my beloved buckwheat pancakes. It may have something to do with why I eventually became a savory breakfast person, preferring eggs, bacon, potatoes, and eventually grits, as I gave up hope that anyone would ever make buckwheat pancakes for me when I ate out.

So when I opened my own restaurant, I wanted to serve us buckwheat lovers proudly and with gusto. Anson Mills enabled us to significantly improve a basic breakfast staple when they introduced a wondrous line of buckwheat flours that are unrivaled by any other on the market. You can make these pancakes with any brand of buckwheat flour you like, but try your farmers' market first to see if you can find a local artisan buckwheat, or go to ansonmills.com if you want them to be extra tasty.

PREP TIME: 45 minutes
EQUIPMENT NEEDED: 12-inch cast-iron skillet, sifter, two 4-quart mixing bowls, wire whisk, ½-cup scoop or ladle, heat-resistant spatula/turner
MAKES: about twelve 4-inch flapjacks

   1½ cups buckwheat flour
   1 cup cake flour or gluten-free flour
   2 teaspoons cream of tartar
   1 teaspoon baking soda
   3 tablespoons granulated sugar
   ½ teaspoon kosher salt
   3 large eggs

2½ cups lowfat buttermilk, or more if you like thinner cakes
¼ cup (½ stick) unsalted butter, melted, plus more for baking
3 to 4 very ripe bananas, peeled and sliced

✸ Preheat a 12-inch cast-iron skillet over medium-low heat. Sift dry ingredients together into a 4-quart mixing bowl. In a separate 4-quart mixing bowl whisk the eggs until frothy, then beat in the buttermilk.
✸ Add the buttermilk mixture to the dry ingredients all at once, and quickly whisk to combine and stir until all lumps are worked out, but be careful not to over-mix. Stir in the butter last.
✸ Use a ½-cup scoop or ladle to dollop the batter into the preheated skillet, then allow the batter to relax and shape itself—no need to spread it out by hand. Dot with sliced bananas. Cook 4 to 6 minutes on the first side. Flip when the very edges of the pancake are bubbling and begin to set. Cook 2 to 3 minutes on the second side, until cooked through. Top with toasted almonds, caramel, and powdered sugar.

Antebellum Rice Waffles

Once while researching the origins of Carolina Gold rice, I stumbled upon a book titled *The Carolina Rice Kitchen* from 1900. It was a stunning revelation in many ways—here was an American cuisine based not on wheat, not on corn, but on rice. It's filled with many useful recipes, but one that really captured my imagination was the rice waffle. Many, many old colonial and antebellum-era cookbooks contain receipts (the literary forebears of recipes) for "wafers," which would eventually become "waffles," and every reasonably well-equipped home kitchen would have a wafer iron or two. In those days, wafers tended toward the thinner and crispier side: the iron was filled with batter then held by hand over a flame or hot coals to do the baking. Early wafers and waffles were treated as breads (which they are) and were just as likely to be eaten with gravy or savory sauces as syrup or sweet preserves.

In order to get just the texture we wanted and to work with our modern waffle irons, I wound up editing and adapting the original recipe pretty significantly, but the revelation of 100 percent rice flour waffles in our history was the most important thing. As a bonus to being exquisitely delicious with a particularly crisp texture, these waffles are gluten-free. In keeping with early American waffle traditions, we often treat these with a savory dish rather than sweet. They've been served with crispy duck confit, fried chicken and cream gravy, and many other combinations of the moment. Of course, you can enjoy them with butter, syrup, and fresh fruit if you like, but try them instead of mashed potatoes sometime when you're cooking up fried chicken.

PREP TIME: 45 minutes
EQUIPMENT NEEDED: sifter, 4-quart mixing bowl, 1-quart mixing bowl, wire whisk, waffle iron
MAKES: 6 waffles in a standard 5-inch or 6-inch home Belgian waffle iron

2½ cups rice flour (we use Anson Mills Carolina Gold rice flour; Bob's Red Mill stone-ground rice flour works as well)
2 teaspoons baking soda
½ teaspoon kosher salt
¼ teaspoon cayenne pepper (optional)
2 large eggs
2 cups lowfat buttermilk
¼ cup (½ stick) unsalted butter

🌱 Sift dry ingredients into a 4-quart mixing bowl. Crack the eggs into a separate one-quart mixing bowl and be sure to remove any bits of shell. Whisk the eggs until smooth, then whisk in the buttermilk until thoroughly combined. Pour the buttermilk mixture into the dry ingredients, and whisk to combine and work out any lumps, then slowly whisk in the butter.
🌱 Bake in a waffle iron according to the manufacturer's instructions. As this batter has no sugar, it is slow to brown and burn, so if you like a crispier waffle, simply cook longer. Great with savory gravy dishes or fresh fruit and syrup.

Salt-Rising Bread

Only in the last couple of years did I become aware of salt-rising bread, and it's easily the most unique and fascinating traditional bread we make at Big Jones, owing to its unusual starter, method of rising, and dense, creamy crumb with the unmistakable aroma of ripe cheese.

The origins of this bread, as with many Southern foods, are murky at best, as is its name—the salt doesn't actually raise the bread, although the addition of salt to the initial starter certainly does inhibit some microbes and encourage others. Some speculate that the name comes from the supposed practice of setting the starter and sponge on a warm bed of salt to maintain the sultry temperatures that cause it to percolate. In my opinion, given its origins in the central Appalachian chain, it seems like a great bread to make when the temperature and humidity are naturally high. Besides, any reasonably experienced home cook could place the starter just the right distance from the hearth to maintain the correct temperature. So, while we may not know exactly how it originated, my personal guess on the origin of the name is with the practice of adding salt to the starter.

Questions about origins and the name aside, this is a fabulously delicious bread with an intoxicating ripe cheese aroma and creamy crumb that lends itself well to being buttered at the table; also, try making grilled cheese with it—you won't believe how good it is. I like to serve it fresh at the table with butter and preserves, or even with a cheese spread such as pimiento cheese or beer cheese. Wrapped tightly in plastic wrap, this bread will keep for several days.

Special notes: This is a bacterial fermentation, not from yeast, so make sure all vessels are thoroughly clean before using them in the recipe, and be sure to clean up thoroughly afterward. And you absolutely must use a rustic whole-grain stone-ground cornmeal for the starter since it comes with essential nutrients that refined cornmeal does not possess.

PREP TIME: 24 hours for starter, 3 hours for rising and proofing, 1 hour for baking

EQUIPMENT NEEDED: 1-quart glass jar, 2-quart heavy glass or stainless-steel pitcher, 1-quart saucepan, digital food thermometer, sifter, wire whisk,

stand mixer with dough hook, rolling pin, two 2-pound loaf pans, large
cake pan or Dutch oven, wire cooling rack

MAKES: two 2-pound loaves

½ pound red potatoes with skin, scrubbed and thinly sliced
2 cups boiling water
2 tablespoons stone-ground whole-grain cornmeal
1 tablespoon granulated sugar
2½ teaspoons kosher salt, divided
1 cup whole milk
¼ teaspoon baking soda
6½ cups all-purpose flour, approximately, sifted before measuring,
    divided
¼ cup lard or unsalted butter, softened to room temperature

⚜ For the starter, place the potatoes in a sanitized 1-quart or larger glass jar
or pitcher, and pour the boiling water over them. Stir in the cornmeal, sugar,
and ½ teaspoon of the salt. Cover with a clean cloth, and place in a spot to
maintain 100°F to 110°F for 24 hours—over a stove or in a basin of regularly
replenished warm water. If you have a dehydrator with temperature control
or a Crock-Pot with a low temperature setting, that works as well. After 20 to
24 hours (depending on temperature), the mixture should be slightly bubbly
and foamy. If not, keep warm and check back every couple of hours until you
can see bubbling or foaming on the surface. The smell should be doughy
with hints of cheese.

⚜ To make the sponge, carefully pour the starter into a 2-quart heavy glass
or stainless-steel pitcher, discarding the potatoes. Heat the milk to 120°F in
a 1-quart saucepan, then add to the starter along with the baking soda and
2 cups of flour. Beat the batter with a whisk to break up any lumps. Cover
loosely with plastic wrap, and again place in a warm spot at 100°F to 110°F. Let
the sponge double in bulk (1 to 3 hours, checking more often as time passes).
It will be light and frothy like the head on a draft beer and smell richly of
ripe cheese. Once the starter is at this stage, you must make the dough and
proceed with baking, or the starter will sour.

⚜ To make the bread dough, pour the starter into the bowl of a stand mixer
with a dough hook, and add the remaining 2 teaspoons of salt and 3 cups of
flour. Mix thoroughly until all flour is incorporated. Allow to rest for 10 minutes to hydrate thoroughly, then proceed with kneading with the dough hook

on medium speed for 2 minutes. Add another ½ cup of flour and all of the lard or butter, and continue kneading another 2 minutes. Every 2 minutes, add another ½ cup of flour while kneading with the dough hook until you have a smooth and elastic dough that is fairly loose but pulls away from the sides of the bowl. Due to the nature of the starter, a little more or less flour may be required than listed in the recipe, so simply be sensitive as kneading goes on to maintain a smooth dough that pulls away from the sides of the bowl cleanly. If it's sticking, add more flour. Once it pulls away from the sides of the bowl, stop adding flour. The dough will feel heavier and more dense than most bread dough—this is due to the nature of the starter. It should be tacky but not terribly sticky: you should be able to handle it cleanly without flouring your hands. Knead for a total of 10 minutes.

❦ Preheat oven to 350°F.

❦ Divide the dough in two, and shape the loaves by rolling each out into a rectangle about 1 inch thick, then roll up and turn the open ends underneath to turn out a loaf that will fit the bottom of a loaf pan. Place in a well-larded 2-pound loaf pan with the crease from rolling on the bottom. Cover loosely with plastic wrap, and place in a warm water (110°F) bath to proof—a larger cake pan or Dutch oven works well for this purpose—changing out the water periodically to maintain a warm temperature. Proof until the dough rises one-third in volume, about 1 hour.

❦ Bake for 45 to 55 minutes, to 195°F internal temperature on a digital food thermometer. For a glistening top, brush with a wash of a large egg whipped with ¼ cup water after the first 25 minutes of baking. Cool on a wire rack for 10 minutes before turning out of the pan to finish cooling on the rack. If not serving immediately, place in a plastic bag when slightly warm, but not hot, to the touch.

Abruzzi Rye Bread

Coming from a long line of German farmers on my dad's side, I've always had a taste for rye bread, and when Anson Mills introduced its Abruzzi rye flour (an Italian heirloom), I wanted to give it a try. The Dutch of Appalachia brought rye with them from Germany, and Italians of the Lowcountry brought rye with them very early during that area's settlement. Rye bread has a rich history in the mountains and Southeast, another example of something that might otherwise seem exotic in Southern food being perfectly natural in another context.

Finding old rye bread recipes to work with wasn't easy, so I engineered this recipe based on ingredients available in the nineteenth century, most notably sorghum molasses, while most all twentieth-century rye bread recipes call for regular sugarcane molasses, reflecting the dominant role sugarcane had begun to play in the dry-goods business.

You can of course use whatever rye flour you have at hand, but if you can, I encourage you to look up Anson Mills. Their Abruzzi rye flour is complex, spicy and earthy, finely textured yet robust. When ordering, take note that the 3 cups you'll need are right at 1 pound of flour.

PREP TIME: 2 hours mixing and rising, 2 hours proofing and baking
EQUIPMENT NEEDED: 1-quart saucepan, digital food thermometer, stand mixer
    with dough hook, 1-quart mixing bowl, rolling pin, 2-pound loaf pan,
    wire cooling rack
MAKES: one 2-pound loaf

    1¼ cups skim milk
    ¼ cup sorghum molasses
    1 teaspoon instant baking yeast
    3 cups finely ground Abruzzi rye flour
    1½ cups all-purpose whole-wheat flour, divided
    2 large eggs
    1 teaspoon kosher salt
    ¼ cup lard (preferred) or unsalted butter, at room temperature

❦ Heat the milk and sorghum in a 1-quart saucepan until lukewarm, about 110°F. Stir in the yeast, and set in a warm place for 10 to 15 minutes, until the yeast activates and forms a foamy mass on top of the milk.

❦ Place the milk mixture in a stand mixer with the dough hook attachment. Add the rye flour, and begin mixing on low speed. Once the rye is incorporated, add whole-wheat flour in thirds, and continue mixing until all is incorporated. Crack the eggs into a separate 1-quart mixing bowl, then add to the dough one at a time, mixing to incorporate each before adding the next. Let dough stand 20 minutes to hydrate. Add the salt, and increase speed to medium to begin the kneading process. The dough will be fairly stiff and heavy. Mix for about 8 to 10 minutes altogether, then test for gluten by stretching between your fingers into a small square pane. If you can stretch it thin enough to see your fingers through the other side without the dough breaking, it is ready to proceed. Return the mixer to medium speed, and add the lard or butter a tablespoon at a time, incorporating well after each addition. Once all is incorporated, the dough is ready to rise.

꽃 Cover the dough with plastic wrap, and set in a warm place, ideally about 100°F, until doubled in bulk, about an hour or more depending on temperature and humidity. Punch down the dough until it reverts back to its pre-risen size. Shape loaf by rolling out into a rectangle about 1 inch thick, then roll up and turn the open ends underneath to turn out a loaf that will fit the bottom of your bread pan. Place in a well-larded 2-pound loaf pan with the crease from rolling on the bottom, cover with plastic wrap, and set in a warm place at about 100°F to proof.

꽃 Preheat oven to 325°F.

꽃 Once the loaf has risen by one-third, wet the sharpest knife you have with cold water and quickly make a slit lengthwise across the top of the loaf, ½ inch deep. Place on the center rack of the oven, and bake to an internal temperature of 185°F on a digital food thermometer, or until a toothpick inserted in the center comes out clean, about 60 to 70 minutes. Allow to rest for 10 minutes before turning out and cooling on a wire rack. If not serving immediately, bag when slightly warm, but not hot, to the touch. Serve with charcuterie, smoked meats, chicken salad, or use for grilled pimiento cheese sandwiches.

Awendaw Spoonbread

One of the museum pieces of Southern food lore, spoonbread dates to the earliest days of European settlement and is immortalized in Sarah Rutledge's *The Carolina Housewife* (1847) under the name "Owendaw Bread." By the twentieth century, it was particularly popular in Appalachia and has a storied history in Kentucky, appearing in many of that state's great cookbooks and garnishing the reputations of some of its finest inns.

There's more than one way to give the savory pudding-like texture to your spoonbread, the most popular being to change the ratios of cornmeal, buttermilk, and eggs to simply make a softer bread. The less common, and we believe best way per Sarah Rutledge's receipt, is the ancient method of combining creamy cooked grits (likely samp in the earliest days) with your cornmeal and milk to make the batter. Ours is lightened ever so slightly with the addition of a touch of baking powder—not a totally authentic spoonbread, but I love the soufflé-like texture you get as a result.

A great spoonbread is light as a soufflé yet rich as the most splendid savory pudding. Even on its own, this can make a light meal with a small salad, but it's great for breakfast, lunch, or dinner, and goes with everything.

PREP TIME: 2 hours
EQUIPMENT NEEDED: 2-quart cast-iron or enamel casserole, 1-quart saucepan, wire whisk, wire mesh skimmer or slotted spoon, 4-quart mixing bowl
SERVES: 4 to 6

1¾ cups whole milk
½ teaspoon cayenne pepper
2 teaspoons kosher salt
½ cup stone-ground hominy grits
½ cup (1 stick) unsalted butter, cut into bits
½ cup sharp cheddar cheese, shredded
4 large eggs
1½ cups lowfat buttermilk
⅓ cup stone-ground fine cornmeal
1 teaspoon baking powder
½ cup sliced green onion, optional
1 cup crackling, optional (page 264)

⚜ Preheat oven to 350°F. Thoroughly butter a heavy 2-quart cast-iron or enamel casserole.

⚜ Place milk, cayenne, and salt in a 1-quart saucepan over medium-high heat, and bring to a boil, whisking occasionally to prevent scorching. Sprinkle the grits into the hot milk and whisk in. Pause, allowing the germ and chaff to rise to the top. Use a skimmer or slotted spoon to skim it off. Resume whisking and continue until the milk thickens measurably, about 3 to 5 minutes. Reduce heat to a low boil and continue whisking regularly to prevent sticking and scorching. The grits will take about 40 minutes to cook: they are done when the larger grits have a nice bite to them but no hard starchy center, and the overall mixture is heavy and creamy. Whisk in the butter and cheese until fully incorporated and creamy. Remove from heat and proceed immediately to the batter.

❦ In a 4-quart mixing bowl, whisk the eggs until frothy, then beat in the buttermilk. Combine the cornmeal and baking powder in a small dish, and then sprinkle over the buttermilk and whisk in. Whisking constantly, slowly pour the hot grits into the buttermilk and beat until smooth. Add the optional green onion and crackling, and pour batter into the buttered casserole. Bake on the top rack of the oven until light and fluffy, yet set in the center and nicely browned, about 50 to 60 minutes. You'll know it's done when the spoonbread jiggles as a whole mass when gently shaken. If it makes liquid waves in the center, it needs more time. Top with butter and serve with jam or sorghum molasses.

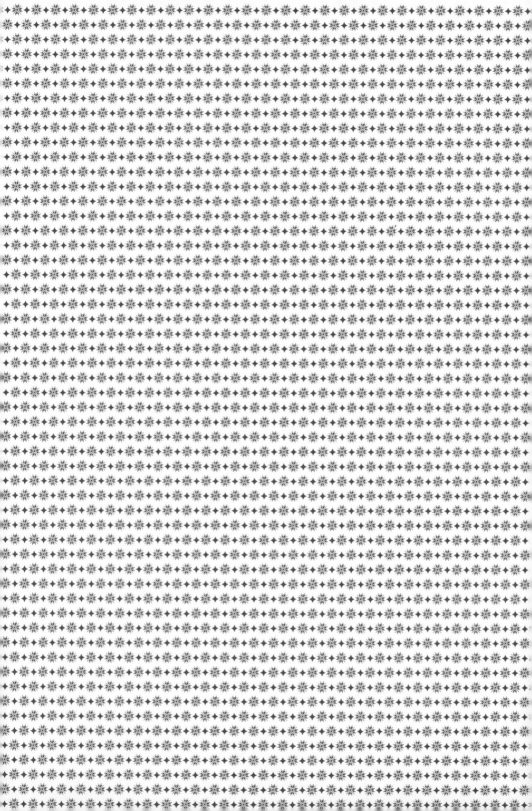

Inspirations from the
Lowcountry

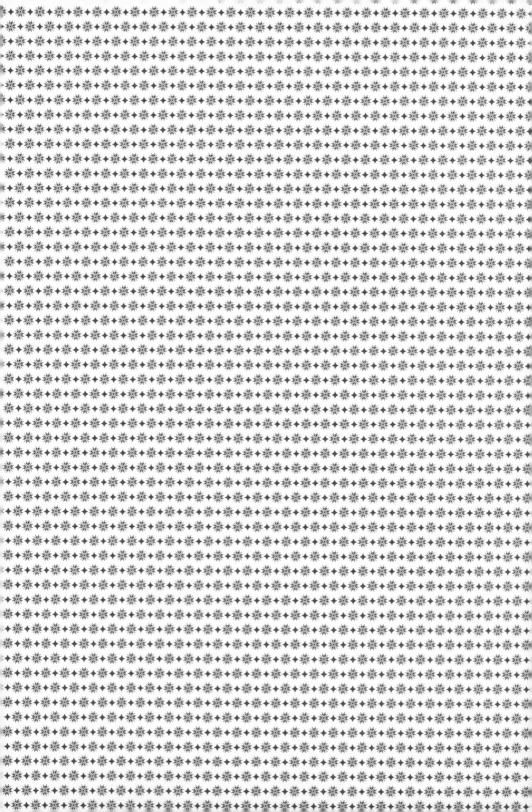

The Lowcountry, as the extensive coastal plain and Sea Islands of South Carolina and Georgia are known, has one of the most distinctive regional cuisines in the whole country, even the entire world. Its cuisine is particularly noteworthy for its ancestral rice industry and what came to be known as the Carolina Rice Kitchen, revived and revitalized through Karen Hess's book of the same name. Rice was being cultivated in the Lowcountry by the late seventeenth century and was to become the cash crop that built the cities of Charleston and Savannah, two of the wealthiest cities in North America by the mid-nineteenth century, which remain two queens of unparalleled beauty.

It's impossible to talk about the Carolina Rice Kitchen without paying respects to the people who were doing the work—enslaved people of African descent. Only by an accumulating body of scholarly work over the last few decades have we been able to realize the epic contributions Africans made to the development of both the rice industry and cuisine of the Lowcountry. It wasn't just slave labor—Africans had been growing rice for more than a millennium and a half along the coast of Africa from Senegal south and east through Nigeria, and had developed epic, monumentally effective methods of growing rice in many different terrains. These are the very people slave merchants bought and sold into slavery in Charleston and Savannah. All known evidence points to the conclusion that it was the ancestral knowledge and keen ingenuity of these people that established and built the mammoth rice-growing systems of the wealthy plantations on which they were enslaved. They contributed what would today be considered intellectual property. They were awarded no patents and shared in none of the wealth, but scholarly research is finally recognizing the important intellectual contributions these slaves made to the building of America.

With the slaves from Africa came *bene* (the ancestral seed of sesame), okra, melons, field peas, guinea fowl, and centuries-old expertise at cooking rice, among many other crops and intellectual contributions. Native Americans were instrumental in their sharing of corn particularly, but also many other crops that would also be part of the Columbian Exchange. It was undoubtedly within this very early recipe exchange in which grits, and even spoonbread, would creep into the Southern kitchen. Many other ethnic groups—from French Huguenots to Germans, Irish, English, and Italians—would settle the Lowcountry and contribute to a cosmopolitan cuisine with a richly local flavor.

Many of the families that populated the Lowcountry during colonization were extensions of families already planting in the West Indies, so Caribbean influences found their way into the cooking, and eventually Charleston's position as a major port of trade meant spices would make their way into kitchens by way of the East India trade; even today a ubiquitous dish such as Country Captain can be traced back to the days when rice was cash money and curry was the hot global ingredient du jour.

Together with the stunning variety and quality of seafood and wild game native to the area, these many global influences combined with a peculiar local climate and geography to germinate a particularly distinctive cuisine. When I discovered these aspects of the Lowcountry's food culture, I realized I was probably missing much more of what the South has to offer. In my personal love affair with the Southern kitchen, if south Louisiana lit the fire, then the Lowcountry fanned the flame.

Benne Oyster Stew

Oyster stew with benne was immortalized in the justifiably famed junior league cookbook *Charleston Receipts*, although preparing oysters with nutty flavors dates at least to Sarah Rutledge's cookbook *The Carolina Housewife* (1847), in which you can find a receipt for groundnut (peanut) stew that includes oysters. We've served benne oyster stew in many permutations, and every one of them has been deemed a knockout by the lucky guests who ordered the classic recipes.

Sesame seeds are usually called benne in the Lowcountry. The West African word for sesame is *bene*, and because of their long history first in slave gardens and eventually in the Big House kitchen, the name stuck. The variety we use is lovingly deemed Sea Island benne by our supplier Anson Mills, which sells a variety of benne that was described in 1804. The ancestral benne are much lower in oil than modern sesame seeds, which are essentially an oilseed crop. Higher in protein, Sea Island benne have a fantastic nutty aroma with lovely bitter undertones on the palate, making them a wonderful foil for briny oysters. You can use regular sesame seeds, but in lieu of true Sea Island benne, look for raw unhulled sesame seeds in a natural foods store.

While at first glance this is a complex recipe—with many crosscurrents of aromatics, textures, salt, umami, and acidity—it's easy to make at home; and once you get good at it, you'll want to make it a staple. That said, read the instructions carefully, and reread them again. The steps are simple but, for optimal layering of flavors, are best followed closely and in order.

Serve this with well-buttered toast and a salad of bitter greens and herbs.

PREP TIME: 1 hour

EQUIPMENT NEEDED: small sheet pan or cookie sheet, 1-gallon heavy-bottomed non-reactive stock pot, long-handled wooden spoon, long-handled slotted spoon, small wire whisk, 1-quart mixing bowl

SERVES: 4 to 6

¼ cup benne seeds
2 tablespoons leftover bacon fat, lard, or clarified unsalted butter
4 ounces slab bacon, cut into ½-inch cubes
2 cups yellow onion, finely diced
3 cloves fresh garlic, crushed and minced
½ cup green bell pepper, finely diced
½ cup celery, finely diced
¼ cup Carolina Gold rice flour
2 cups whole milk
2 bay leaves
½ teaspoon dried thyme leaves
½ teaspoon ground nutmeg
¼ cup brandy
½ cup dry Madeira
Juice of 1 lemon
2 tablespoons Louisiana-style hot sauce
1 teaspoon freshly ground black pepper
2 teaspoons kosher salt, or more to taste
3 dozen shucked select oysters, with liquor reserved
1 cup heavy whipping cream
½ cup (1 stick) unsalted butter, chilled and cut into bits

⚜ Toast the benne seeds on a dry sheet pan in a 350°F oven until just slightly browned and aromatic, about 10 minutes. In a 1-gallon heavy-bottomed non-reactive stock pot, place the reserved bacon fat or alternative and the diced bacon, and render over low heat, stirring occasionally with a wooden spoon. Gradually increase the heat as the bacon renders, eventually frying until crisp and well browned in its own fat. Remove bacon with a slotted spoon and reserve with the benne seeds.

⚜ Working with the rendered fat in the pot, increase heat to high and add onions. Cook, stirring constantly with a wooden spoon, until the onions lightly caramelize to an amber hue, about 8 minutes. Add the garlic, green bell pepper, and celery, and continue cooking until vegetables are well rendered and translucent. Remove from heat temporarily.

⚜ Combine the rice flour and milk in a 1-quart mixing bowl, whisking out any lumps, then stir into the pot and return to medium-high heat. Gradually bring to a boil, whisking often as scorching is a risk. As the mixture boils, it will thicken slightly. Reduce heat if necessary to maintain a low boil. Add the bay leaves, thyme, nutmeg, brandy, Madeira, and reserved benne seeds and bacon, and return to a low boil. Simmer 5 minutes, stirring often, then add the lemon juice, hot sauce, pepper, and salt. Add the reserved oyster liquor and return to a boil, then add the cream and return to a boil yet again. Whisk well. Taste for seasoning and add more salt if desired. Add the oysters and chilled butter, stirring well to melt the butter. Remove the bay leaves, and serve at once. If you prefer your oysters well done, return to a boil for 1 minute before serving.

She-Crab Soup

One of the most famous dishes of the Lowcountry and an absolute delight when prepared with fresh ingredients and a little bit of care, she-crab soup is a recipe we save for special occasions, never having put it on the regular menu. It's that good, and that special.

She-crab soup's origins are almost certainly tied to Scottish settlers, who brought with them a taste for partan bree, a simple soup of crab, milk, and rice. In the fabulously wealthy climes of Charleston, this basic porridge took on more and more sumptuous and decadent forms, incorporating the unusually rich roe of the female crab, cream, butter, and sherry or Madeira wine.

These days, many lackluster restaurants offer she-crab soup in forms that are hardly accurate representations of this historic dish. Particularly lazy kitchens will use roux to thicken the soup rather than a puree of rice porridge, ignoring the affinity crab and rice have for one another and also adding an unnecessarily rich thickener while crabmeat and dairy are already sufficiently rich.

I like to go the extra mile when making she-crab soup and use Carolina Gold rice, but you can use any medium- or long-grain rice for this recipe, although Arborio or carnaroli rice is a better option if you don't have Carolina Gold. Carolina Gold rice has a starchy texture that is unusually fine and will make a silky puree. Arborio and carnaroli are even starchier and will make an even smoother puree, but they lack the great pure grain flavor of Carolina Gold. Aromatic rice such as basmati, jasmine, or even Charleston Gold add delicious flavor contributions but make a less refined puree. I've always found Carolina Gold to offer the best balance, and with respect to the Carolina Rice Kitchen, it's undoubtedly the most historically accurate rice to use.

Other sloppy recipes call for gobs of heavy cream or, even worse, commercially processed soup bases. With crab, milk, and a little butter, believe me, it's rich enough.

Truly accurate versions of she-crab soup will include the roe of the crabs used to make the soup, so if you're lucky enough to score some female crabs with roe, simply use the roe as part of the crabmeat called for in the recipe, still going for a total of 8 ounces of crab.

As far as wine goes, I usually reach for dry Madeiras because I think they help lighten the flavor more than sherry does, but you should feel free to use sherry if you prefer, or if that's what you have on hand.

PREP TIME: 1 hour

EQUIPMENT NEEDED: 2-quart or larger saucepan, long-handled wooden spoon, blender

SERVES: 4 to 6

2 tablespoons (¼ stick) unsalted butter
1 cup yellow onion, finely chopped
½ cup celery, finely chopped
1 teaspoon Spanish paprika
¼ teaspoon cayenne pepper

½ cup Carolina Gold rice

2 bay leaves

4 cups whole milk, divided

8 ounces cooked lump crabmeat

¼ cup dry Madeira or sherry

1 tablespoon kosher salt

1 tablespoon freshly squeezed lemon juice

❧ In a 2-quart or larger saucepan, melt the butter over medium-high heat until foaming. Add the onions and celery, and sauté, stirring constantly with a wooden spoon, until the vegetables are translucent and aromatic. Add the paprika and cayenne pepper, and sauté another half minute, until the aroma of the spices is released. Add the rice, bay leaves, and 1 cup of the milk, and reduce the heat to medium.

❧ Stirring regularly, bring to a boil and continue to cook as the rice swells and cooks through. As the rice absorbs the milk, continue to add more milk ½ cup at a time to maintain the consistency of runny oatmeal, adding more milk as the porridge becomes too thick, and returning to a boil. Continue to stir often and well as this combination will have a tendency to scorch; stirring will also help release the starches on the grains of rice and create a creamier texture.

❧ Once all the milk is incorporated, continue to heat at a low boil until the rice is cooked so well it is mushy when pinched between your fingers. Add the crabmeat, wine, and salt, and return to a low boil for 1 minute, stirring often. Stir in the lemon juice.

❧ Remove from the heat and allow to cool for 15 to 20 minutes. Remove the bay leaves. With the lid of your blender tightly in place, puree in batches, starting first on low speed and gradually increasing the speed to blend to the desired consistency. Some folks like this with a little texture, or you can puree longer for a silky puree. Serve at once with buttered toast and a garnish of fresh lemon and herbs.

Carolina Gold Rice and Boiled Peanut Perlau

I was never a big fan of risotto until I made it with Carolina Gold rice. At the risk of getting in trouble with the more militant fans of Italian cuisine, my feeling was always that Arborio rice, while contributing a marvelous texture, falls flat in the flavor department. Not so with Carolina Gold— this staple of the historic Carolina Rice Kitchen packs lots of flavor into each grain. Carolina Gold is a medium-grain rice, and it's phenomenally versatile, with a firm core to the grain that allows for separated-grain dishes like pilafs, pilaus, perlaus, and purloos; and a soft, starchy exterior that makes for great risottos if stirred while cooking.

This perlau is a summer regular of ours and is typically served with salmon at Big Jones, as the fresh peanut harvest typically begins as wild Alaskan salmon runs reach their summer peak. Besides salmon, this is also magnificent with roast or grilled chicken or guinea fowl.

You can certainly boil your own peanuts according to my recipe in this book (page 172), or look up the Lee Brothers Boiled Peanut Catalog—they ship anywhere in the country!

PREP TIME: 40 minutes
EQUIPMENT NEEDED: 2-quart saucepan, long-handled wooden spoon
SERVES: 4 as a main course or 8 as a side dish

6 tablespoons (¾ stick) unsalted butter, divided
½ cup shallots, finely minced
4 cloves garlic, mashed and minced
1 cup Carolina Gold rice
3 cups unsalted fish or chicken broth
¾ cup frozen English peas, defrosted
1 teaspoon kosher salt
½ teaspoon cayenne pepper
¾ cup shelled boiled peanuts

✦ Melt 2 tablespoons of the butter in a 2-quart saucepan over medium-high heat until foaming. Add the shallots and garlic, and sauté to sweat well, stirring constantly with a wooden spoon, but do not brown. Add the rice and sauté, toasting the grains until the rice releases its aroma, 1 to 2 minutes. Add 1 cup of the broth, and reduce heat to medium. Stir often but gently so as not to break the rice grains yet also to release some creamy starch from the grains into the broth. Return to a boil and cook until nearly all broth is incorporated, about 6 to 8 minutes. Add one more cup of broth, and continue cooking and stirring until once again most of the rice is incorporated, about 6 to 8 minutes. By now the rice is nearing fully cooked and is turning very sticky. Add the peas and the final cup of broth, and continue cooking and stirring until rice is tender and the perlau starts to come together—loose and creamy, but it should hold its shape somewhat when dropped from a spoon, very slowly dissolving back into the pot. Add the salt, cayenne, and boiled peanuts, then the remaining butter, stirring constantly until the butter is melted and the perlau is creamy. Serve at once.

Pickled Shrimp

We first made pickled shrimp to serve with deviled eggs, something we still stick to on many occasions. Shrimp are a very rich protein themselves, so this preparation in which they are marinated in a vinegary pickle before serving—kind of like a seviche of the South—is special because it gives them a refreshing, mouthwatering quality so they can pair with rich foods. I've always been mighty fond of combining shellfish with meats, and this is one of the best ways to do so, since the shrimp will add that layer of complexity only seafood can lend, but the marinade keeps it from becoming too rich or cloying.

I love these served with cold cuts and cheese—try them with some sliced tasso, pimiento cheese, and benne crackers (this plate will sound quite familiar to longtime guests) and a smear of good homemade mayonnaise. Chopped up and dressed with a little high-quality sesame oil, they make a fantastic salad dressing, or chop them up and add them to potato salad. No one will believe how good it is. Pickled shrimp also make a delicious garnish for Bloody Marys, and the leftover brine is a tasty way to spike your Bloody Mary mix.

PREP TIME: 90 minutes

EQUIPMENT NEEDED: 1-quart saucepan with tight-fitting lid, 4-quart stock pot, 4-quart or larger colander, mixing bowl, 1-quart canning jar or non-reactive container with tight-fitting lid

MAKES: 1 quart

STAGE ONE, PREPARE THE MARINADE

1½ cups distilled white vinegar

¾ cup water

1 tablespoon yellow mustard seeds

4 whole cloves

4 whole allspice berries

2 teaspoons whole black peppercorns

2½ teaspoons kosher salt

2 tablespoons granulated white sugar

 In a 1-quart saucepan, bring the vinegar and water to a boil with the mustard seed, cloves, allspice, peppercorns, salt, and sugar. Cover tightly, remove from heat, and allow to cool to room temperature while steeping, about 1 hour. In the meantime, prepare the shrimp.

STAGE TWO, COOKING AND PICKLING

2 quarts cold water

2 tablespoons kosher salt

6 bay leaves

2 medium yellow onions, peeled, one coarsely chopped, the other finely julienned, separated

1 teaspoon crushed red pepper

2 pounds raw shrimp, 40–50 or 50–70 count, peeled and deveined

Zest of 2 lemons (yellow part only) carefully peeled with a paring knife and finely julienned

1 tablespoon fresh ginger, peeled and minced

 In a 4-quart stock pot, bring the water to a boil with the salt, three of the bay leaves, the coarsely chopped onion, and red pepper, and allow to infuse for 10 minutes at a low boil. Add the shrimp, stir well, remove from the heat, and rest for 1 minute, then stir again. The shrimp should be gently cooked, pink, and a rich opaque white color (or pink depending on your shrimp).

Strain into a colander at once, and rinse with cold water to stop the cooking. Reserve the shrimp, and discard the cooked pieces of onion.

🦐 Rinse the julienned onion briefly under cold running water to remove the smelly sulfur aromas, then toss in a mixing bowl with the cooked shrimp, the remaining three bay leaves, lemon zest, and ginger, then pack into a 1-quart non-reactive storage container or jar with lid and cover with the marinade. The marinade might not quite cover the shrimp, but will after the shrimp absorb the brine and relax into the pickle. Cap tightly and refrigerate for at least 1 day before serving, or up to 2 weeks.

Creamy Grits

We cook up hundreds of pounds of grits a month, yielding big pots of hot, creamy cereal, so many people call us the grits experts. There are actually few recipes that are simpler or easier to master at home. The keys to good grits are the grits themselves (you want a stone-ground slow-cooking true hominy grit) and lots of stirring. Use a non-reactive pot since aluminum or iron pots can lead to discoloration. Many restaurant recipes call for whole milk or even half-and-half in addition to an injection of heavy whipping cream. I've always deemed this excessively rich, as some butter and cheese are rich enough as is. We want to taste the floral earthiness of the grits themselves, so it's best not to envelop them in a shroud of creamy milk fat. I've found that skim milk yields the best balance of dairy richness and earthy corn goodness, but if all you have on hand is whole milk, use half whole milk and half cold water.

We use Anson Mills coarse-ground white grits and recommend them without hesitation since they are certified organic and made from 100 percent heritage varieties of corn.

PREP TIME: 45 minutes
EQUIPMENT NEEDED: 2-quart non-reactive saucepan, sturdy wire whisk, wire
    mesh skimmer or slotted spoon
SERVES: 4 to 6

    1 quart skim milk
    2 teaspoons kosher salt

⅛ teaspoon cayenne pepper
1 scant cup coarsely ground hominy grits
2 ounces shredded sharp cheddar cheese
¼ cup (½ stick) unsalted butter, cut into small bits

🌱 In a 2-quart non-reactive saucepan, heat milk over medium-high heat just to a boil, stirring often. Add salt and cayenne, then add the grits in a steady stream, stirring constantly with a wire whisk. Allow to settle for a moment, then use a skimmer or slotted spoon to skim off the chaff that floats to the top of the milk before resuming stirring. Stir constantly over medium heat until mixture thickens slightly. Continue to stir often as grits cook, which will take 20 to 40 minutes depending on the thickness of the grind. The grits are done when the largest pieces are al dente but with a creamy center, not hard and starchy. Stir in the cheese and then the butter. Taste and add more salt or cayenne if desired, and serve at once.

Shrimp and Grits

One of the South's most distinctive dishes, shrimp and grits has ridden the wave of Southern cuisine to new heights of prominence nationally, popping up on menus from coast to coast and from south to north. When we opened our doors with this tasty combination in April 2008, we had no idea that we were on the leading edge of a trend—we just love the dish and think it tells a wonderful story about how the coastal South has fed itself for centuries.

I'm not the most-qualified food anthropologist around, but in my experience shrimp and grits is a very different animal in the Lowcountry than it is on the Gulf Coast—most versions I've seen in the west consist of some version of Creole or Cajun barbecued shrimp served over grits, whereas in the east it's more likely to be stewed or fricasseed in broth or gravy, with ham, bacon (or even in some cases—*gasp*—sausage), mushrooms, or other vegetables. I took a distinctively Louisiana ingredient—tasso—and used it in a gravy-based version of the dish, because I like the intense smoke and spicy complexity that tasso adds to the gravy. It also ensured that we would have a grits and gravy dish on the menu—a broad category of Southern dishes to be sure, but one I felt needed representation.

You're likely to get the best results by following three broad steps: (1) Prepare the gravy and maintain at a low simmer on the back burner while you cook the grits. (2) Cook the grits. (3) Return the gravy to the front burner, and cook the shrimp. This will allow you to serve the shrimp when they are just cooked and plump.

PREP TIME: 45 minutes
EQUIPMENT NEEDED: 12-inch cast-iron skillet, long-handled wooden spoon, long-handled slotted spoon
SERVES: 4 to 6

- ¼ cup (½ stick) unsalted butter
- ¼ cup tasso or other smoked ham, finely chopped into ⅛-inch pieces
- 3 tablespoons all-purpose flour
- ¼ cup yellow onion, finely diced
- 2 tablespoons celery, finely diced
- 2 tablespoons green bell pepper, finely diced
- 2 cloves garlic, smashed and minced
- ¼ cup shiitake mushrooms, stemmed and thinly sliced
- 1½ cups good strong chicken stock, unsalted
- ½ teaspoon dried thyme leaves
- ½ teaspoon freshly ground black pepper
- 1 bay leaf
- 1½ teaspoons kosher salt, or more to taste
- 1 tablespoon Worcestershire sauce
- 1 pound small Gulf of Mexico shrimp, 40–50 or 50–70 count, peeled and deveined

❧ In a 12-inch cast-iron skillet, melt the butter over medium-low heat until it begins to foam, then add the diced tasso or ham. Increase the heat to medium, and fry the tasso in the butter, stirring constantly with a wooden spoon until lightly browned and aromatic, about 4 to 6 minutes. Remove the skillet from the heat temporarily while you remove the tasso with a slotted spoon and set it aside.

❧ Return the skillet and butter to medium heat, then add the flour, stirring constantly with a wooden spoon, until the flour is lightly browned, relaxed, and creamy, not pasty. Being careful of splatter, add the onion, celery, bell pepper, and garlic to the roux, stirring constantly, until the vegetables are well sweated and translucent, about 4 to 6 minutes. Add the mushrooms, and cook until they sweat and turn soft, another 3 to 4 minutes.

🦐 Stirring constantly, add the chicken stock a little at a time and gradually increase heat to high. Bring to a boil while stirring regularly. Add the reserved tasso plus the thyme, pepper, bay leaf, salt, and Worcestershire. Reduce heat to a simmer, then cook for about 4 to 6 minutes to allow everything to harmonize.

🦐 Stir constantly while adding the shrimp, and continue stirring while the shrimp cook, about 2 to 3 minutes. The shrimp are done cooking as soon as they turn pink and opaque. Remove from heat, take out the bay leaf, and serve at once; don't try to hold or they will overcook.

Reezy-Peezy, ca. 1780

This simple dish of peas and rice is the one that first captured my imagination and led me down the path of historically dated dishes on the menu. When Anson Mills introduced Sea Island red peas in 2009, I was hooked. These delicious field peas originated in Africa and traveled to the Lowcountry very early in the slave trade. One of the older strains of crowder pea, together with Carolina Gold rice, they constitute the earliest American version of the dish we have come to know as hoppin' john.

Slaves knew the dish by a different name, reezy-peezy. Some believe the name was lent by Italian rice farmers who were brought into the Lowcountry to help develop a rice-growing system and brought the old Venetian dish *risi pisi* with them. How much the Italians actually taught the budding plantations isn't exactly known; however, the bulk of knowledge and expertise that set up the phenomenally successful rice industry in the Lowcountry was brought by the slaves themselves—it was African intellect and muscle. While the origin of the dish's name might possibly be Italian, there can be little doubt that it is African through and through: it was a staple in slave kitchens for generations, at harvest and New Year's celebrations, during which they'd eat their ancestral peas with rice middlins—the grains that were broken during milling and wouldn't be shipped abroad for sale and were thus sometimes left to slave rations.

In order to bring this dish to entrée proportions, I pair it with seasonal market vegetables cooked over the wood fire, since this comes as close in spirit to slaves cooking one of their most traditional dishes at home with vegetables from their gardens—which slaves in the Lowcountry were allowed to keep on their own time. I did take one leap away from this ancient tradition, using laurel-aged Charleston Gold rice, a recently developed aromatic rice. For a novel texture, we cook the rice and shape it into a cake so that it can be grilled over the fire along with the vegetables.

In the early days of American rice cultivation, there were no seed dealers or stores, and every plantation had to maintain its own seed bank, storing three years' worth of seeds from harvest in the event of crop failure. To preserve the seed rice, it was stored in oak barrels lined and layered with laurel leaves, the wild bay relative native to the Deep South. At the end of three years, if your crops were successful, you were free to either sell the rice for seed, mill it and sell it, or, even better, eat it. The rice picks up the most wondrous vanillin and wood aromas from the barrel; herbaceous green, grassy, and leafy aromas from the laurel. Plus each individual grain would be cured into a more tightly bound package, making it cook into a distinctively delicate texture. Charleston Gold, an aromatic rice variety distinct from Carolina Gold, makes the best laurel-aged rice and is the variety that Anson Mills uses to make this gem of a grain.

Each year when we have local farmers' market vegetables as beautiful as slaves would have grown in their own gardens, I put reezy-peezy on the menu. It's not the only dish by which we can remember what they have left us as a nation—virtually every Southern dish has either African origins or evolved from European cooking under the skilled hands and watchful eyes of slaves. But it's one of my favorites, as peas and rice have fed generations of southerners, seeing many a family—black and white—through hard times, and have since earned a special place on the Southern table for all of us today.

The date 1780 links this dish to a time and place when you could have found these very peas and rice together in a bowl in the South—it gives it added meaning in my opinion, opening dialogue with many customers on a daily basis, and is a chance to teach Southern culinary history.

PREP TIME: 4 hours for pea gravy and rice cakes (may be done ahead of time), 45 minutes for mixed grill

EQUIPMENT NEEDED: two 2-quart saucepans with tight-fitting lids, long-handled wooden spoon, 4-quart mixing bowl, 9-by-9-inch cake pan, gas or charcoal grill, pastry brush, grilling tongs and spatula, serving platters

SERVES: 4 to 6

SEA ISLAND PEA GRAVY
1 tablespoon vegetable oil
1 cup shallots, minced
2 tablespoons fresh garlic, minced
1 cup dried Sea Island red peas
3½ cups unsalted mushroom broth, plus more as needed
2 tablespoons sherry vinegar
1 teaspoon freshly ground black pepper
1 tablespoon Spanish paprika
2 teaspoons kosher salt
2 bay leaves

❧ In a 2-quart or larger saucepan, heat the oil until smoking, then add the shallots and garlic. Sauté, stirring constantly with a wooden spoon, until the shallots are translucent and just start to brown, about 3 to 4 minutes. Add the remaining ingredients, and bring to a boil. Reduce to a simmer and cook, stirring regularly, for 3 to 4 hours, until the peas are long since cooked, begin to fall apart, and have thickened into a gravy. If the mixture becomes too thick or dry, add a little more broth or water as needed. Check seasoning and add more salt, cayenne, or vinegar if desired. Remove bay leaves. Serve at once or refrigerate up to 1 week.

❧ While the peas are cooking, make the rice cakes.

LAUREL-AGED CHARLESTON GOLD RICE CAKE
2 tablespoons first-press sesame oil, untoasted
½ cup shallots, minced
1½ cups laurel-aged Charleston Gold rice or Carolina Gold rice
2 cups cold water
1 bay leaf
1 teaspoon kosher salt

In a 2-quart or larger saucepan, cook the shallots in the sesame oil over medium heat until translucent, 5 to 6 minutes. Add remaining ingredients, bring to a boil, cover tightly, and reduce heat to a simmer. Steam until rice is evenly cooked extra tender—you're looking for rice that is slightly overcooked and soft, which will take 20 to 25 minutes. Remove from heat and allow to steam further, covered, an extra 15 minutes. Turn out into a 4-quart mixing bowl. While still steaming hot, use the back of a wooden spoon to beat the rice, working downward into the bowl to avoid tossing rice out of the bowl, until the rice forms a cohesive, yet grainy, mass.

Butter and line a 9-by-9-inch cake pan with plastic wrap, then turn the beaten rice out into the cake pan and cover with plastic. Wearing kitchen gloves, carefully press and form the rice into a square cake just under an inch thick, about ¾ inch. Make sure plastic wrap is sealed tightly around the edges of the rice, cool to room temperature for 1 hour, and refrigerate overnight.

The following day, cut into 2-inch or 3-inch squares depending on your desired number of servings.

THE MIXED GRILL

2 to 3 king trumpet (matsutake) mushrooms, or other meaty mushroom such as porcini or portobello
1 spring onion or cipollini onion, with green top, skinned
1 baby zucchini, cymling, or summer squash per person
1 rice cake per person
1 recipe Sea Island pea gravy
Extra-virgin olive oil, for basting
Kosher salt
Freshly ground black pepper
2 heads radicchio or endive
Basic vinaigrette, for dressing the radicchio or endive
Chow-chow (page 219), on the side
Pickle juice from chow-chow, on the side

Have pea gravy hot and ready on the back burner of the stove during grilling, so it's ready to pull the final dish together. At home this is easiest served family style, with a platter of each ingredient ready for guests to dish themselves, rather than plating individually.

Prepare your charcoal or gas grill to moderate heat, enough to cook the vegetables through before they overly char. If you have a grill thermometer, about 350°F at the cooking surface is ideal.

🌱 Split the king trumpet mushrooms lengthwise, and trim any other vegetables into a grill-friendly thickness, ½ inch or slightly more. Place each vegetable and the rice cakes on a large serving tray so they can be basted before grilling. Using a pastry brush, brush the mushrooms, onion, squash, and rice cakes with olive oil, and season with salt and pepper. Arrange the rice cakes and vegetables over the grill, observing where the hottest spots are and arranging the thickest parts of the vegetables over those. Depending on the thickness of your vegetables, they will take 6 to 10 minutes to cook. Once the vegetables are nearly finished, begin to move to the cooler sides of the grill to hold while you cook the radicchio or endive. Dress the radicchio or endive with vinaigrette, salt, and pepper, and set over the hottest spot on the grill. Cook just to wilt, and hopefully get some char on the edges, about 30 seconds to 1 minute per side, so watch closely. Arrange everything on serving platters and serve up with the pea gravy, plus chow-chow, pickle juice, and extra olive oil as condiments.

Mustard Barbecue Sauce

Since I'm putting this recipe down in writing, it feels a bit as if I'm just asking for trouble, wandering into the world of South Carolina barbecue. If you've ever had whole hog barbecue done in any one of the Carolina styles by a capable pitmaster, you already understand that barbecue can be a transcendent experience and thusly raises heated passions.

My family's German ancestry may be what seared into my tongue a taste for mustard. While my goal is to tell as many Southern stories as I can through food, I often gravitate toward the German influences in Southern cooking because of their unique (and delicious) contributions to the cuisines of the Lowcountry, Appalachia, Kentucky, and south Louisiana in particular. In the sea of regional Carolina barbecues, the mustard-laden sauce common in central and coastal South Carolina stood out to me as particularly unique and interesting among the many Southern barbecue sauces. To boot, the added pungency from good mustard helps cut the richness of my favorite cuts of whole hog barbecue—the jowl, lower belly, and collar.

Almost every recipe you'll come across for this sauce from other sources will call for American yellow mustard. I opted for Creole mustard for a few reasons. Creole mustard is a German contribution to south Louisiana's foodways; its brown mustard seed and whole-grain composition undoubtedly make it more like mustards Germans would also have brought with them to the east Carolinas during the eighteenth century. Thus, I believe it is likely closer to the roots of the mustard barbecue in spite of the yellow mustard that is commonplace today. As a matter of personal preference as well, the heavy turmeric flavor you get in yellow mustard is just too bitter. I prefer to stick with the clean, pure mustard flavor of Creole mustard. You can, of course, use your favorite mustard in the recipe. If you can't find Creole mustard, you can use a German Dusseldorfer mustard, or look for a brown mustard such as Koops' or Gulden's.

Serve this with smoked pork, especially smoked pork shoulder—or if you are truly ambitious, barbecued suckling pig or even whole hog.

PREP TIME: 1 hour

EQUIPMENT NEEDED: 4-quart non-reactive saucepan with tight-fitting lid, long-handled wooden spoon, blender

MAKES: 6 cups

1 tablespoon vegetable oil
2 cups yellow onion, coarsely chopped
4 cloves garlic, crushed
2 teaspoons crushed red pepper
¼ teaspoon ground cloves
2 bay leaves
2 teaspoons dried thyme
2 teaspoons freshly ground black pepper
3 cups distilled white vinegar
2 cups pork stock or water
¼ cup Worcestershire sauce
½ cup Creole mustard
1 tablespoon kosher salt

❦ In a 4-quart non-reactive saucepan, heat the vegetable oil over high heat until a piece of onion dropped into the pot sizzles rapidly. Add the onions and garlic, and sauté, stirring constantly with a wooden spoon, until the vegetables give up their liquid, turn translucent, and just start to brown, about 5 to 6 minutes. Add the crushed pepper, cloves, bay leaves, thyme, and black pepper, and sauté a moment until the spices give up their aroma, about another 3 to 4 minutes. Add the vinegar, pork stock or water, Worcestershire, mustard, and salt, and bring to a boil. Reduce heat to a simmer, cover with a tight-fitting lid, and simmer for 30 minutes. Remove from heat, take the lid off the pot, and allow to cool for 30 minutes or until lukewarm before proceeding.

⚜ After removing the bay leaves, puree mixture in batches in your blender. Be sure to start your blender on low speed and gradually increase to high. Puree until smooth. Place in a tightly sealed container in the refrigerator until needed. Will keep for several weeks in the refrigerator.

Sea Island Benne Cake

While we've become known for our historically inspired recipes, oftentimes our dishes are inspired by ingredients, pure and simple. That's even better when an ingredient is a heritage crop that was long forgotten in spite of its being uniquely Southern. This is why I love working with Anson Mills—they are regularly coming up with long-lost heritage crops of the South, the Lowcountry in particular, from Purple Cape beans and Sea Island peas to laurel-aged rice and this gem: bennecake flour.

A staple of slave kitchens in the Lowcountry, bennecake is the product of Sea Island benne, an heirloom sesame that followed slaves from Africa to the Lowcountry, and which bears so little resemblance to modern sesame it would be misleading to call it such. Modern sesame is an oilseed developed to maximize oil content, while this early heirloom benne was much higher in protein and has a more pronounced nutty flavor with quite a nice tangy green vegetal bitterness.

To make bennecake flour, they would simmer the seeds in water, then decant them to draw off the water and oil. The oil would be used in other cooking, and the seeds would then be dried and pounded into a fine flour for cookies, pones, and such. I have found bennecake flour makes wonderful biscuits, waffles, cookies, and this delicious cake, basically a sponge cake. The flavor of benne and honey are pure magic together, although you'll want a fairly rich honey such as wildflower or gallberry, because the benne's strong nutty flavor will overwhelm more delicate honeys such as clover, sourwood, or tupelo.

Ice this cake with roux icing. If you want to give the finished cake an extra badass layer of flavor, make a roux with the flour in the recipe and just enough butter to wet it, and cook the roux to peanut-brown before adding the milk and boiling. It will add a nutty, toasty layer of complexity that really sets off the icing. Always be sure to chill the boiled milk thoroughly before proceeding to make the icing.

PREP TIME: 90 minutes for the cake, 30 minutes for the roux icing, 20 minutes to ice the cake

EQUIPMENT NEEDED: three 8-inch cake pans, cookie sheet, two 4-quart mixing bowls, sifter, stand mixer with flat beater attachment or hand mixer, wire whisk, rubber spatula, wire cooling rack

MAKES: one 8-inch three-layer cake

> 1 cup Sea Island benne (see "Notes on Sources")
> 1½ cups sifted all-purpose flour
> 1 cup sifted bennecake flour
> 1 teaspoon baking soda
> 1 teaspoon kosher salt
> 1½ cups granulated sugar, divided
> ½ cup (1 stick) unsalted butter, at room temperature
> ½ cup vegetable oil
> ½ cup rich honey—wildflower or gallberry
> 5 large eggs, separated
> 1 tablespoon pure vanilla extract
> 1 cup lowfat buttermilk

🌾 Preheat oven to 325°F. Butter and flour three 8-inch cake pans and reserve. Spread the benne seed evenly on a dry un-oiled cookie sheet, and bake in a 325°F oven until lightly toasted and fragrant, about 15 minutes. Allow to cool on a counter or baking rack while you prepare the rest of the batter.

🌾 Place the flours, baking soda, and salt in a 4-quart mixing bowl, then sift together to combine thoroughly.

🌾 In a stand mixer with the flat beater attachment or a hand mixer, cream the butter and 1 cup sugar together with the egg yolks until light and fluffy. Then beat in the vegetable oil a tablespoon at a time, incorporating thoroughly before each next addition. Continue beating while you add the honey and vanilla, beating until creamy and thick. Reducing speed to low, gently mix in the toasted and cooled benne seeds.

♔ In a separate bowl whip the egg whites with a wire whisk to soft peaks, sprinkle with the remaining ½ cup sugar, and beat until peaks are nearly stiff.

♔ With a rubber spatula, fold by hand the combined flours and the buttermilk into the yolk mixture one-third at a time, starting with flour, then buttermilk, then flour, until all is incorporated, constantly turning the bottom over the top to ensure a smooth batter. Fold in the egg whites in thirds, being careful not to overwork the batter.

♔ Divide the batter between three buttered and floured 8-inch cake pans, and bake in a 325°F oven until they pass the toothpick test, 30 to 40 minutes. Cool 10 minutes on a wire rack before turning the cakes out onto the cooling rack. Wrap lightly with plastic wrap, and refrigerate or freeze thoroughly before icing with roux icing.

Roux Icing

Roux icing—aka butter roux icing or boiled milk icing—is one of those preparations whose roots are murky, with the specifics probably forever lost to the ages. What we can be somewhat sure of is that this particular icing became increasingly popular during the Great Depression, possibly as a means of stretching a household's butter, an expensive ingredient during lean times. It appears in many cookbooks during the 1930s and '40s; as the 1950s and '60s rolled on, it became increasingly rare in print, overtaken by the much simpler preparation of cream cheese icing—a use that was aggressively and successfully promoted by cream cheese manufacturers during those decades as industrial processed foods encroached upon traditional foodways.

While a well-made cream cheese icing is magnificent and worthy of every cook's repertoire, it's a shame that it overtook roux icing so completely that roux icing is virtually unheard of today. Roux icing is rich, spectacularly so, as is cream cheese icing, but it also has the most beguiling velveteen texture lent by the boiled flour. This gives it a lightness that seems inconceivable given the calories involved. Rather than coating the palate and overwhelming the senses, it glides across it as if on air, making its gentle vanilla perfume all the sweeter. Roux icing has an elegance to which cream cheese icing can never pretend. When you have a cake that is nuanced in flavor and you want an elegant white icing, this is the one. When you have a rich, decadent cake that you want to throw over the top, you might think about cream cheese icing.

For this icing to turn out well, it is essential that you're working in a relatively cool room (ideally 65°F to 70°F). If it's summertime and hot outside, have your air-conditioning on.

PREP TIME: 20 minutes for the boiled milk, 1 hour to chill (may be done ahead of time), 20 minutes to prepare icing

EQUIPMENT NEEDED: 1-quart saucepan, wire whisk, stand mixer with flat beater attachment

ICES: one 8-inch three-layer cake

1½ cups whole milk
¼ cup plus 2 tablespoons all-purpose flour
1 teaspoon kosher salt
2 cups (4 sticks) unsalted butter, at room temperature, cut into 1-inch pieces
1½ cups granulated sugar
1 tablespoon vanilla extract
¾ cup sour cream

❦ Place the milk, flour, and salt in a 1-quart saucepan over medium-low heat, and whisk thoroughly to incorporate and work out any lumps of flour. Slowly bring to a boil, whisking constantly to prevent flour from sticking to the bottom and scorching. It will take 10 to 15 minutes for the mixture to boil.

❦ Once the mixture has boiled, it will be very thick. Beat well with your whisk, then set aside to cool for a few minutes. Once it's at room temperature (15 to 20 minutes depending on the size and shape of your saucepan), cover with plastic wrap and refrigerate for at least an hour, or up to 5 days before using.

❦ Place the 1-inch pieces of butter and the sugar into the bowl of a stand mixer. Using the flat beater attachment, begin mixing on low speed until the butter and sugar are combined. Gradually turn up speed to high, and cream the butter and sugar together until the mixture is light and fluffy but the sugar granules are not yet completely dissolved, about 5 minutes.

🌾 Turn mixer to medium speed, and add the vanilla extract. Then, a heaping tablespoonful at a time, beat in the chilled boiled-milk mixture. Return the mixer to high speed, and beat until the mixture is light and fluffy, with the sugar granules completely dissolved so the icing is light, airy, and super smooth. This will take 10 to 15 minutes.

🌾 Once the icing is light, fluffy, and smooth, beat in the sour cream. Taste and add a little more salt if you like. Ice your cake at once.

🌾 Pro baker's tip: it's easier to ice frozen cake than freshly baked! If you do choose to freeze your cake before icing it, allow time for the iced cake to rest at room temperature for a couple of hours before serving, so it can thaw all the way to the center.

Sea Island Benne Ice Cream

This was the first recipe I made when we received our inaugural delivery of Anson Mills heritage Sea Island benne. I've always been a huge fan of those delicious sesame and honey candies you can find in Middle Eastern markets and thought that this simple flavor profile would score big with two very Southern ingredients: honey and Sea Island benne. When I put out word to our social media audience that a Big Jones cookbook might be in the works, one of our longtime customers who's also a first-rate cook and food blogger asked for this recipe to be included, and I had to oblige.

Sea Island benne ice cream is rarely offered anymore because we do so much else with benne, but I definitely want to share this recipe because you should absolutely make it. It's dynamite. Many of our Sea Island benne recipes will not turn out well if made with regular sesame seeds, but this one surely will, so make the substitution if need be. You can even use black sesame seeds if you want, which will bleed color and yield an eerie, haunting gray ice cream that's just delicious.

PREP TIME: 30 minutes for custard base, 30 minutes for freezing
EQUIPMENT NEEDED: cookie sheet, 2-quart non-reactive saucepan, wire whisk, 4-quart mixing bowl, fine-mesh strainer, 2-quart or larger ice cream freezer
MAKES: 1½ quarts

½ cup Sea Island benne (see "Notes on Sources")
½ cup granulated sugar
½ cup bright honey, such as sourwood or clover
2 cups heavy cream
2 cups skim milk
2 teaspoons pure vanilla extract
1 teaspoon kosher salt
6 egg yolks

♛ Toast the benne on a cookie sheet in a 350°F oven for 12 minutes and cool before using. Place the sugar, honey, cream, milk, vanilla, and salt in a 2-quart non-reactive saucepan and whisk to combine, then slowly bring to a low boil over medium heat, stirring regularly. Separate the 6 egg yolks into a 4-quart mixing bowl and whisk by hand until smooth. While whisking, add a tablespoon of the hot milk mixture to temper the yolks, whisk to incorporate, then add a bit more, and add the remaining mixture in a thin steady stream, whisking constantly. Whisk periodically while cooling for a half hour. Strain the custard through a fine-mesh strainer, and stir in the toasted benne seeds. Cover tightly and refrigerate for at least 6 hours or overnight before freezing according to your ice cream freezer's manufacturer's instructions.

Coconut Cream Cake

Because of things like this cake, I have a sweet tooth.

There are nearly as many recipes for coconut cake as there are bakers in the South. Here, you have the recipe that is one of our most requested year-round, even though we only serve this cake a few days a year. If you want to make a good impression with your own home cooking, this cake is a good place to start.

The South is a wonderland of cakes, and while a good coconut cake is treasured across the region, early receipt books place coconut on the East Coast even before coconut cake appeared as a recipe in its own right in Annabella Hill's *Mrs. Hill's New Cook Book*, written in Georgia in 1867. Coconut appears in Harriott Pinckney Horry's *A Colonial Plantation Cookbook* from 1770 (South Carolina Lowcountry) and Mary Randolph's *The Virginia Housewife* from 1824 (Richmond, Virginia). Mary Virginia Hawes

Terhune's *Common Sense in the Household,* written in Richmond in the late 1860s, included cocoanut cake and ambrosia, and was the household standard cookbook for many East Coast households of the day. So, while the epicenter of this cake is not likely right in the Lowcountry, the Southeast is the broader region, and we all owe a debt of gratitude.

Over the course of the twentieth century, countless variations of coconut cake became traditional on many Southern holiday tables, so I put it on our first Thanksgiving menu and a Big Jones classic was born. Each year as the holidays approach and folks call for their Thanksgiving or Christmas Eve reservations, we are asked to confirm that this very cake will be on the menu. While we might tinker with the recipe a bit, I can't imagine ever taking this utter delight off of our signature holiday menus.

PREP TIME: 90 minutes for the cake, 30 minutes for the cream cheese icing, 20 minutes to ice the cake

EQUIPMENT NEEDED: three 8-inch cake pans, sifter, two 4-quart mixing bowls, stand mixer with wire whip attachment, rubber spatula, wire whisk or hand mixer, wire cooling rack

MAKES: one 8-inch three-layer cake

> 2 cups all-purpose flour, sifted before measuring
> 1 teaspoon baking soda
> 1 teaspoon kosher salt
> 2 cups granulated sugar
> ½ cup (1 stick) unsalted butter, at room temperature
> 5 large eggs, separated
> ½ cup vegetable oil
> ½ cup pecans, ground in the food processor to the size of uncooked grains of rice
> 1 cup unsweetened shredded coconut
> 1 cup lowfat buttermilk

꽃 Preheat oven to 325°F. Butter and flour three 8-inch cake pans and have at the ready. Sift the flour, measure, and then resift into a 4-quart mixing bowl with the baking soda and salt, and set aside.

꽃 In your stand mixer with the wire whip attachment, cream 1 cup of the sugar with the butter until light and fluffy, beginning on low speed and gradually increasing to high speed, about 4 to 5 minutes. Reduce speed to low, and with the mixer running, add the egg yolks one at a time until all are incorporated. Increase speed back to high, and beat until light and fluffy, 4 to 5 minutes. Add in the oil in a steady stream, a little at a time, and continue to beat until creamy and light, another 2 to 3 minutes.

🐚 In a separate mixing bowl, either with a wire whisk or a hand mixer, whip the egg whites to soft peaks. Add the remaining cup of sugar, and beat to firm but not stiff peaks, and have at the ready.

🐚 Fold the pecans and coconut into the creamed butter and yolk mixture. Fold in one-third of the flour mixture, followed by one-third of the buttermilk, and repeat until all flour and buttermilk are incorporated, being careful to work out any lumps of flour. Fold in whipped egg whites a third at a time. You should have a light, fluffy cake batter.

🐚 Divide batter between three prepared cake pans, and bake on the center rack of your preheated oven until a toothpick comes clean, 35 to 40 minutes. Cool in the cake pans on a wire rack for 10 minutes before turning cakes out to cool on the wire rack. Gently wrap in plastic wrap and refrigerate or freeze thoroughly before icing with cream cheese icing. For an extra flourish, dust the sides of the frosted cake with crushed pecans and toasted sweetened coconut.

Cream Cheese Icing

Another of my not-so-secret childhood weaknesses: I used to go to the trouble of making carrot cake just so I'd have an excuse to make this icing. We all know it, most of us love it, and while many pastry elites might deem it a boorish preparation more fit for plebes than those with sophisticated palates, I disagree and maintain that this popular and easy icing has a proper place in every cook's repertoire. I will say I believe it's horribly overused and encourage you to think of making a roux icing in many instances where you want a white icing; but occasionally you do want a rich, over-the-top icing that makes a decadent cake seriously killer, as with my Coconut Cream Cake. For more nuanced cakes with delicate flavors, use a roux icing.

PREP TIME: 30 minutes
EQUIPMENT NEEDED: stand mixer with wire whip attachment, rubber spatula
ICES: one 8-inch three-layer cake

1 cup (2 sticks) unsalted butter, at room temperature
1 cup powdered sugar, sifted before measuring
1 pound cream cheese, cut into 1-inch pieces
1 teaspoon kosher salt
2 teaspoons pure vanilla extract
3 tablespoons milk (skim, whole, and lowfat all work fine)

❦ In the bowl of your stand mixer with the wire whip attachment, combine the butter and sugar on low speed, then turn to high speed and beat until light and fluffy, about 5 to 6 minutes. Periodically raise the mixer and scrape down the sides with a rubber spatula for even mixing. Reduce speed to low, and add the cream cheese in bits, incorporating after each addition, then return speed to high and beat the whole until light and fluffy, about 5 to 6 minutes. Add the salt, vanilla, and milk a little at a time, and beat until smooth, 1 to 2 minutes. Ice your prepared and chilled cake at once—this icing is difficult to use when chilled, and must be refrigerated if not being served right away. Refrigerate frosted cake until 1 hour before you are ready to serve, then set out to allow icing to soften.

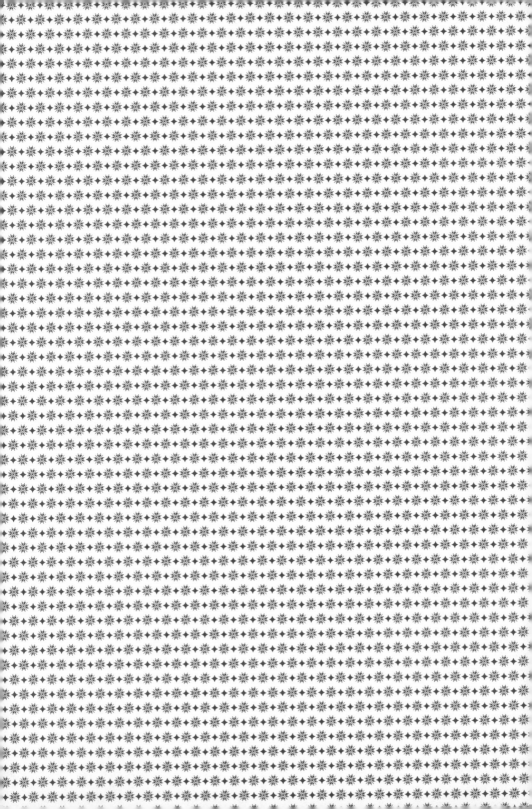

South Louisiana

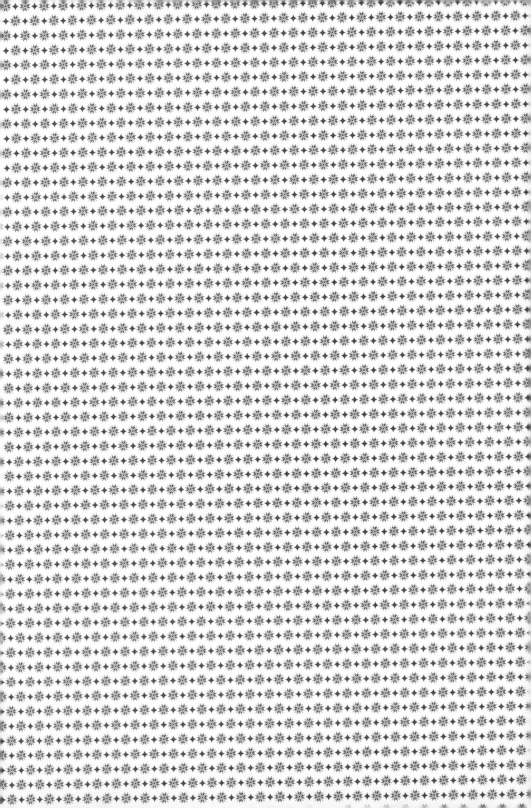

It's safe to assume many non-southerners or would-be southerners first develop a taste for Southern cooking through the lens of south Louisiana, most likely via New Orleans, as it is a popular tourist destination and the culinary traditions in the Big Easy are unrivaled in the United States.

The cooking of this land of bayous, swamps, levees, and the big river is often lumped into a catch-all term, Cajun/Creole, which is a moniker I despise because it fails to recognize the beautiful nuances of those two very distinct cuisines. While it's true that the Cajuns and Creoles share many dishes in common, this was rarely the case in the past; the two cuisines only started to converge somewhat during the mid-twentieth century as newspapers and television from the big city started to make their way out into the country, and Cajuns going to work on oil rigs in the Gulf brought home a taste for seafood, which previously was something you'd see on many a Creole table, but rarely on a Cajun one.

So what makes Creole and Cajun cuisines distinctive? As with any other regional cuisine, the first place to look for clues is in the history and foodways of the area's ethnic groups. The Creoles populated New Orleans and plantations upriver; by the late nineteenth century, people of African descent, French, Spanish, Italian, German, Irish, and Native American could all be considered Creole if they blended into the French language–based culture of New Orleans and surrounding areas. Because of the varying degrees of assimilation, the primary influences on Creole cuisine and culture are French and African, with more minor contributions from Germans, Italians, Spanish, and today Latinos and Vietnamese. Nonetheless, because the urban culture and tastemakers were largely driven by the demands of New Orleans' planter and merchant classes, Creole cuisine is urbane, sophisticated, rich, and draws upon a wide range of ingredients. The original Cajuns were a penniless group of Caucasians kicked out of Canada by the British Crown. They lived a hardscrabble, subsistence life out in the bayous and swamps of south Louisiana, drawing upon Native American influence and, to a lesser extent, African and a little peppering of German from the farmers who settled upriver from New Orleans along what became known as the German Coast. Being of modest means, the cuisine is simpler and more rustic, yet in many ways even more exotic than its Creole counterpart from New Orleans because Cajun cooking evolved during a long period of relative isolation.

According to Marcelle Bienvenu's history of Cajun cuisine, *Stir the Pot*, much of what we know today as Cajun cooking is the result of marketing and even a bit of hucksterism on the part of people seeking to capitalize on the growing fame of Cajun country cooking. While the cuisine continues to evolve, as does any regional cuisine, the basics still ring true. Pork is king of meats in most of Acadiana, as Cajun country is often called, although in some areas beef was an important meat. Chickens, or yardbirds, were more often kept for eggs than meat, but older hens would often find themselves in the gumbo pot along with sausage and any other bits deemed worthy. It's hard to imagine something as iconic as rice in Cajun cooking actually being a relative newcomer to the Cajun table. The Cajun rice culture emerged in the twentieth century, as the rice industry—which expanded dramatically in the Delta region following the collapse of the rice industry in the Lowcountry after emancipation—took hold and rice was promoted locally; this provided opportunities to grow the crop as well as consume it. Even the iconic boudin, the liver-and-rice sausage that is one of Cajun cuisine's signature dishes, was made with cornmeal (surely in a fashion not unlike the Carolinas' livermush) until sometime in the early twentieth century.

An important event in Cajun cuisine has historically been the boucherie, or butchering party: large, festive, multi-family gatherings during which hogs were brought out into the yard and butchered, each part of the animal being processed and put to good use. Boucheries typically took place in winter because the butchering was done outdoors and the cold weather helped preserve the meat while processing was done. At the end of the day, there would be boudin, head cheese, smoked sausages, sometimes tasso, and, by the twentieth century, often andouille, plus fresh cuts that would be salted or pickled to preserve them until they would be used in the kitchen.

Wild game was important in many Cajun households and has been historically abundant in the area's wild country, from alligator to frog legs, duck, deer, and anything else that moves. Frog legs and duck especially seem to be part of many time-honored family recipes you might still encounter today in households that hunt and cook.

Crawfish, that icon of the French Quarter's Cajun caricature, didn't become an important food in Acadiana until the 1950s at the earliest, although many Cajuns enjoyed their sweet meat much earlier. Typically associated with slave cabin and sharecropper scavenging in earlier generations, prior to the 1950s few Cajuns would admit publicly to enjoying them because crawfish were poor folks' food, and to admit eating them was to subscribe oneself to a lower social status. By the 1970s, with the rise of Cajun Paul Prudhomme to national fame as a chef, crawfish became a symbol of Cajun cooking, and eventually crawfish étouffée became one of the most popular dishes in Cajun restaurants.

Creole cooking is the offspring of the many influences previously mentioned. It evolved in the hands of highly skilled cooks of African descent, first as slaves during the antebellum period and then as servants in New Orleans' and rural plantations' wealthy households. Through the twentieth century, this Haute Creole cooking continued to evolve in the hands of chefs in some of the world's most famous restaurants to serve elite guests with the money to spend on fine cuisine. Consequently, much Creole cooking can be rich, decadent, and expensive.

In contrast, Creolized African American cooking in New Orleans is invariably inexpensive at no cost to flavor—it's one of my favorite microcuisines in the South, with unique takes on gumbo and hot sausage, po' boys, red beans and rice, cornbread, delicious uses for pig parts such as feet and ears, and simple yet soulful vegetable dishes. It's a special privilege to be invited to dinner in a Tremé household that cooks.

What are some differences between Creole and Cajun that I can point to as examples? Gumbo, for one—as I explained earlier, it's a wildly regional dish. For starters, Cajun roux tend to be much darker, and seafood is not often found in the Cajun gumbo pot, at least not the historically accurate one. Cajuns also tend not to use so much okra in gumbo. Okra is a distinctively African influence and followed slaves into Creole foodways, thus came naturally to the households of Creoles of African descent and eventually became an important ingredient in Haute Creole seafood gumbos. Since Cajuns couldn't afford slaves—or, later, servants—okra came late to their table and still plays a minor role.

Creole gumbos will most often have okra in the event they have seafood, no okra if it's meat-based. However, Creole gumbo, at least in my observations, tends to have seafood in it, and seafood gumbos will often include tomatoes, rare in a Cajun gumbo. Creole roux are generally lighter than Cajun ones if they have a roux at all, and Creole gumbos are invariably thicker than Cajun gumbos, which are often thin and brothy. Confused yet? That's gumbo. There really aren't any rules, just some traditions and guidelines that reflect different influences.

You can also look at the preparation of something such as bread pudding—it didn't really exist in Cajun country until media brought Creole influences out into the bayous. Does that make bread pudding a Cajun dish or a Cajun/Creole dish? Just as a Yankee making grits in Chicago is still making Southern food, I'd say a Cajun making bread pudding in Lafayette is still making Creole food.

These two very distinctive cuisines make south Louisiana as exciting as any other culinary region on earth, and it's always been a challenge to adequately represent both the Cajuns and Creoles on our menus, but here are a few of our most popular recipes from south Louisiana.

Crawfish Boudin Fritters

Another one of the recipes we've served regularly since day one, crawfish boudin fritters might actually be considered another kind of croquette, since historically croquettes could be made with either potato or rice binders. I don't know when the Cajuns got creative with boudin, using base ingredients other than pork, but I think I actually prefer crawfish boudin over pork. In Cajun country, boudin is most often stuffed in natural hog casings, and to eat it you break the casing and squeeze the filling out, either directly into your mouth if you're properly hard-core, or onto a plate to eat like rice dressing, since it's a fairly loose and soft sausage. For more proper occasions or to serve as finger food at parties, boudin is sometimes shaped into balls and deep fried, the inspiration for this preparation.

I'll say it many times throughout this book, but please only use American crawfish. Most domestic crawfish is from Louisiana, and that's what we use at Big Jones. If you see the imported stuff, pass it over and change plans. Friends don't let friends eat imported crawfish. For sources, see "Notes on Sources" (page 267).

PREP TIME: 1 hour to make the boudin, overnight to chill, 1 hour to bread and fry
EQUIPMENT NEEDED: 2-quart saucepan with tight-fitting lid, 4-quart cast-iron Dutch oven, long-handled wooden spoon, long-handled fork, cookie sheet with edges or jelly roll pan, small ice cream scoop, 2-quart mixing bowl, wire whisk, 9- or 10-inch pie pan, countertop deep fryer (optional

or use the 4-quart Dutch oven), digital clip-on thermometer, slotted spoon

MAKES: 15 to 20 fritters, serves 6 to 8

2 cups long-grain rice cooked in 3 cups water
1 tablespoon vegetable oil, plus 2 to 3 quarts for frying, divided
1 cup yellow onion, finely minced
1 teaspoon fresh garlic, minced
2 teaspoons kosher salt
1 teaspoon freshly ground black pepper
¼ teaspoon cayenne pepper
½ cup green onion tops, finely chopped
1 pound crawfish tail meat, coarsely chopped
3 large eggs
¾ cup cold water
1 pound dried French bread crumbs

❦ Cook the rice in a 2-quart saucepan with a tight-fitting lid, and have hot at the ready to make the boudin.

❦ In a 4-quart cast-iron Dutch oven, heat 1 tablespoon of the vegetable oil over high heat until smoking, then add the onion and garlic. Working quickly and stirring constantly with a wooden spoon, sauté to sweat well but do not brown the onions. This will take less than 2 minutes. Add the salt, black and cayenne peppers, green onion, and crawfish. Sauté until the crawfish renders a bit, giving up its liquid to the pot. Turn off heat and stir a few moments more. Fluff the rice with the tines of a fork, and add to the pot, stirring in well. Using the back of a wooden spoon, mash the rice into the crawfish a bit until everything begins sticking together like a rice dressing, but don't overdo it— you want a nice rice grain to the finished dish, not a mushy mess. Transfer to a cookie sheet with edges or a jelly roll pan, and spread out an inch thick to cool for a half hour, uncovered. Cover tightly with plastic wrap and refrigerate for at least 1 hour or overnight before breading and frying.

❦ Use a small ice cream scoop to shape the boudin into balls of about 3 tablespoons each. Gently roll between the palms of your hands to smooth on all sides, and place on a cookie sheet with plenty of space between each ball. In a 2-quart mixing bowl, beat the eggs until frothy with a wire whisk and then whisk in the water. Fill a 9- or 10-inch pie pan with bread crumbs, and hold any extra bread crumbs in reserve.

꙳ Roll each ball first in bread crumbs, and gently roll between your palms again to work in the bread crumbs; then roll in the egg wash, wetting all sides, and roll in the bread crumbs again. Roll a little more firmly after the second dip in bread crumbs, using your fingers and palms to finalize the shape of the fritter. Return breaded balls to the cookie sheet and continue until all have been breaded, then refrigerate, covered loosely with plastic wrap, until ready to fry.

꙳ Use a home deep fryer or 4-quart cast-iron Dutch oven with a digital clip-on thermometer for frying. Fill with 3 inches of vegetable oil. Heat oil to 325°F and watch temperature closely to maintain as close to this frying temperature as possible. Gently drop boudin balls in a few at a time, making sure there is plenty of space between each ball—don't overcrowd or they may not brown evenly. Turn occasionally while cooking. Fry for 5 to 6 minutes, until a deep rich golden-brown color. Remove with a slotted spoon and drain on paper towels. Keep in a low-temperature oven while you fry any remaining fritters. Serve hot with rémoulade (page 84) or cayenne mayonnaise.

Gumbo Ya-Ya

Gumbo Ya-Ya means different things to different people, although I have seen more than one translation giving the meaning of "Ya-Ya" as "everyone talking at once," which I always took to mean there could be just about anything in that gumbo pot. While our gumbo's base is always chicken and andouille sausage, I went with the broader term Gumbo Ya-Ya for its menu designation as kitchen odds and ends are often thrown into our gumbo pot—for instance, if we've been working on a steak dish and have beef trim sitting around, or in other cases veal, rabbit, or duck. We do not, because of allergies, ever add seafood to the Gumbo Ya-Ya, but you should feel free to add any other type of meat or seafood that strikes your fancy, as that's kind of the point of gumbo. If it runs, swims, crawls, flies, scampers, lies in wait, or just sits there getting fat, you can put it in gumbo.

About a year after we opened, I took a fateful trip out to Cajun country, ostensibly to eat boudin at as many places as I could on the Southern Foodways Alliance's Boudin Trail. But in the course of that journey, I was exposed to some roux that was darker, smokier, and more ballsy than any I'd attempted to date. It was at a small market in Port Barre. It tasted like char, and its bitterness stung just a little like a hot black espresso. I was hooked and began experimenting with darker and darker roux, sometimes taking them up to such a charred state that the finished product had a bite like bitter baking chocolate. This proved to be a little too dark even for me, so I pulled back a little bit on the darkness—but it's still way darker than you'll find almost anywhere in New Orleans, where the Creole roux are typically lighter, though still very brown.

Having settled on this very dark, almost black roux, our gumbo has since been the most divisive dish I've ever served on a menu. You either love it or you hate it. Its fans are legion, but not a week goes by without at least one dish of gumbo coming back to the kitchen for being "burnt." Never mind that we know what we're doing when we make our roux and that there is a very distinctive difference between charred and burned; folks take their most familiar reference point when describing their objection, so we take the verbiage in stride.

When making your roux, you will know if it's burned because the smell is nasty. If it smells nutty, smoky, chocolaty, or a lot like full city roast coffee, you're on the right track. The biggest telltale sign as far as appearance goes is black specks: if you've got black specks in your roux and it smells like fire, it's time to start over.

You'll have to experiment for yourself and decide how dark you like your roux. As I said, we like it very, very dark. You might like it lighter, looking for a milk chocolate color on the roux as opposed to dark chocolate or coffee. The great thing about the method here is that by adding the vegetables to the roux when you've achieved your desired color, you can stop the cooking of the roux at precisely the color you like—the addition of the cold vegetables will drop the temperature of the pot by a couple hundred degrees. Be careful though as it will still be hot enough to give you third-degree burns! You can then season, add stock, and build your gumbo up from there.

If you try to cook your roux separately and cool it before adding it to the pot where you have sautéed your vegetables, keep in mind that residual heat will keep cooking the roux long after you take it off the fire, so you will need to keep stirring for some time, and you may not get exactly the color you're looking for.

We serve this with steamed rice at Big Jones and encourage you to do the same. Hard-core Cajuns will actually plop a dollop of potato salad in their gumbo. Don't knock it till you try it—it's pretty freaking awesome.

PREP TIME: 3 hours

EQUIPMENT NEEDED: 10-by-18-inch baking sheet with edges, 2-quart bowl, 9-inch pie pan, 8-quart heavy-bottomed stock pot, large measuring cup, long-handled wooden spoon, 4-quart colander, 4-quart stock pot, small ladle

MAKES: 6 quarts

3 pounds andouille sausage, skin removed and diced

1 whole roasting chicken, 3 to 3½ pounds

2 quarts cold water

Enough vegetable oil that when combined with rendered chicken and andouille fat, you have 1½ cups

2 cups all-purpose flour

4 cups yellow onion, finely diced

1 cup green bell pepper, finely diced

1 cup celery, finely diced

¼ cup fresh garlic, mashed and minced

¼ cup Cajun seasoning (recipe follows)

4 bay leaves

2 tablespoons Worcestershire sauce

¼ cup Louisiana-style hot sauce

1 tablespoon kosher salt, or more to taste

☙ Preheat oven to 375°F.

☙ Remove the casing from the andouille by scoring one side of the sausage with the tip of your knife and peeling the skin away. Chop andouille into bite-size pieces, arrange in a single layer on an oiled baking sheet with edges, and place on top rack of oven. Bake until sausage is nicely browned and has rendered clear, reddish oil. If the oil in the pan is still milky or watery, return to the oven and bake longer. This will take approximately 45 minutes. Once well browned and rendered, carefully pour off the fat and reserve to use for the roux. Hold the sausage aside.

☙ Skin the chicken and debone completely. Chop the meat into bite-size pieces, and reserve in the refrigerator in a 2-quart bowl, covered, until needed. Place the skin in a 9-inch pie pan in the oven, and bake until fat is rendered and clear, the skin crispy, 60 to 90 minutes. Pour off the chicken fat, combining with the andouille fat, and reserve to make the roux. Discard the skin or chop and season with salt and pepper to garnish the gumbo when finished.

Place the bones in an 8-quart stock pot, and cover with 2 quarts cold water. Place over medium-high heat, and bring to a boil, using a small ladle to skim the top of any scum or foam that rises. Once boiling, reduce heat to a low boil and simmer stock while assembling the rest of your ingredients. Simmer for a total of an hour or more—this may be done ahead of time.

❦ Place the rendered chicken and andouille fats in a large measuring cup, and add enough vegetable oil to make 1½ cups total fat. In an 8-quart heavy-bottomed stock pot, heat the oils over medium-high heat until just smoking. Immediately turn off heat, and add flour to the hot fat, sprinkling it in gradually to avoid splatter, and stir with a wooden spoon. Turn the heat back up to medium, and continue cooking and stirring. Once flour starts to brown, gradually turn heat down to medium-low, but continue browning the flour, stirring constantly, until dark brown, the color of milk chocolate. This takes 30 to 40 minutes. Take the roux a little longer and darker if you like smoky gumbo, less so if not. Stir constantly to avoid burning. If you burn the roux, you'll know by the awful smell and will have to start over. Once you have the color you want, add the vegetables directly to the hot roux—be careful of the hot splatter! Stir in the onions, peppers, and celery. Cook, stirring constantly, until vegetables are soft, 6 to 8 minutes or longer depending on how much heat you're using—at this stage, medium heat is best.

❦ Strain the stock though a 4-quart colander into a 4-quart stock pot, discarding the bones. Add the stock, garlic, Cajun seasoning, browned andouille, reserved chicken, and bay leaves to the stock pot with the roux and vegetables. Set heat to medium-high, and bring to a boil, stirring often. Reduce heat to a simmer, and simmer until chicken is cooked and tender, which will take 15 to 20 minutes. Add Worcestershire, hot sauce, and salt, then check seasoning, adding more salt, pepper, or hot sauce if desired. Skim any excess oil from the top of the gumbo with a small ladle, and serve at once with Creole boiled rice (page 68).

Cajun Seasoning

This is the basic workhorse seasoning we use in many recipes. It makes quite a bit, so store it in an airtight container in a dark spot or in a spice tin. Be sure to use the best spices you can get your hands on—this makes all the difference.

¼ cup kosher salt
¼ cup celery salt
½ cup Spanish paprika
2 tablespoons cayenne pepper
¼ cup granulated garlic
¼ cup granulated onion
2 tablespoons dried thyme leaves
2 tablespoons ground basil
2 tablespoons ground oregano

⚜ Combine thoroughly and store in an airtight container.

Creole Boiled Rice

If you look up rice in enough old cookbooks, you'll notice the preferred method of cooking was the same as we use today for pasta, which is to boil it until done in a large surplus of seasoned water. Steaming rice, the most common form of preparation today, was often referred to in historic cookbooks as "the Chinese method." It's true that steaming retains a bit more nutrition, but there's something special about the discrete grains obtained by the traditional Creole method that I wanted to print a recipe for you to try. Especially with okra gumbos, the texture is just perfect.

PREP TIME: 40 minutes
EQUIPMENT NEEDED: 6- to 8-quart stock pot, long-handled wooden spoon, fine-mesh colander, serving bowl
MAKES: 4 to 5 cups, serves 4 to 6

1 gallon water
3 tablespoons kosher salt
½ teaspoon cayenne pepper
1 pound long-grain rice
3 tablespoons unsalted butter, cut into 3 to 4 pats

⚜ In a 6- to 8-quart stock pot, bring the water to a boil over high heat. Add the salt, cayenne, and then the rice. Turn heat down to medium to maintain a low boil, and cook, uncovered, stirring regularly from the bottom with a wooden spoon to make sure rice isn't sticking, until the rice is tender, 15 to 30 minutes depending on the rice. Strain through a fine-mesh colander like you would with pasta, turn into a serving bowl, and top with butter. Serve at once.

Gumbo z'Herbes

Long before Big Jones's doors even opened, I wondered what traditional options we'd have for Lent, given that Chicago is a very Catholic town. I soon started coming across recipes for Gumbo z'Herbes, a delicious gumbo that substitutes a multitude of greens for meat. Of course, most old-school receipts for Gumbo z'Herbes also call for a ham bone, which always amused me. Apparently a bone isn't considered meat in some parts.

It didn't take much experimentation to come up with a fully vegetarian version. By adding extra onion and a touch of tomato paste for their savory amino acids, and smoked paprika for a little smoke, you're unlikely to miss the ham bone.

You should absolutely use any cooking greens you want for this recipe, as in some parts of the country traditional greens such as turnips might be hard to come by certain times of year. Kale is an acceptable substitute, as is chard or spinach.

PREP TIME: 2 hours

EQUIPMENT NEEDED: 6- to 8-quart heavy-bottomed stock pot, long-handled wooden spoon, small ladle

MAKES: approximately 3 quarts, enough for a small party or several meals for a small family

1 cup vegetable oil
1 cup all-purpose flour
3 cups yellow onion, finely diced
2 ribs celery, finely diced
1 cup green bell pepper, finely diced
6 cloves garlic, mashed and minced
1 bottle (6 ounces) Louisiana-style hot sauce
1 tablespoon granulated garlic

2 tablespoons granulated onion

1 tablespoon freshly ground ground black pepper

2 tablespoons smoked paprika

1 teaspoon dried thyme leaves

1 quart mushroom stock, unsalted

4 packed cups finely chopped greens, including mostly collards, turnip
greens, and/or mustard greens; you can also use some parsley, rad-
ish, or carrot tops—the more greens the better

1 cup shiitake mushroom caps, thinly sliced

2 bay leaves

1 small can (6 ounces) tomato paste

2 tablespoons kosher salt

A few dashes Worcestershire sauce is optional, or you can use a good-
quality soy sauce

❦ In a 6- to 8-quart heavy-bottomed stock pot, heat the vegetable oil over medium-high heat until just smoking. Immediately turn off heat, and add flour to the hot fat, sprinkling it in gradually to avoid splatter, and stir with a wooden spoon. Turn the heat back up to medium, and continue cooking and stirring. Once flour starts to brown in 4 to 5 minutes, gradually turn heat down to medium low, but continue browning the flour, stirring constantly, until dark brown, the color of milk chocolate, another 45 minutes. Stir constantly to avoid burning. If you burn the roux, you'll know by the awful smell and will have to start over.

❦ Once you have the color you want, it's time to add the vegetables. Turn off the heat, and using a long-handled wooden spoon, stand back to avoid splatter while carefully adding the onions, celery, and bell peppers to the pot, then stir well. Return heat to medium, stirring constantly, until the vegetables sweat well and turn soft, 6 to 8 minutes. Add the garlic, hot sauce, and spices, then turn off the heat, and stir for a minute or two. Allow the roux to rest off the heat for 10 minutes to infuse. Add half the stock, and turn heat back to high. Stir to incorporate the roux to the stock, and bring to a low boil, stirring constantly, at which point the mixture will be very thick. Add the rest of the stock and return to a boil, then reduce heat to a simmer.

❦ Add the greens and mushrooms a cup at a time, adding the next cup after the previous is wilted and soft, stirring well before and after each addition. Once all greens are added and have wilted, add the bay leaves, tomato paste, and 1 tablespoon of the salt. Stir the pot well, reduce to a simmer, and simmer 1 hour uncovered, stirring regularly. Skim off and discard any fat that rises to the top, using a small ladle. After an hour, add the rest of the salt to your taste and Worcestershire or soy if desired. Serve over hot boiled rice.

Crawfish Étouffée

Étouffée is another perfect example of a distinctively regional Southern dish that is often subjected to the preconceived notions of authenticity that develop when folks have a limited experience with one regional variation. With étouffée, it's most likely to be an exposure to the New Orleans Creolized versions that are very often roux-based and tomato-heavy. In Cajun country, where crawfish étouffée originated, it often has no roux and might consist of nothing but butter, wine, onions, and maybe a few spices. Interestingly, early Creole recipes for smothered fish or shellfish more closely resembles this Cajun recipe than current Creole versions.

Legend (or facts, if you choose to believe the highly credible story) has it that the term *étouffée*, which means "smothered" in Acadian French, was first assigned to a dish of crawfish smothered in butter and wine in the late 1920s at the Hebert Inn in Breaux Bridge, when a French-speaking guest wandered into the kitchen and inquired what was cooking for dinner. In full French-speaking mode, the Hebert sister who was cooking replied simply that she was smothering crawfish, which came out as *étouffée*. Variations of this basic preparation exist from the 1790s in the Creole cooking of the region, more commonly using shrimp than crawfish. Talk about blurring the lines between Cajun and Creole!

Until the 1920s and '30s, crawfish were considered lowly laborer food and were still associated more with slave or sharecropper cooking than proper white folks' food. By the 1930s and '40s, more Cajuns started to "come out" as crawfish eaters, and south Louisiana cooking has never looked back.

PREP TIME: 30 minutes
EQUIPMENT NEEDED: 10-inch cast-iron skillet, long-handled wooden spoon
SERVES: 4 to 6

½ cup (1 stick) plus 2 tablespoons (¼ stick) cold unsalted butter, cut into ½-inch-thick pats and divided

½ cup yellow onion, finely diced

¼ cup green bell pepper, finely diced

¼ cup celery, finely diced

3 cloves garlic, mashed and minced

½ cup dry, fruity white wine

1 nice-size sprig of fresh thyme

1 pound of picked crawfish tails, with fat and juice

½ teaspoon cayenne pepper, or to taste

1 to 2 teaspoons kosher salt, or to taste

2 tablespoons freshly squeezed lemon juice

2 tablespoons Worcestershire sauce

¼ cup parsley, finely chopped

⚜ In a 10-inch cast-iron skillet over medium-high heat, melt 2 tablespoons butter until foaming but not brown. Add the onion, bell pepper, celery, and garlic all at once, and stir constantly while cooking until they sweat and turn translucent and soft but not brown, 2 to 3 minutes. Add the white wine and thyme, and bring to a boil while stirring regularly with a wooden spoon. Maintaining a brisk boil, reduce the wine by half, 2 to 3 minutes. Add the crawfish, pepper, and some of the salt, and return to a boil, stirring often. The crawfish will render some additional juice—continue at a brisk boil for 2 minutes to reduce until only ¼ inch of liquid remains in the bottom of the skillet. ⚜ Reduce heat to medium, and stir in the remaining ½ cup of butter, stirring constantly until all is melted and steaming hot. Remove from heat immediately once the butter has all melted and you see steam rising from the skillet. Do not boil or the sauce will break! Remove the thyme sprig, and season with lemon juice, Worcestershire, and parsley, plus additional salt and pepper as desired. Serve it up at once with hot steamed rice.

Barbecued Shrimp

One of my absolute favorite ways to enjoy crustaceans, the typical south Louisiana barbecued shrimp rarely has anything to do with a grill much less a wood fire, and is probably named simply for the piquant sauce with which it is served. This is a dish that is often passed off as Cajun in restaurants that seek to capitalize on the public's appetite for foods branded as such, but it's almost certainly Creole in origin. As I mentioned earlier, until recent decades there was little history of seafood in Acadiana, probably due to inadequate and expensive transportation and storage of highly perishable items such as fresh shrimp. While many Creoles in New Orleans and on plantations could make arrangements for any such item they wanted with less regard for cost, transportation and storage to concentrated markets such as New Orleans were far more efficient and cost effective than trying to distribute to a diffuse rural market.

Recipes also bear the mark of Creole cooking in other ways. It's easy to draw a line from receipts in Creole cookbooks for "smothered" fish or shellfish that called for gob-smacking quantities of butter and wine in addition to onions, fresh herbs, and other aromatics. Sometime in the twentieth century, heavy cream began to find itself in many of the recipes, as did Worcestershire and bracing quantities of spices, and at some point the dish became distinctive in its own right.

I enjoy this most when prepared with large, head-on Gulf of Mexico white shrimp. True aficionados enjoy the shrimp, shell and all, and I'll encourage you to give it a try. Crunching the shell amid the tangy sauce and shrimps' natural juices is a singular experience and delicious beyond words. Of course, if you can't fathom as much, you may certainly use peeled and deveined shrimp for this recipe: just add them at the end and cook them minimally so they are not tough. Serve with lots of French bread or toast for sopping up the outrageously tasty sauce.

PREP TIME: 30 minutes
EQUIPMENT NEEDED: 12-inch cast-iron skillet, long-handled wooden spoon
SERVES: 4 to 6

1 cup (2 sticks) plus 2 tablespoons (¼ stick) unsalted butter, chilled
    and cut into tablespoon-size bits, divided
¼ cup shallots, minced
4 cloves garlic, mashed and minced
1 tablespoon Creole seafood seasoning (recipe follows)
2 teaspoons freshly ground black pepper
1 teaspoon kosher salt
¼ cup fruity, dry white wine

½ cup Worcestershire sauce

2 tablespoons freshly squeezed lemon juice

1 3-inch sprig fresh rosemary

1 pound 8- to 12-count Gulf white shrimp, shell-on and head-on

French bread or toast, for dunking

※ In a 12-inch cast-iron skillet over medium-high heat, melt 2 tablespoons of the butter until foaming but not brown. Add the shallots and garlic, and sauté, stirring constantly with a wooden spoon, until the shallots are translucent, soft, and aromatic but not brown, about a minute. Add the Creole seafood seasoning and black pepper, and sauté a moment, until the spices give up their aroma, between 30 seconds and 1 minute. Add the salt, wine, Worcestershire, lemon juice, and rosemary, and bring to a boil. Reduce until the liquid thickens slightly, 3 to 5 minutes. Add the shrimp, and cook 1 to 2 minutes on each side, until they have turned pink throughout their heads and tails. Reduce heat to medium, and begin adding the rest of the butter bit by bit, swirling and rocking the entire skillet constantly to cook evenly and melt the butter throughout the pan, swirling it in as it melts. As each new addition of butter is nearly melted away, add another, continue stirring, and repeat until all butter has been added and melted into the sauce. Continue heating and stirring gently until steam rises from the pan, but do not boil or the sauce will break! Carefully transfer the shrimp to a serving bowl, and pour the sauce over the shrimp. Serve at once.

Creole Seafood Seasoning

This is the basic workhorse seasoning we use in many recipes. It makes quite a bit, so store it in an airtight container in a dark spot or in a spice tin. Be sure to use the best spices you can get your hands on—this makes all the difference.

6 tablespoons celery salt

½ cup Spanish paprika

2 tablespoons cayenne pepper

¼ cup granulated onion

2 tablespoons dried thyme leaves

1 tablespoon ground basil

1 tablespoon ground oregano

꽃 Combine thoroughly and store in an airtight container.

Red Beans

Red beans and rice is a dish of Creole origin, but it was also adopted by some parts of Cajun country as big-city newspapers and their recipes made their way into Cajun country during the early decades of the twentieth century. As simple as this combination is, it's been one of the most challenging dishes for me to master, since there are so many variables. It's true, you can cook up some beans with some seasonings, simmering them until they're nice and creamy, and serve them over rice with delicious results. But for me, beans and rice presented a special challenge to make the simple sublime.

In my recipe for pickled pig's feet (page 261), I discuss the use of pickled pork and how I arrived at pig's feet particularly. Of equal importance is the addition of way more onion than you might have thought prudent. In fact, I tell cooks just starting out on sauces and soups at Big Jones, "If you're not sure you've added enough onion, add more onion. If you're pretty sure you've added enough onion, add more onion. If you think you've added too much onion, add a little more." When cooked, one of onions' major by-products is glutamic acid, a non-essential amino acid that is nonetheless responsible for the fifth taste, *umami*. This is the Japanese word for savory. Onions will make your beans more savory, so why not pile them in? Tomato paste adds still more glutamic acid and helps slightly with thickening.

If your provisions are on the more conventional side, you can eliminate the pig's feet and substitute a couple tablespoons of white distilled vinegar and omit the pigskin. Your beans will still be mighty delicious.

PREP TIME: 2 hours prep, 5 hours braising time

EQUIPMENT NEEDED: 1-gallon heat-proof container, 2-gallon cast-iron or enamel Dutch oven with tight-fitting lid, 2-quart saucepan, long-handled wooden spoon, 8- to 12-ounce bowl, 12-inch cast-iron skillet,

cheesecloth, butcher twine, wire cooling rack, long-handled tongs
MAKES: 4 quarts

1 pound dried small red beans
2 quarts chicken or pork stock, plus 2 to 3 cups more as needed
Enough pigskin to line a 2-gallon Dutch oven—skin from one belly
    side is usually perfect (optional)
8 ounces smoked hog jowl or bacon, cut into ½ inch dice
3 cups yellow onion, finely diced
6 cloves garlic, mashed and minced
1 cup green bell pepper, finely diced
1 cup celery, finely diced
1 pickled pig's foot (optional) or 2 tablespoons distilled white vinegar
1 small can (6 ounces) tomato paste
1 teaspoon dried thyme
1 teaspoon rubbed sage
1 teaspoon cayenne pepper
1 tablespoon freshly ground black pepper
1 tablespoon Spanish paprika
4 bay leaves
1 tablespoon kosher salt, or more to taste
2 tablespoons Louisiana-style hot sauce
2 tablespoons Worcestershire sauce

꽃 Place red beans in a heat-proof 1-gallon container. Bring 2 quarts chicken or pork stock to a boil, and pour over the red beans. Allow to soak and cool for an hour while you prepare the rest of your ingredients.

꽃 Preheat oven to 325°F.

꽃 Line a 2-gallon cast-iron or enamel Dutch oven with a tight-fitting lid with fresh pigskin, draping the excess skin over the sides of the pot while you add the ingredients for the braise. (If you are making the red beans without pigskin, you may skip this step.)

꽃 In a 2-quart saucepan over medium-low heat, cook the smoked pork jowl or bacon, stirring regularly with a wooden spoon, especially at the beginning as you are waiting for the fat to begin rendering. As the fat renders, you can turn the heat up to medium, and the pieces of pork will begin frying in their own fat. Continue cooking and stirring until the pork is nicely browned and crisp, 10 to 12 minutes total cooking time. Set the browned bacon aside in a small 8- to 12-ounce bowl, and reserve the rendered fat for the next steps. If any brown bits remain in the saucepan, deglaze with a little stock and use a wooden spoon to scrape the leftover bits up into the stock, and pour this into the Dutch oven.

☙ In a 12-inch cast-iron skillet over high heat, heat half the reserved jowl or bacon fat just until smoking, and add the onions and garlic. Cook, tossing and stirring constantly with a wooden spoon to prevent burning, just until lightly caramelized and the onions are amber in color. Transfer quickly to the Dutch oven. Add the remaining half of the bacon fat to the sauté pan, and heat just until smoking. Then add the bell pepper and celery, and sauté until well rendered and just beginning to brown. Add to the Dutch oven. If any brown bits remain in the sauté pan, deglaze with a little stock and add to the Dutch oven.

☙ Wrap the pig's foot in one layer of cheesecloth, and tie off the ends with butcher twine. This will allow you to keep the many pin bones in the foot out of the beans. Place the foot in the Dutch oven, add the soaked beans including the soaking liquid, the reserved browned bacon, the tomato paste, and all of the seasonings, hot sauce, Worcestershire, and vinegar if you are not using pickled pig's foot. Add only 1 tablespoon of salt—you can add more to taste after cooking. Use a wooden spoon to make sure all the ingredients are settled into the pot, and add any more stock necessary to just cover the contents by a ½ inch. If using pigskin, fold the excess skin up over the top of the beans. Place the tight-fitting lid over all.

☙ Set the Dutch oven on the middle rack of the oven at 325°F, and cook for 5 hours. Remove from oven, and place on a wire rack to cool. Allow to cool for 30 minutes before opening the lid. Uncover, and use a pair of tongs to remove the pig's foot, which will still be wrapped in cheesecloth. Return the lid to the pot, and cool the pig's foot on a plate at room temperature until cool enough to handle, 20 minutes. Remove cheesecloth, and carefully remove the many bones, saving all skin, meat, fat, and tendons, which will all be very tender and delicious. Chop these edible feet parts, and add them back to the Dutch oven and stir into the beans, discarding the bones. Use the back of a wooden spoon to mash up the beans somewhat until creamy. Add a little hot stock if too thick, and re-season with more salt, pepper, hot sauce, or Worcestershire as desired. Carefully ladle the beans into a serving dish, leaving the cooked pigskin behind, either to discard or eat on its own. Serve with Creole boiled rice (page 68), cornbread (page 4), and voodoo greens. Refrigerates well for up to 1 week.

Voodoo Greens

Our most frequent, year-round customers know that while our greens are always good, early summer is the absolute peak time for them, followed by late fall. That's when we have the optimal mix of tender young sweet collards and pungent young mustards and turnip greens available. During winter, when we're buying collard greens from California—or if we're lucky, Georgia or Mississippi—the greens are less tender and less pungent (a factor of picking for transportation and storage, not terroir); though some folks like the simple taste of pure collard greens, and it's hard to fault them for that.

You can make this recipe with any mixture of greens—or any one green—you like, but if you can swing this particular mix of leafy vegetables, give it a try; it makes for a very special pot of greens. My personal favorite is pulling young turnips—greens, taproots, and all—scrubbing them well, and cooking the whole plant, root, leaves, and stems. They have to be young, or the turnips won't cook through by the time the greens are done and the stems will likely be tough as well. Pick them young, less than 2 inches in diameter, and it's one of the most delicious vegetable preparations you can imagine, at least if you like turnips. I've seen this done in the Delta as well, one of the reasons I love that region as much as I do.

PREP TIME: 90 minutes

EQUIPMENT NEEDED: 4-quart stainless-steel or enamel stock pot with tight-fitting lid, wooden spoon

MAKES: 12 cups, serves 6 to 12

1 bunch collard greens, washed and stems removed
1 bunch turnip greens (or kale in a pinch), washed and stems removed
1 bunch mustard greens, washed and stems removed
Green tops from 3 carrots, washed and heavy stems removed, finely chopped
2 tablespoons lard or bacon grease
2 cups yellow onion, thinly sliced lengthwise
2 tablespoons fresh garlic, mashed and minced
2 teaspoons crushed red pepper

½ cup apple cider vinegar
½ cup cold water
1 smoked ham hock
1 tablespoon kosher salt
2 tablespoons Worcestershire sauce

🌱 To prep the greens, take the larger, woody stems from all the greens and wash thoroughly. Drain but do not shake dry, as the extra moisture will help wilt the greens. Chop the greens into 1-inch strips. Chop the carrot tops more finely, into ½-inch bits, being careful to remove the woody bits.
🌱 In a 4-quart stainless-steel or enamel stock pot with a tight-fitting lid, heat the lard or bacon grease over medium heat until hot but not smoking—a grain of rice dropped in the oil should sizzle briskly. Add the onions and garlic, and sauté to sweat and cook, stirring often, until onions have sweated and just begin to brown, 8 to 10 minutes. Turn off the heat for a moment, and add as many greens as you can fit in the pot, then add the red pepper, apple cider vinegar, and water. Turn heat back to medium and cook patiently, as the greens on the bottom of the pot wilt. Every 3 to 4 minutes, use a wooden spoon to reach the bottom of the pot and turn the cooked greens over the top and raw greens underneath, then punch the whole pot of greens down to make room for more greens. Add as many greens again as will fit into the pot, and repeat until all greens are in the pot. Add the ham hock, salt, and Worcestershire, then cover the pot tightly. Reduce heat to medium low to maintain a low boil. Return every few minutes to turn the greens over.
🌱 Continue to cook until all the greens are thoroughly cooked and tender, which will take 30 minutes for young, tender greens or up to an hour for larger, woodier greens. Taste for seasoning and add more salt, pepper, or vinegar if desired. Serve with hot cornbread (page 4) for dipping in the vinegary potlikker.

Brown Butter Roasted Palm Hearts

When we have this dish on the menu, we often have to explain to perplexed guests that palm hearts are indeed a Southern ingredient, just not one you see too often these days. Early cookbooks from the Carolina Lowcountry always contain recipes for "swamp cabbage," a name that might have been given because of the rank, fetid odor palm heart takes on when it's turning, just like cabbage. It's also good prepared most ways that cabbage is, and when really fresh, it's one of the most magnificent vegetables.

Swamp cabbage was so popular at one time that it threatened the survival of one of the Southeast's signature flora, the palmetto palm, and its harvest was banned. In Florida the native palms endured the same fate, their harvest being banned after feeding early generations of cattle bushmen working and foraging the central and northern Florida backwoods.

Hearts of palm then made one of those funny inversions that some foods do from time to time—it went from being cheap (free for the taking, really) to being rare, expensive, and highly prized since suddenly it had to be imported from Central and South America, a costly proposition for such a perishable foodstuff.

Hearts of palm remain expensive, and their commercial harvest threatened some palm populations across much of the Western Hemisphere until a couple of species were discovered that reproduce by suckers, so you can harvest the young suckers rather than killing the whole plant. One peach palm, for instance, can put off as many as forty suckers, a boon to growers who wanted to create a sustainable palm industry. We buy our palm hearts direct from a little producer on the Big Island of Hawaii, where they grow peach palms in a sustainable, low-impact manner among many other native tropical plants. Ask your specialty produce store if they can special order it for you.

Many recipes for palm salads call for highly acidic or mayonnaise-based dressings, and I wanted something different. Working with some commodities of the early Columbian Exchange—pineapple, lime, and peanuts—this warm salad emphasizes the buttery, nutty aromatics achieved when palm hearts are roasted. It's always popular when it's on the menu, usually in winter when local produce is scarce.

PREP TIME: 90 minutes

EQUIPMENT NEEDED: 12-by-18-inch sheet pan with raised edges or a jelly roll pan, 4-quart mixing bowl, metal spatula, 1-quart saucepan, small ladle, fine-mesh strainer, 12-inch cast-iron skillet, digital food thermometer, long-handled basting spoon, long-handled slotted spoon, wire draining rack with sheet pan with raised edges, 4-quart mixing bowl

SERVES: 4 to 6

   1 tablespoon vegetable oil
   ½ pound raw shelled peanuts
   1 tablespoon cold water
   3 teaspoons salt, divided
   ½ teaspoon cayenne pepper
   ¼ cup granulated sugar
   1½ cups (3 sticks) unsalted butter
   1 pound fresh hearts of palm, sliced ½ inch thick at a 45-degree
      diagonal (canned are not an acceptable substitute)
   ½ very ripe fresh gold pineapple, cored and sliced lengthwise into long
      planks, ½ inch thick
   ¼ cup dark brown sugar
   2 tablespoons freshly squeezed lime juice
   2 tablespoons honey
   2 tablespoons untoasted first-press sesame oil
   1 cup fresh pea shoots or tendrils, to garnish

🌴 Preheat oven to 325°F.

🌴 Oil a sheet pan with raised edges or a jelly roll pan with 1 tablespoon vegetable oil and set aside. In a 4-quart mixing bowl, toss the peanuts, water, 1 teaspoon salt, and the cayenne pepper to wet and season the peanuts, then sprinkle in the granulated sugar and toss to coat the peanuts. It will look like the peanuts are coated in wet sand. Spread evenly on the oiled sheet pan, and bake in the oven, moving them around often with a metal spatula to ensure that they cook evenly, until evenly golden brown, 30 minutes. Remove from oven and continue to toss the peanuts while cooling to prevent them from sticking together in one mass.

❦ Place the butter in a 1-quart saucepan over high heat until butter is melted and foaming. Use a small ladle to skim the foam off the top and any other scum that rises. Once boiling, reduce heat to medium and continue to boil, using a small ladle to skim the surface often, until the buttermilk boils off and you are left with clarified butter. Continue cooking until the butter browns to a rich amber color, then remove from heat at once. Strain through a fine-mesh strainer.

❦ Place the browned butter in a 12-inch cast-iron skillet over medium heat until too hot for your finger but not so hot that the hearts of palm sizzle when added. We're looking to wilt them. If you have a thermometer, 165°F is ideal. Add the palm hearts and 1 teaspoon salt, and turn up the heat to medium high for a couple of minutes to let the temperature come back up. Once the hearts of palm just start to sizzle, tilt the pan toward you to pool butter in the near side of the pan, then use a large metal basting spoon to turn the hot butter over the top of the palm hearts, basting constantly until they are tender but retain some bite, 5 to 6 minutes. Use a slotted spoon to remove the palm hearts, draining the butter back into the pan. Drain the palm hearts on a wire rack placed over a sheet pan with raised edges. Retain in a low-temperature oven to keep warm.

❦ Increase the heat on the butter in the sauté pan to medium high and add the pineapple. Baste in the same manner of the hearts of palm, allowing more heat to caramelize the pineapple slightly, 6 to 8 minutes. Once the pineapple has browned slightly, tilt the pan toward you, sprinkle the brown sugar over the pineapple, and baste in the brown butter until the sugar melts and coats the fruit. Use a slotted spoon to remove and drain on the wire rack with the hearts of palm.

❦ To serve, place the warm palm hearts and pineapple in a 4-quart mixing bowl, then add the peanuts and the remaining teaspoon of salt and toss. Add the lime juice, honey, and sesame oil, and toss to coat evenly. Place on a serving platter and garnish with fresh pea greens.

Debris Gravy

In both Cajun and Creole cooking, there are recipes called debris. At Cajun boucheries, or butchering days, debris was a dish into which parts like the hearts, kidneys, and spleens would make their way, to be simmered in a rich gravy until tender and eaten with grits. When butchering beef, tripe might also find its way into the dish. In Creole parlance, it usually refers to a gravy made from the drippings and bits of shredded beef that are found in the pan after roasting beef. You'll see it in po' boy shops in which it serves to slick roast beef po' boys, or in delis where in addition to lubricating po' boys, it might be served up with grits or mashed potatoes.

The common thread between Cajun debris and Creole debris gravy is that it's usually a dark gravy made with a brown roux. Here we take the name and hopefully honor it well, but when I wanted a tasty gravy to serve with biscuits for brunch, I also wanted something along the lines of the old "possum" or sausage gravy I grew up with. This gravy is usually milk-based and seasoned high with salt and pepper, and most often included pork sausage (or in the old days, quite possibly possum). We often have head meat left over after we cure our hog jowls for jowl bacon, and we always have kidneys, hearts, and ham bits and pieces around, making for a nice rich porky base, to which I've added andouille sausage to spice things up a bit. This is perfectly appropriate to serve for breakfast or supper with biscuits, popovers, toast, grits and greens, or rice.

PREP TIME: 90 minutes

EQUIPMENT NEEDED: 9-inch pie pan, 2-quart saucepan, long-handled wooden spoon

MAKES: 5 cups, serves 4 to 6

½ cup andouille, diced
½ cup raw bacon, diced
½ cup ham trimmings, diced
¼ cup clarified butter or fresh lard
¼ cup plus 2 tablespoons all-purpose flour
½ cup yellow onion, minced
¼ cup celery, minced

2½ cups whole milk

½ cup cooked hog's head, heart, kidney, or tongue, diced

2 teaspoons coarsely ground black pepper

1 teaspoon crushed red pepper

2 teaspoons kosher salt, or more to taste

¼ cup heavy whipping cream

꙳ Preheat oven to 350°F.

꙳ Place andouille, bacon, and ham on a 9-inch pie pan and spread evenly. Bake in the oven until well browned and rendered fat is clear, 30 to 40 minutes. Drain rendered fat into a 2-quart saucepan, and reserve the browned meats.

꙳ Add the clarified butter or lard to the saucepan with the rendered fat, and cook over medium-high heat until a bit of flour tossed in sizzles. Stirring constantly with a wooden spoon, sprinkle in the flour, then reduce heat to medium and continue stirring as the roux cooks. Be careful to stir and scrape the entire bottom and sides of the pan to prevent scorching. As soon as the color starts to turn, reduce heat to medium low, and continue cooking and stirring until a dark blond or tan color is reached, 12 to 15 minutes total cooking time.

꙳ Being careful of splatter, add the onion and celery to the roux, and continue to cook, stirring constantly, over medium heat until the vegetables turn soft, 4 to 5 minutes. Stirring constantly, pour in the milk and maintain medium heat while returning to a boil, 4 to 5 minutes. Add the reserved browned meats, the hog's head or organ meats, and season with the black and red peppers and salt. Maintain heat on medium while stirring occasionally from the bottom of the pan to prevent scorching, until the gravy returns to a boil, 5 to 7 minutes. Finish by stirring in the heavy cream and serve at once.

Rémoulade

Even though we often change seafood dishes on our menu, I don't think there's ever been a lunch or dinner menu at Big Jones that didn't involve rémoulade, a staple of the Creole table. A long history and a city full of ambitious cooks have led to many variations of this sauce. The common threads are mayonnaise, mustard, some sort of pickle, and hot peppers—

be they in fresh form or as dried cayenne pepper or hot sauce. I'd add that horseradish is also essential. From there, the variations are many, and even in our own kitchen, it could be any one of three recipes we use regularly. This is our first and flagship rémoulade, and my favorite—perhaps as much for sentimental value as the tart, spicy tang it laces any dish with which it's served.

PREP TIME: 20 minutes
EQUIPMENT NEEDED: 2-quart mixing bowl, wooden spoon
MAKES: 2 cups

1 cup mayonnaise
2 tablespoons Creole mustard
1 tablespoon Cajun seasoning (page 67)
2 tablespoons Louisiana-style hot sauce
2 stalks green onion, washed and sliced very thin, green tops only
¼ cup dill pickles, finely chopped
1 tablespoon finely grated fresh horseradish root (may substitute prepared horseradish from a jar in a pinch)
1 tablespoon Worcestershire sauce

⚜ Place all ingredients in a 2-quart mixing bowl, and stir with a wooden spoon until evenly combined. Cover tightly with plastic wrap and refrigerate for 1 hour before serving, or up to 1 week.

Eggs New Orleans

Far and away the most popular brunch dish we have ever served, Eggs New Orleans is my salute to Haute Creole, or the high, fancy Creole cooking associated with the merchant and planter classes and later the city's incredible restaurant scene.

Most folks don't know where Eggs Benedict originated, and some assume it must come from New Orleans because of its history there. Actually, it originated in New York, though it is undeniable that the dish, as much through its many elegant variations as the original itself, reached its critical mass in New Orleans and became an American classic. The basic formula of protein and/or a vegetable preparation with poached eggs and some form of toast and a creamy butter sauce has spawned many variations, some of which are classics in their own right.

I love a good crab cake, poached eggs are comfort food to me, and béarnaise is one of my absolute favorite sauces in the world: they all sing together like angels. This was all a natural to me. While the original Eggs Benedict was likely served with buttered toast, in more recent generations the American standard has been with an English muffin, and some Creole restaurants in New Orleans served it on rusks, or crispy toast rounds. Never shy to do something just a little bit different but more importantly *à la minute*, fresh, homemade, and for an interesting textural contrast, I opted for popovers, which make cozy nests for the crab cakes and eggs, rather than platforms as with muffins or toast.

Potatoes O'Brien (page 92) or creamy grits (page 38) are both good choices for sides, but there's something extra special about the marriage of corn and crab, so I tend to go for grits with Eggs New Orleans.

PREP TIME: 1 hour to prep crab cakes the day before, 1 hour for popovers and béarnaise, 30 minutes to prepare the dish
SERVES: 6

Popovers (page 7)
12 poached eggs, instructions follow
Crab cakes (recipe follows)
Béarnaise sauce (recipe follows)

꙳ Prepare popover batter according to instructions, and refrigerate up to 3 days before you want to make Eggs New Orleans. Prepare crab cake mixture up to 1 day in advance and refrigerate.

꙳ Have oven preheated and put popovers in the oven 1 hour before you plan to serve. Start your poaching pot (instructions follow). Next, make the béarnaise sauce, and maintain over a bowl of hot, but not boiling, water while you cook the crab cakes. Once cooked, set the crab cakes aside on a cookie sheet. Reheat them in the oven while you poach the eggs. The oven will still be hot from baking the popovers.

꙳ To serve, place each popover upright (the bottom of the popover will be smaller than the puffy, popped-over top), and gently open the popover from the center of the top, exposing the feathery, airy center. Place a crab cake in the center of each one, nestling it into the center. Set a poached egg atop each one, and cover with béarnaise sauce. Serve at once.

Poached Eggs

Good poached eggs are one of the basics of brunch, and even though there's a bit of a trick to them, they are easily mastered with a little practice. There are two primary methods of poaching eggs practiced in the restaurant industry: the deep-pot method and the shallow-pot method. We'll focus on the shallow-pot method here because it's the method we use at Big Jones. We poach eggs this way because the volume of eggs we poach on a Sunday morning is more readily executed consistently by this method, where each egg is visible in the poach pot at a mere glance.

Absolutely fresh farm eggs are a must because they have the most albumin in the whites, which is the protein that helps the eggs stand up in a nice, rounded dome shape rather than going flat on the bottom of the poaching pan. For the same reason of albumin content, large eggs will perform better than extra-large. So, if you buy from a farmer who doesn't grade their eggs by size, select the smallest ones for poaching.

PREP TIME: 15 minutes

EQUIPMENT NEEDED: 3-quart enamel casserole or stainless-steel braising dish, digital clip-on thermometer, 3-inch mini kitchen strainer, 1-quart mixing bowl, round-bottom teacup, slotted spoon, serving platter for holding eggs

1 tablespoon unsalted butter
10 cups (2½ quarts) cold water
2 teaspoons distilled white vinegar
12 farm-fresh large eggs

⚜ Butter the inside of a 3-quart enamel casserole or stainless-steel braising dish, fill with the cold water and vinegar, and place over high heat. Using a clip-on thermometer, set the temperature of the water to 190°F, controlling the heat with the burner settings.

⚜ Hold a small kitchen strainer over a 1-quart mixing bowl, and carefully crack an egg into the strainer, and allow the runny part of the white to run through the strainer into the bowl to be discarded. Carefully roll the egg into a round-bottom teacup, and then very gently tip the cup over the surface of the steaming water, and let the egg gently roll out and drop into the poaching water. Repeat with remaining eggs, but limit each batch to 6 to 8 eggs to allow space between each egg and to avoid a large swing in water temperature. In order to achieve uniform doneness on each egg, we drop the first egg at six o'clock, the second at eight o'clock, and so-on, so everyone in the kitchen knows which egg was dropped first, and which last. Therefore, you are able to remove the eggs, clockwise starting from six o'clock, in the order in which they were dropped, so each gets the same amount of cooking time.

⚜ After 3 minutes, the eggs should be done, firm around the edges with a jiggly, soft, runny yolk in the center. Check them at 2 minutes if you like them especially runny, or cook 4 to 5 minutes for medium-well to well-done yolks. Gently use a slotted spoon to scoop up each egg from underneath. We teach our cooks to literally scrape the poaching pan underneath the egg to get under it, to avoid poking the egg and breaking it. Gently lay each egg onto a serving platter to hold while you poach any remaining batches. To reheat, simply dip back into the poaching water for 20 seconds before serving.

Crab Cakes

I love crab cakes because they are so versatile, besides including crab, my absolute favorite seafood. Due to crab's sweet, complex flavor, the meat pairs well with a broad range of accompaniments, and they are equally satisfying enjoyed any time of day. Our crab cakes are probably best known as one of the components of Eggs New Orleans, our most popular brunch dish, but they are also one of our most popular appetizers on the dinner menu. Most people associate crab cakes with Maryland and the Chesapeake Bay region. However, our recipe was inspired by a receipt from *Creole Cookery* (1885) by the Christian Woman's Exchange of New Orleans, in which the receipt is titled "A Nice Way to Serve Crabs."

Sometimes, depending on the composition of the overall dish, we crust the cakes in benne seeds. The rich, nutty flavor pairs beautifully with crab, and you get the added bonus of a nice crunch on the exterior. To crust your crab cakes in benne, simply coat in benne seeds instead of bread crumbs before frying them up. Besides Eggs New Orleans, our favorite pairings are rémoulade, sweet corn relish, or hearts of palm.

PREP TIME: 30 minutes to prepare the mix, 30 minutes for cooking
EQUIPMENT NEEDED: 4-quart mixing bowl, wire whisk, wooden spoon, pie pan, 12-inch cast-iron skillet, ¼-cup ice cream scoop, metal turning spatula
MAKES: twelve 2-ounce crab cakes

2 large eggs
2 teaspoons kosher salt
2 tablespoons Louisiana-style hot sauce
1 tablespoon prepared Creole, Dijon, or Dusseldorfer mustard
1 tablespoon Worcestershire sauce
¼ cup mayonnaise
¼ cup onion, minced
2 tablespoons carrot, minced
¼ cup celery, minced
2 tablespoons red bell pepper, minced
1 clove garlic, mashed and minced
1 pound American lump crab meat, either freshly picked or
    pasteurized, chilled
4 cups plus ½ cup French bread crumbs, divided
Clarified butter or vegetable oil for pan-frying

♆ Beat the eggs well with a wire whisk in a 4-quart mixing bowl. Add the salt, hot sauce, mustard, Worcestershire, and mayonnaise, and whisk until smooth. Add the onion, carrot, celery, bell pepper, and garlic, and stir in with a wooden spoon until evenly combined. Add the crab meat and ½ cup of bread crumbs, and toss gently until evenly combined, but do your best to avoid breaking up the lumps of crab meat too much. Cover tightly with plastic wrap. Refrigerate at least 1 hour or up to 3 days before using.
♆ Place the remaining bread crumbs in a pie pan to bread the crab cakes.
♆ To cook, add enough clarified butter or vegetable oil to a 12-inch cast-iron skillet to just coat the bottom of the pan. Cook over medium heat until a bread crumb tossed in the pot sizzles. With a small ice cream scoop, scoop up ¼ cup of crab meat mixture at a time and drop into the pan of bread crumbs, then roll gently in bread crumbs for a light coating, shaping into a ball as

you roll. You're not looking for a heavy coating here—just a light dusting, so you will still be able to see the crab mixture through the bread crumbs. Place the cake gently into the heated, oiled skillet. Flatten the cake with the back of your cooking spatula just a touch, until it's the shape of a fat round disc, like a hockey puck that could go on a diet. Working quickly, continue making more cakes until you skillet is full but not overcrowded—you may need to make two batches.

❦ Allow the cakes to cook on the first side for 6 minutes—if they begin to brown too heavily, reduce the heat. After 6 minutes they should be a full rich brown but not burning. Turn gently and cook another 4 minutes, increasing the heat on the second side if necessary to brown. They are done when they are springy to the touch and not mushy, and a toothpick inserted in the center comes out clean. Serve at once with rémoulade (page 84).

Béarnaise

Famed gourmand and author James Beard once said, "I believe that if I ever had to practice cannibalism, I might manage if there were enough tarragon around." While that witticism is always good for a belly chuckle, it's also a ringing endorsement of one of my favorite herbs, and absolutely the best herb with many meats and especially eggs. Perhaps that's why béarnaise is the greatest sauce in the world to me, bar none. Yes, even more so than mayonnaise.

Actually the offspring of hollandaise, the French mother sauce of emulsified butter and egg yolk, béarnaise has the added hook of fresh tarragon, shallots, wine, and vinegar. It's at once creamy, buttery, and sweet from the shallots, a little bit tart, a little fruity from the wine, and mightily herbaceous. Nothing is better with a skillet-seared steak, poached chicken or fish, or eggs. It's the great harmonizer of our Eggs New Orleans and Eggs Benedict, but you should feel free to make this sauce any time you want something awesome. Sometimes you just don't have to reinvent the wheel.

PREP TIME: 30 minutes
EQUIPMENT NEEDED: 2-quart saucepan, 1-quart saucepan, wooden spoon,
    2-quart stainless-steel bowl, wire whisk

MAKES: 1½ cups—enough for 6 servings of Eggs Benedict or Eggs New Orleans

¾ cup (1½ sticks) plus 1 tablespoon unsalted butter, chilled and cut into teaspoon-size bits, divided
3 tablespoons shallots, minced
2 tablespoons fresh tarragon, minced, or 1 tablespoon dried
¼ cup dry white wine
¼ cup white wine vinegar
1 tablespoon Louisiana-style hot sauce
4 large egg yolks
½ teaspoon kosher salt, or to taste
Freshly ground black pepper to taste

❦ Prepare the base of a double boiler by placing 1 inch of water in a 2-quart saucepan, and bring to a simmer over medium heat. Maintain the simmer while you proceed with the recipe.

❦ In a 1-quart saucepan, melt 1 tablespoon butter over medium heat until foaming but not browning, and add the minced shallots. Sauté the shallots, stirring constantly with a wooden spoon, until they sweat, turn translucent, and soften, 2 to 3 minutes. Add the tarragon, wine, vinegar, and hot sauce, and increase heat slightly to bring to a boil. Reduce until thick and syrupy and only a few tablespoons of liquid remain, 3 to 4 minutes at a rolling boil. Set aside for a moment while you finish setting up the double boiler.

❦ In a 2-quart stainless-steel bowl, beat the egg yolks with a whisk until smooth. Add a tablespoon of the wine and shallot mixture to temper the egg yolks, and whisk thoroughly to combine. Add the remaining wine and shallot mixture slowly, in a steady stream, while whisking constantly until all is combined.

❦ Raise the heat under the 2-quart saucepan to bring the water to a low boil, monitoring the heat closely to maintain this low boil. Place the bowl with the egg yolk mixture over the boiling water, and whisk constantly. Begin adding the butter bit by bit, continuously whisking and adding another bit of butter as the previous one melts into the egg yolk mixture.

❦ Once all the butter is incorporated, continue whisking to cook the eggs to the point where they are creamy yellow in color rather than the slightly darker, translucent color of raw egg yolks, and the mixture is steaming and coats a spoon thickly, 6 to 8 minutes total cooking time. Add the salt and pepper, taste and re-season to your liking. May be held for a short period over the steaming water in the saucepan off the burner, if stirred regularly. Serve with Eggs Benedict or Eggs New Orleans as the sauce.

☙ If your sauce breaks, simply place another egg yolk into a separate 2-quart mixing bowl, and while whisking constantly, slowly pour the broken sauce onto the egg yolk until it comes back together, return to the double boiler, and continue cooking.

Potatoes O'Brien

Simple is the name of the game here, and the success of our brunch potatoes from our very first brunch service left me confident that there's no need to change these—they're simply not broken. Perhaps ironically, they are claimed to have originated out East rather than in New Orleans, but they fit right in.

When I first moved to Chicago and went to brunch at a few places, I realized I would have to make proper shredded breakfast potatoes a mission of mine, after being served the boiled red potato chunk mistake that often passes for brunch potatoes in Chicago. With eggs, I want the finer texture of shreds and a nice crispy crunch to make my plate come alive, and these are much easier to scoop up on your fork with a bit of omelet or runny egg yolks.

Baking the potatoes first accomplishes two things: it cooks them so they can be shredded and kept for service without browning, and it also dries them out and gives you some of that fluffy baked potato texture, the better to absorb some of that delicious butter you'll be frying them in. If you want to be extra decadent, use a mixture of bacon fat and butter—something we're not able to do at the restaurant as we want our potatoes ready for a vegetarian customer on a moment's notice.

PREP TIME: 1 hour to bake the potatoes, overnight to refrigerate, 30 minutes
    to cook
EQUIPMENT NEEDED: baking sheet pan, box grater, 12-inch cast-iron skillet,
    cooking spatula
SERVES: 4 to 6

2 pounds medium russet potatoes, about 5 to 7 potatoes

¼ cup clarified butter

1 cup yellow onion, finely diced

½ cup green bell pepper, finely diced

Kosher salt and freshly ground pepper to taste, about 1 teaspoon salt and ½ teaspoon freshly ground pepper is a good start; you can add more at the table if desired

☙ The day before you want to make your breakfast potatoes, preheat oven to 350°F. Puncture each potato three to four times with a fork to allow steam to escape while baking. Place on a baking sheet on the top rack of the oven, and bake until potatoes are tender when pierced through with a fork, 45 to 60 minutes. Remove from oven and cool to room temperature for an hour or so. Refrigerate overnight or up to 5 days in a covered airtight container.

☙ When you're ready to finish the dish, cut the potatoes in half lengthwise and use a box grater to shred, starting with the open cut side of the potato and using the largest shredding side of the grater. Getting a little peel in with the shredded potatoes is ideal, but you will find as you shred the peel will naturally separate from the starchy interior. Discard the leftover skins, or save to fry later as potato skins.

☙ In a 12-inch cast-iron skillet, heat the clarified butter over medium-high heat until a bit of potato dropped into the pan sizzles rapidly. The butter will be foamy and just beginning to brown. Add the potatoes in an even layer, being careful to gently layer them so they will be fluffy when cooked, rather than pressed. Evenly distribute the onions and peppers over the top, and season with salt and pepper. Reduce heat to medium, and cook until well browned on the bottom, as dark or light as you like. This will take 5 to 8 minutes. Turn gently with a cooking spatula and cook for only 2 minutes on the second side, then transfer to a serving platter or individual plates. Keep warm, uncovered, in a low oven until ready to serve.

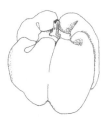

Bread Pudding

When you're opening a Southern restaurant, high on the list of probable desserts is bread pudding. In fact, while I often shy away, or at least try to, from doing what's expected, bread pudding is one that's hard to avoid for one good reason: almost any kitchen cooking American food will have bread sitting around, past its prime. In the fall and winter, we will often make stuffing to serve with fowl, and we grind our share for bread crumbs and make croutons to boot.

The coolest thing about bread pudding is that you can take a stale leftover and make a sticky, sweet, gooey, drunken hot mess of awesome. On a cold night in winter, few desserts can rival the comfort of a pan of bread pudding fresh out of the oven, and on the hottest summer day, a chilled and sliced bread pudding is mightily refreshing, especially with cool whipped cream and some sliced ripe peaches fresh from the orchard.

Generations of bread pudding recipes have this one pretty well figured out, so I'm not looking to build a new Rome here, and we stick with the basics: flavorful bread, fresh farm eggs, great cream, top-quality spices (see "Notes on Sources"), and enough bourbon to give a horse a nice warm buzz. I fall into the camp that puts raisins in bread pudding; if that's an abomination to you, feel free to leave them out.

Seasonally, in winter I tend to increase the alcohol by adding rum in addition to the whiskey while upping the nutmeg content and adding a little clove to make the pudding extra festive and warming. Other good options are various candied fruits and fresh or candied ginger. In the summer you can serve it cold with fresh fruit and whipped cream, but most of the year a tangy fruit compote and ice cream are in order.

PREP TIME: 30 minutes to prepare the custard, 1 hour to overnight for
    soaking, 1 hour for baking
EQUIPMENT NEEDED: wire whisk, 4-quart mixing bowl, wooden spoon, 13-by-9-
    inch (3-quart) casserole dish with tight-fitting lid, wire cooling rack
SERVES: 8 to 12

    6 large eggs
    1 cup granulated sugar

½ teaspoon kosher salt

1 teaspoon ground Korintje cinnamon

½ teaspoon ground nutmeg

1 cup heavy whipping cream

1 cup whole milk

6 tablespoons of good, strong bourbon

2 teaspoons natural vanilla extract

5 cups 2- to 3-day-old Sally Lunn (page 6), cut into ½-inch cubes

1 cup golden raisins

¼ cup (½ stick) plus 1 tablespoon unsalted butter, cut into small bits, divided

¼ cup dark brown sugar

❦ Beat the eggs well with a wire whisk in a 4-quart mixing bowl. Add the sugar, and beat until smooth and creamy, 2 to 3 minutes, then whisk in the salt, cinnamon, and nutmeg. One at a time, whisk in the cream, milk, bourbon, and vanilla, combining well after each addition. Add the bread and raisins, toss well with a wooden spoon, and use the back of the wooden spoon to tamp the bread back into the custard, as it will have a tendency to float. Cover with plastic wrap, and refrigerate for 1 hour or overnight.

❦ Preheat oven to 325°F.

❦ Prepare the 13-by-9-inch casserole by rubbing it with 1 tablespoon of the butter. Transfer the soaked bread and all of the custard mixture to the casserole, and once again use the back of a wooden spoon to tamp the bread down into the custard mix, smoothing the top as much as possible. Dot the top with the remaining ¼ cup butter, and sprinkle brown sugar evenly over the top.

❦ Bake, covered, on the bottom rack of the oven for 45 minutes. Remove the lid, and place the pudding on the top rack of the oven, then continue baking until set in the center (a toothpick will come out clean) and the top is nicely browned and crusty, another 40 to 45 minutes. Cool on a wire rack until slicing and serving warm, or refrigerate to enjoy cold.

Cherry Bavarian Cream

Often called simply "Bavarian" in many old cookbooks, including *Creole Cookery* (1885) by the Christian Woman's Exchange of New Orleans, a Bavarian cream is a light, dreamy dessert perfect for a hot summer day with fresh summer fruit. Ever since I can remember from my youngest days, I've always had a real propensity to reach for red fruits during summer, save for the occasional blueberry binge. Strawberries, cherries, and watermelons all seem the most refreshing when it's hot outside, perhaps not so much because of any intrinsic qualities, but because of the things we tend to make with them, my favorite summer desserts: strawberry shortcake, cherry delight (a strangely delightful redneck version of a mousse pie), and of course iced watermelon straight out of hand.

You can make this recipe with many different fruits, but my favorites are, not surprisingly, cherries and strawberries. Besides serving with fruit and whipped cream, any old cookie will do, especially snickerdoodles. Avoid pineapple or passion fruit when making Bavarian cream or any gelatin-based recipe, since those fruits both contain an enzyme that will "digest" the gelatin, leaving you with a flat mousse.

PREP TIME: 1 hour

EQUIPMENT NEEDED: small soup bowl, 2-quart saucepan, wire whisk, two 4-quart stainless-steel bowls, double boiler, rubber spatula, wire cooling rack, 9-inch 6-cup ring mold or Bundt pan

MAKES: one 9-inch 6-cup ring mold or Bundt pan

2 envelopes unflavored gelatin
¼ cup iced water
2 tablespoons maraschino liqueur or kirschwasser, optional
1 pint tart cherries (fresh or frozen and defrosted), pitted and coarsely chopped
3 cups heavy cream, well chilled, divided
1 cup granulated sugar
1 teaspoon kosher salt
6 large egg yolks
Fresh sweet cherries and whipped cream, to garnish

꽃 Soften the gelatin in the iced water in a small bowl for 30 minutes. In a 2-quart saucepan over low heat, heat the optional maraschino liqueur or kirschwasser, cherries, 1 cup of the cream, the sugar, and salt, stirring regularly with a wire whisk, to a low boil. Add the soaked gelatin to the cream, return to a boil, mix well, and remove from the heat.

꽃 Whisk egg yolks well in a 4-quart stainless-steel mixing bowl. Temper the yolks by whisking in a tablespoon of the hot cream mixture, then add the rest of the cream in a thin, steady stream while whisking constantly. Place custard over a double boiler, and cook, stirring constantly with a rubber spatula, until it heavily coats a spoon, 15 to 20 minutes.

꽃 Cool the custard on a wire rack until barely warm to the touch. In a separate 4-quart mixing bowl, whip the remaining 2 cups of heavy cream to firm but not stiff peaks. Fold into the cooled custard in thirds with a rubber spatula. Pour into ring mold, cover, and refrigerate overnight before using. Most modern ring molds have special unmolding instructions. If using a vintage mold, invert serving plate over the mold and dip the mold into a basin of clean warm water for 15 to 20 seconds and invert. Garnish and serve with fresh sweet cherries and whipped cream.

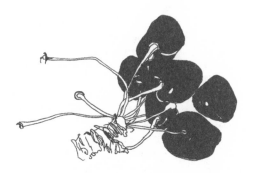

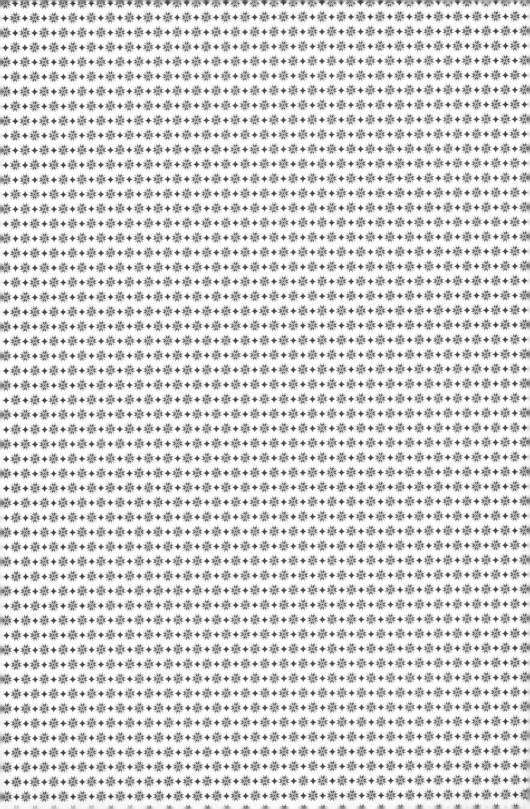

The
Appalachian Highlands

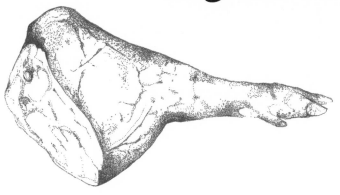

Appalachia is one of the most storied yet misunderstood tracts of land in America. Beautiful beyond words with a complex topography and incredible biological diversity, it was blessed (or cursed, as it were) with seemingly endless forests of timber ripe for cutting, and some of the richest deposits of coal on earth. But before the timber and coal industries came to plunder the mountains, there were the various tribes of Algonquin and Cherokee before English, then Ulster (Scotch-Irish Protestants) and German settlers, laying the foundation for a particularly unique food culture.

Appalachian foodways developed the way they did as much because of the climate, soil, and small-scale farming culture that the challenging landscape would allow, as for the ethnic groups that combined their traditional tastes with the realities of mountain life.

The regional cuisine that evolved in the mountains is unique amid the broader South in that the African influence was minimal. The mountainous landscape did not lend itself to large-scale plantations, so wealthy planters didn't venture into the region and bring slaves with them. Instead, Appalachia became populated with folks who were the very model of Thomas Jefferson's "yeoman farmer," the strong, independent, small farmer who was at the center of the nineteenth-century agrarian romanticism embraced by politicians and writers in both Europe and America.

As far as the day-to-day cooking goes, what became the norm defines much Southern cooking today—Appalachia is easily as influential, if not as respected, as Louisiana or the Lowcountry in laying the foundation for a broader Southern cuisine. Country ham, smoky bacon, sawmill gravy, biscuits, and fried chicken are but a few of the icons of Appalachian cooking that belong in the proverbial museum of Southern cooking. However, while these dishes are certainly important, they present a very narrow view of Appalachian cooking.

Your typical small-scale farmer in Appalachia would let pigs out in the woods to fatten themselves up and bring them in for butchering as winter set in. Hog meat, lard, fatback, cracking, streak o' lean, and literally every part of the pig were important sources of calories in winter when fresh foods were scarce. Most farms would have a dairy cow, but beef as meat was not common, as female births typically went on to provide dairy, while male births were taken as calves for veal; every competent homemaker knew how to take the stomach of the calf and prepare and preserve it to make cheese with the rennet that naturally occurred in the stomach's lining. Animal fat could be used to make fuel, candles, and soap, in addition to providing calories; a whole range of fruits and vegetables was grown in kitchen gardens and orchards and skillfully preserved for winter use by fermenting, canning, or drying. Native Americans showed early settlers how to exploit the rich and abundant wild foods of the region, from wild nuts to pokeweed, cornflower, ramps, frogs, and the many species of wild mushrooms.

These were highly intelligent, industrious people, nothing like the redneck bumpkins commonly portrayed in popular media. By the time media had consolidated in the late nineteenth and early twentieth century, Appalachia was an unfortunate shadow of its former self, suffering pillage by extraction industries of coal and timber. Many families signed deals that left them tenants on their formerly family-owned plots, which were promptly razed for timber or coal. It was a classic case of big industry picking apart small landowners one by one. To the extent that mistrust or even disdain of "city slickers" or outsiders took hold in Appalachia, it would be because they were once promised the moon and instead left a barren landscape that would take generations to recover. Those fortunate enough to escape the pillage became extra protective of their neck of the woods.

The extreme poverty that followed the extraction industries into the mountains certainly had its impact on the evolution of the region's foodways. While every successful small farm would always practice "waste not, want not," by using everything possible—whether it was odds and ends of fabric, parts of a pig, vegetables, fruits, or saving the drippings from the fry pan—this ethic became even more important. Sauces such as sawmill gravy and redeye gravy were born as ways to stretch the leavings in a fry pan into something substantial that would stick to your ribs.

Both of those gravies are substantially richer when you encounter them in restaurants than they were when they took hold in poverty-stricken households of Appalachia. Sawmill gravy was so named because of its association with mill workers, usually poorly paid workers from families who used to farm the land that was being clear-cut. This gravy often consisted of nothing more than water added to the pan drippings to stretch them. On a good day, you might add milk. On a Sunday, maybe cook up sausage and build it right into the gravy to serve with biscuits—but the point is, this was how you could feed a family with next to nothing. Redeye gravy probably began as nothing more than leftover coffee not going to waste by adding it to the pan drippings after frying country ham and boiling it into a sauce.

The more I learn about the people of Appalachia and its cooking, the more I'm smitten. Their story is one of heartbreak and perseverance, back-breaking labor, and yet supremely delicious food. Moonshine and mountain music, two other stories in and of themselves, surely made the Appalachian life a bit easier to take.

Sautéed Ramp Greens with Benne

Native to the eastern North American forests from South Carolina to Canada, the ramp, a perennial wild onion, has been particularly popular in the cooking of the Upland South, where mountain hollers will often turn green even before the last snow melts. These early spring vegetables poke their leaves up through the ground to soak up early spring sunshine before the trees fill in their leaves and cast their shadow on the forest floor. They look and taste just like common onions, but with a bit of added funk from their hibernation below the forest floor. The onion aromas are sharp in the bulbs, and a trained palate will also detect humus and raw soil in the smell and taste of these delectable wild edibles.

Ramps can be cooked many ways, but we always separate the bulbs and the greens because the greens cook quickly and will be mush by the time the bulb is cooked, the lone exception being when grilling them, as you can position the bulb over the hot spot and trail the greens away to cook more slowly.

Typically, we pickle the bulbs and cook the greens as a quick sauté. When cooking pungent greens like this, or fleshy eggplant in the summer, my old background in Southeast Asian food comes forward: we get a dish that seems as Asian as it is Southern, though notice we're using Worcestershire instead of soy or oyster sauce. In a high-heat sauté such as this, the resulting flavor is surprisingly similar in the finished dish. We serve this as a side for the table, and it pairs well with just about anything.

Chances are if you live near a forest in the eastern part of the United States or Canada, you live near a ramp patch. But if you don't have access to a forest you're permitted to forage, they appear at farmers' markets in the very first weeks of the season, even leading asparagus by several days.

Grocery stores and produce markets that focus on quality and variety also source them from all over their range from south to north, so if you know where to look, you might find them from early April through mid-May.

PREP TIME: 20 minutes
EQUIPMENT NEEDED: colander, 12-inch sauté pan, long-handled tongs
SERVES: 4 to 6

2 quarts green ramp tops, washed and drained
1 tablespoon vegetable oil, for sautéing
½ teaspoon crushed red pepper
2 teaspoons Sea Island benne
2 teaspoons Worcestershire sauce
2 teaspoons freshly squeezed lemon juice
½ teaspoon kosher salt, or more to taste

꽃 Wash ramps thoroughly, removing the bottoms for another purpose, as they will not cook as fast as the greens do. Drain in a colander in a clean sink, but do not dry completely as the added moisture will help the greens steam and wilt—just be sure they're not sopping wet.

꽃 Heat the oil in a 12-inch sauté pan over high heat until smoking. Add the ramp greens, which should sizzle and pop, so stand back and use a long-handled set of tongs. Sprinkle the red pepper and benne over the top of the greens. Use the tongs to turn over and check the greens on the bottom—when they are just charring, they are ready to turn. Turn the greens, add the Worcestershire and lemon juice, then toss to coat evenly with these seasonings and wilt the greens further. When the greens are well coated, not quite fully wilted, and a deep, rich green color, remove to a serving bowl and taste for seasoning. Add salt, pepper, or lemon to taste, and serve at once.

Grilled Asparagus with Cottage Cheese and Lemon

In Appalachia, asparagus is often known by its moniker "spar grass," and likely arrived in the region with Ulster farmers who knew it as a reliable early spring producer—one of the best options to get fresh vegetables on the table after a long winter of "leather breeches" (dried string beans) and fermented or pickled vegetables.

Asparagus is unique among vegetables in that it has nearly a hundred different identifiable aromatics, making it perhaps the easiest vegetable with which to pair flavors. We've done it many ways, and this is the most popular. There's something addictive about the complex, assertive green vegetable flavor of asparagus cut cleanly with lemon, with some fresh cottage cheese to lend creaminess and a little crispiness from toasted bread crumbs. On certain spring evenings, I'd eat a pile of this myself as a whole meal.

PREP TIME: 30 minutes for the toasted bread crumbs, 30 minutes for asparagus

EQUIPMENT NEEDED: serving platter; 1 cup hickory, apple, or cherry wood chips, soaked in cold water for 20 minutes; charcoal or gas grill; long-handled tongs

SERVES: 4 to 6

    1 bunch asparagus
    1 tablespoon extra-virgin olive oil
    ½ teaspoon kosher salt
    ½ teaspoon crushed red pepper
    ½ cup large-curd cottage cheese
    Juice and zest of ½ lemon
    ¼ cup toasted bread crumbs (recipe follows)

⚜ Wash asparagus and cut any tough woody parts from the bottom of the stalks, usually 1 to 2 inches, and reserve for vegetable soup or stock. Arrange stalks over a serving platter, and drizzle with the olive oil, kosher salt, and red pepper, and toss to coat evenly.

❦ Prepare your grill with charcoal, or if using a gas grill, turn it to a medium-high flame and make sure you have lava rocks evenly dispersed on which to smoke the wood chips. When the charcoal has burned down to red-hot coals, evenly disperse your wood chips over the coals.

❦ Arrange the asparagus on the grill over the hot coals and cover, making sure the vents on the grill are open to encourage the grill to burn hot. Remove the cover every minute to toss and turn the asparagus with long-handled tongs, checking its progress. Cook until evenly blistered and just beginning to char, tender but still with a bite, 4 to 6 minutes. Transfer to a serving platter, crumble the cottage cheese evenly over the asparagus, and evenly sprinkle the lemon juice and zest, followed by the bread crumbs and the finishing salt. Serve at once, while the asparagus is still piping hot, the cottage cheese cold, and the bread crumbs crispy.

TOASTED BREAD CRUMBS

1 cup very coarsely ground stale French or Italian bread
2 tablespoons (¼ stick) unsalted butter, melted, plus more for buttering your cookie sheet
½ teaspoon kosher salt
½ teaspoon freshly ground black pepper
½ teaspoon granulated garlic
1 tablespoon freshly grated hard cheese, such as Parmesan, Romano, or your favorite such local cheese

❦ Preheat oven to 325°F. Liberally butter a cookie sheet with edges, or use a cake pan since butter will melt and may run to the edges of the pan. Place the bread crumbs in a small mixing bowl and toss while drizzling in the melted butter, then the salt, pepper, garlic, and grated cheese, tossing well to combine. Evenly sprinkle the mixture over the cookie sheet, place on the top rack of the preheated oven, and bake, tossing with a spatula every 3 to 4 minutes, until evenly golden brown. Allow to cool thoroughly before storing in an airtight container at room temperature for up to 1 week.

Pimiento Cheese

Some call it the caviar of the South; I just call it a delicious and versatile spread. While the exact origins of pimiento cheese are hard to pinpoint, we do know that it was a staple in high-class tearooms across the country in the early twentieth century; by the 1920s a thriving pimiento industry had sprung up around Griffin, Georgia, which was supported by growers throughout the Carolina and Georgia Piedmont.

A bit of serendipity, working-class style, led it to become a staple in lunch boxes in the textile industry that was thriving in this same area. Workers were encouraged to make time to eat on the job when they could, rather than taking structured lunch or meal breaks. Of the many kinds of traveling sandwiches you can imagine were popular, such as chicken salad and ham salad, pimiento cheese became an icon, something particularly unique to the Appalachian Piedmont as the popularity of pimiento cheese waned in the tearooms and cocktail parties around the county. What at one time could have been considered American in a more broad sense gradually became a Southern peculiarity, albeit a marvelous one.

When tasting a great pimiento cheese, it's hard to imagine such a thing could ever fall out of fashion. However, given the direction that American foodways took after World War II in particular, with the rise of processed foods, it is probable that the commonly encountered pimiento cheese took a turn for the worse quality-wise, with processed cheese and "salad dressing" standing in for real cheddar cheese and mayonnaise, both significantly more expensive ingredients. This could explain the decline in popularity, and possibly also the resurrection of pimiento cheese during the first part of the twenty-first century, as chefs and regular folks alike began expecting more integrity in their food. Once again, pimiento cheese is made with proper cheddar and good mayonnaise together with real pimientos.

A well-made pimiento cheese is unquestionably rich yet with enough tanginess to make it addictive rather than cloying, slightly sweet from the pimientos, and retaining just a little of the texture of the grated cheese, making each bite feel a little bit different on your tongue—always a way to invite yet another bit to try and see just what might be next. With crackers, on bread, stuffed in celery, baked into grits, on a burger, or on a toasted cheese sandwich, make yourself a great pimiento cheese and you will be hooked.

The basics of pimiento cheese are grated cheddar cheese, roasted or canned pimientos, and good mayonnaise. I like to add a little Worcestershire and hot sauce for spice and intrigue. As far as the mayonnaise goes, we use our own homemade mayonnaise from the recipe in the pantry section of this book (page 215). Duke's is the favored store-bought mayonnaise in the Piedmont and is the best choice for canned mayonnaise because of its high egg content and low sugar content. In a pinch, you can use Hellman's.

PREP TIME: 30 minutes
EQUIPMENT NEEDED: box grater, 4-quart mixing bowl, wooden spoon
MAKES: 1 pound

- ¼ cup mayonnaise
- ¼ cup cream cheese
- 1 teaspoon crushed red pepper
- 1 tablespoon Louisiana-style hot sauce
- 1 tablespoon Worcestershire sauce
- ½ cup canned pimientos, peeled, seeded, and minced
- 8 ounces sharp cheddar cheese, shredded on the large side of a box grater
- ½ teaspoon kosher salt

⚜ Place the mayonnaise, cream cheese, and red pepper in a 4-quart mixing bowl, and use the back of a wooden spoon to mash together until smooth. Work in the hot sauce and Worcestershire, then add the pimientos, cheddar cheese, and kosher salt, and toss as if it were a salad—by turning from the bottom over the top: you're looking for a light mixture, not a dense, pasty one. Once everything is evenly distributed, taste for seasoning and add more salt or hot sauce to taste. Cover and refrigerate at least 4 hours before serving or up to 1 week.

Hominy

One of the most important preparations in the history of Southern cooking, hominy maintains its dominant position as the base of true grits even as whole hominy has declined in popularity over the past couple of generations. I think true grits and whole hominy are so delicious, we serve them both regularly at Big Jones.

Early European settlers learned to make hominy from the Native Americans—we know that much. What we don't know is what first inspired Meso-Americans to cook dried corn with ashes and then eat the result. Surely there was some trial and error, but we can all thank those early food adventurers for giving us one of the most delicious and nutritious grain preparations at our disposal.

The chemical process that turns corn into hominy is fascinating. The corn is made more digestible, on the one hand; plus more of the important dietary minerals calcium and potassium, as well as protein, are made available. It effectively takes a starchy grain and turns it into a nutritional powerhouse. The flavor enhancements are awesome—the earthy, sweet soil fragrance that leaps from freshly cooked hominy is glorious, with beautiful floral notes that remind us of vanilla and fruit blossoms.

Hominy is dried and ground to make grits, but cooked then freshly ground hominy is what we know as *masa*, the dough used to make corn tortillas and Mexican tamales. In both Latin American cultures where it is known as *pozole* and in early American kitchens in which it was simply known as hominy stew or soup, whole hominy shows its ultimate potential as a hearty and delicious way to make a complete meal out of this simple, inexpensive preparation.

PREP TIME: 2 hours for lime treatment, 2 to 4 hours cooking
EQUIPMENT NEEDED: 4-quart non-reactive stock pot with tight-fitting lid, long-handled wooden spoon, slotted spoon, 4-quart colander
MAKES: 1 quart whole hominy, or 2 quarts fully cooked

1 pound whole kernel dried field corn, about 3 cups
1 quart cold water
¼ cup pickling lime (available at Mexican supermarkets or in online

stores specializing in canning supplies, Mrs. Wages is the most common brand)

1 to 2 tablespoons of salt, to taste

4 bay leaves

❦ Place the corn in a 4-quart non-reactive stock pot, and cover with the cold water. Stir corn vigorously, and allow to settle. Use a slotted spoon to skim off any bits of debris or dead kernels that float to the top. Repeat a few times until nothing floats after stirring.

❦ Add the culinary lime, being careful not to get in eyes or to breathe the powder. Place the pot over a low flame, and gradually bring to a boil. Reduce heat to maintain a low boil, and cook for 30 minutes. Then remove from heat, cover, and let stand 2 hours.

❦ Place pot in a clean sink under cool running water. Flush out clouded liquid and transfer to a colander. While constantly rinsing under running water, vigorously rub kernels between your hands and continue to rinse until all hulls have been removed and the water below runs clear.

❦ At this point, you can proceed straight to cooking, or you can refrigerate in an airtight container for up to 1 week before cooking, or dehydrate to be ground for grits.

❦ To cook, cover with 8 cups of water or stock, season with 1 to 2 tablespoons (your taste) salt and 4 bay leaves, and cook at a low boil for 2 to 4 hours or longer depending on your variety of corn (older heritage grains generally take longer), until cooked through, but with some bite left. You can tell the hominy is cooked when there is no longer a starchy uncooked core in the grain.

Succotash

One of the South's signature vegetable dishes, succotash dates to pre-Columbian times and is likely one of the first dishes early settlers learned from Native Americans. Interestingly, it more likely originated in the Northeast than the South, but it's been a staple on the Southern table for centuries. In recent generations, it typically means sweet corn fried with some type of shell bean (lima beans classically in many minds) and stewed with peppers, often including tomatoes, onions, or salt pork. An easy and quick stove-top dish, it's come to know many variations and continues to be the subject of many a Southern cook's creativity. Our version is fairly straightforward and couldn't be easier to make. You'll usually find lima beans easier to obtain, but I like to make this with crowder peas when they are in season as fresh shell beans.

Keep in mind you can make this dish any time of year, but for it to truly sing, make it in late summer when you have great fresh sweet corn, shell beans, and peppers so fresh, their perfume lingers in your head when you smell them. Prepared with market-fresh ingredients, this succotash is sweet, savory, crunchy, and creamy, making for a satisfying side dish with roasted or grilled pork, fowl, or fish.

PREP TIME: 30 minutes, plus 20 minutes if using fresh beans
EQUIPMENT NEEDED: 1-quart saucepan, 12-inch cast-iron skillet, long-handled
    wooden spoon
SERVES: 4 to 6

¾ cup frozen or fresh shelled lima beans or crowder peas
2 tablespoons bacon fat or unsalted butter
¼ cup tasso or other smoked ham, diced
¼ cup yellow onion, finely diced
¼ cup red bell pepper, finely diced
2 teaspoons fresh garlic, mashed and minced
2 cups fresh sweet corn kernels, cut from the cob (about 2 to 3 ears'
    worth) or frozen (defrost before using) with cleaned cobs reserved
1 tablespoon Worcestershire sauce
1 tablespoon Crystal hot sauce
¼ cup chicken stock, pork stock, or heavy cream if you're
    feeling decadent
1 teaspoon kosher salt
Sliced green onion, to garnish

❦ *If using frozen lima beans or crowder peas, defrost before using and proceed to next paragraph.* If using fresh, place the lima beans or crowder peas in a 1-quart saucepan, and cover with cold water. Place over high heat and bring to a boil, then reduce heat to a simmer and cook until tender, 15 to 20 minutes. Rinse under cold running water to stop the cooking and drain.

꽃 Melt the butter or bacon fat in a 12-inch cast-iron skillet over medium-high heat. Add the tasso or ham, cooking until lightly browned, 3 to 4 minutes. Then add the onion, bell pepper, and garlic, stirring constantly with a wooden spoon, until well sweated and translucent, 2 to 3 minutes. Turn heat to high and add the sweet corn. Fry the corn, tossing often to prevent burning, until sweated and aromatic, 3 to 4 minutes. If you used fresh corn on the cob and still have the cobs, use the back of a knife to scrape any remaining juice from the corncobs into the pan, then discard the cobs. Stir well, reduce heat to medium, and add the lima beans or peas, Worcestershire, hot sauce, and stock, stirring constantly, until the liquid reduces and thickens to a gravy-like consistency, another 3 to 4 minutes. Taste and season with salt if desired. Serve at once and garnish with sliced green onion.

Old Virginia Fried Steak, ca. 1824

Chicken-fried steak is another one of those iconic Southern dishes I resisted serving at Big Jones. The few times I did put it on the menu in the early days—using a nice, thick-cut sirloin we butchered ourselves and fried up to a nice bloody medium—it was met with many howls because some people just wanted that square, pounded round steak thing you get at the Waffle House with eggs, to which my response was always, "Really, you want me to make *that*?" Unwilling to compromise what I thought was a great way to fry steak (round steak, in my opinion, is far better utilized for long-braised gravy dishes such as Louisiana's grillades, or simply turned into ground beef), it went off the menu for good.

I always keep my eyes open for older versions of modern classics. When I came across the recipe for veal cutlets in Mary Randolph's *The Virginia Housewife* from 1824, I found a very early version of fried steak that bore little resemblance to the version served at truck stops and diners across the country. It was elegant and refined, yet given the receipt's provenance, it is as Southern as a pig pickin'.

The Virginia Housewife was published in Richmond, Virginia, which is at the fall line of the James River, marking a boundary between the Tidewater region and the Virginia Piedmont, or upcountry leading to the mountains. For the purposes of this book, I've included it in Appalachia, but it could easily be viewed as a coastal dish considering the history. In any case, it's easy to imagine that this receipt may have ultimately inspired what we know today as chicken-fried steak.

Please be careful how you source your veal—there is still rampant mistreatment of animals in the veal industry. In fact, while the ideal is to avoid "industry" whenever you're selecting food, when selecting veal it is essential. Get to know a small dairy farmer who pastures calves with their mothers, and you'll have the good stuff: it will be pink, nowhere near the anemic whitish color of industrial veal. If you have any small dairy farms and meat lockers in your area, it's worthwhile to seek out local pastured veal—it will almost always be tastiest in early summer when the calf's mother is dining on the lushest pasture of the year, and the calf is munching a little of the fresh green grass as well in addition to his mother's milk. If you can't find pastured veal, you can substitute grass-fed round or sirloin steak.

During brunch we serve this with creamy grits (page 38), and at dinner I reach for barley and cream, also their best at the same time as veal, and make a creamed barley dish with early sweet peas and mushrooms. This is filling, made for an early supper on a day of leisure.

PREP TIME: 1 hour

EQUIPMENT NEEDED: three 10-inch pie pans, meat tenderizer (mallet), 12-inch cast-iron skillet, clip-on thermometer, long-handled tongs, long-handled wooden spoon, wire rack or serving plate lined with paper towels

SERVES: 4

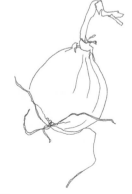

2 cups all-purpose flour
4 cups bread crumbs from low-sugar bread, such as French bread or panko
4 large eggs, beaten well
¼ cup cold water
4 veal leg cutlets, about 4 ounces each
Kosher salt
Freshly ground black pepper
Lard or vegetable oil for pan frying, enough to fill
    ¾ inch deep in iron skillet
1 cup onion, sliced very thinly lengthwise
1 cup shiitake mushrooms, very thinly sliced
2 tablespoons Worcestershire sauce

¼ cup veal or beef stock
¼ cup dry sherry such as Amontillado or Fino
½ cup heavy whipping cream
Juice of ½ lemon

❦ Place the flour in one pie pan, the bread crumbs in another, and the eggs and water in a third pie pan, mixing the eggs and water together well. Loosely wrap one of the cutlets in plastic, with the muscular grain vertical, and pound out with the mallet until an even ½ inch thick. Unwrap the steak and repeat with the other three pieces. Season the cutlets liberally with salt and pepper on each side, then one at a time, dip first in the flour, then dip both sides in the egg mixture, and return to coat both sides with bread crumbs. Repeat until all steaks are well breaded, gently brushing with your fingers to smooth any lumps of breading.

❦ Heat the lard in your cast-iron skillet over medium-high heat until hot but not smoking, 325°F on a clip-on thermometer. Without overcrowding the skillet (you can fry more than one batch), add the steaks to the hot fat and fry, reducing heat to medium, until well browned and golden on the first side, 3 to 4 minutes; then gently turn with long-handled tongs to cook on the second side until browned, another 2 to 3 minutes. Transfer to a wire rack or paper towels to drain while finishing the rest of the steaks. Once all steaks are finished, drain off and discard any leftover fat but a couple of tablespoons, also trying to retain in the pan any bits of breading that have browned.

❦ Continuing over medium heat, add the onions to the skillet and sauté, stirring often with a wooden spoon, until wilted and just beginning to brown, 6 to 8 minutes. Add the mushrooms and sauté to sweat and release the aroma of the mushrooms. When the smell of mushrooms rises, add the Worcestershire, stock, and sherry, and increase heat to high. Reduce the liquid until thick and syrupy, with the onions and mushrooms well coated. Add the cream and lemon juice, and bring to a boil. Reduce for another minute or two just until it seizes into the consistency of a light gravy. Season with salt and serve at once over the fried steaks with creamy grits (page 38) or creamed barley.

Chicken-Fried
Morel Mushrooms

I remember my first taste of morel mushrooms quite vividly. We spent one of the first warm days of spring at my Uncle John and Aunt Dorothy's farm out near Ferdinand, Indiana. We younger kids were left back at the house with supervision while the adults and older kids fanned out into the woods with empty bread bags and the charge to bring them back full of mushrooms, and they were successful. I have no idea what the haul was that day, but there were several bread bags full, enough that both of our large families had our fill for dinner with more to take home.

Our favored method of cooking these delectable wild fungi was to bread them and fry them in lard or bacon or ham drippings. Our deep southern Indiana version was dipped in regular "sweet" milk before dredging, while farther south these types of preparations likely involved buttermilk. Nonetheless, it's still my favorite way to enjoy morels, and it's a great way to prepare any number of mushrooms. The important thing is to use mushrooms with thin bodies such as hen of the woods, black trumpet, chanterelle, or oyster mushrooms; or if you use thicker mushrooms such as portobellos or matsutake, slice them into ½-inch thick slabs before cooking them.

We'd always make a gravy with the bits left in the pan—what is commonly called sawmill gravy in Appalachia. Enjoy this dish with creamy grits, mashed potatoes, or even biscuits for a unique biscuit and gravy dish, and a green salad of early lettuce or wild greens such as dandelions to counter the richness of the mushrooms and gravy.

PREP TIME: 30 minutes
EQUIPMENT NEEDED: two 2-quart mixing bowls, 10-inch cast-iron skillet, clip-
   on thermometer, long-handled tongs, plate lined with paper towels
SERVES: 4 to 6

   1 pound morel mushrooms
   1 cup buttermilk
   2 cups all-purpose flour

3 tablespoons stone-ground cornmeal

1 teaspoon baking powder

2 teaspoons kosher salt

2 teaspoons freshly ground black pepper

1½ cups lard or vegetable oil

❦ Preheat oven to 300°F.

❦ To clean the morels, cut them in half lengthwise, making one long clean slice from the cap down through the open bottom of the stem, exposing the hollow center. Inspect both sides of the mushrooms for bugs and debris. Use a soft, clean washcloth to rub away any dirt or debris, but refrain from washing under water as this can make the mushrooms soggy.

❦ Pour the buttermilk in a 2-quart mixing bowl. In a separate 2-quart bowl, combine the flour, cornmeal, baking powder, salt, and pepper.

❦ Heat a 10-inch cast-iron skillet over medium-high heat, and melt the lard or vegetable oil, heating until a bit of flour dropped into the pan sizzles vigorously, 325°F on a clip-on thermometer. Dip each piece of mushroom in the buttermilk, very gently shake off excess buttermilk, and dip in the flour mixture, gently tossing to coat evenly. Bread all the mushrooms, and reserve on a plate before proceeding.

❦ Place the mushrooms in the hot lard in a single layer, leaving enough space between for hot lard to bubble up in between. Depending on the size and shape of your mushrooms, you may need to make two batches. Reduce heat to medium, and cook on the first side to golden brown, 4 to 5 minutes; then gently turn with a long-handled tongs, and cook to brown on the second side, another 2 to 3 minutes. Place on a plate lined with paper towels to drain, and hold in your preheated oven while you fry the second batch and then make the gravy.

❦ Once all the mushrooms are fried and warming in the oven, drain off excess lard (die-hard Southern cooks save this to be used again—my grandma kept it in a coffee can on the back of her stove), leaving just the brown bits in the bottom of the pan and a couple tablespoons of the lard for making sawmill gravy.

Sawmill Gravy

So named for its common use in lumber camps during the late nineteenth century when great tracts of the Appalachian forest were being cut to help build America's rapidly growing cities, sawmill gravy could most easily be described as a pan gravy made with leftover bits after pan-frying. This was a delicious and simple way to make sure no last bit of food went to waste, not even the pan drippings.

In particularly hard times, the gravy might be made with little more than water boiled up with the pan drippings, whatever would catch everything and get it onto the plate and into hungry bellies. These days milk is the most common base for sawmill gravy, or you can use whatever kind of stock you have on hand.

PREP TIME: 15 minutes
EQUIPMENT NEEDED: 10-inch cast-iron skillet, long-handled wooden spoon,
    serving bowl or gravy boat
SERVES: 4 to 6

2 to 3 tablespoons lard in addition to whatever solid bits are left in the
    pan after frying mushrooms, pork chops, chicken, etc.; excess lard
    or cooking oil can be drained off for later reuse
1 tablespoon all-purpose flour
1½ cups whole milk
½ teaspoon kosher salt
¼ teaspoon freshly ground black pepper

☙ In your cast-iron skillet after frying, heat the remaining lard and leftover bits over medium-high heat and add the flour. Cook, stirring constantly with a wooden spoon, until the flour browns to a rich tan color. Add half the milk, stirring constantly until mixture boils and thickens. At this point it will be somewhat pasty. Add the remaining milk, stirring constantly, until it returns to a boil. Add salt and pepper. If the gravy is too thin, allow to boil down for a few minutes until thickened to a desired consistency. Transfer to a bowl or gravy boat, and send to the table right away.

Turnip Greens with Potato Dumplings

Potatoes were an important crop that took root in Appalachia with both German and Ulster immigrant groups, and in some parts were nearly as important as corn. The German in me loves a good potato dumpling, and these are a rustic, easy dumpling with roots in both southern Germany and Appalachia, not unlike traditional Italian gnocchi in composition. Prepared just right, they are toothsome and hearty yet tender and light all at once—quite a treat.

Turnips were an important crop on many Appalachian farms, especially among the Dutch (as the Germans were known locally), and the tops were used as well as the roots so nothing would go to waste. There are also varieties of turnips grown specifically for their greens, and these are especially delicious and make a great counterpoint to the soft, velvety dumplings. Ham or other salt pork enriches the dish, but if you're vegetarian, you can eliminate the ham or even add some mushrooms if you like.

Look for turnip greens by the bunch at the market. If you're lucky enough to find young turnips, especially the Japanese variety called hakurei, with the greens attached, you can peel the turnips and add them to the pot with the greens for an even more substantial meal. This makes a wonderful side dish with fried chicken or pork chops, or a satisfying light supper on its own.

If you're unable to find turnip greens, you can substitute kale, collards, or mustard greens. The result won't quite be the same, but will be delicious nonetheless.

PREP TIME: 1 hour for the dumpling dough, 1 hour for the braise
EQUIPMENT NEEDED: baking sheet pan, clean dry towel, potato ricer or tamis, 4-quart mixing bowl, wooden spoon, 4-quart Dutch oven with tight-fitting lid, long-handled tongs
SERVES: 4 to 6

1 pound russet potatoes, about 2 to 3 medium potatoes
3 teaspoons kosher salt, divided

1 to 1¼ cups all-purpose flour, divided

2 bunches turnip greens, with large woody stems removed

¼ pound smoked country ham (or substitute bacon), diced into ½-inch pieces

1 cup yellow onion, thinly sliced lengthwise

½ cup white wine vinegar

2 cups unsalted chicken stock

1 teaspoon freshly ground black pepper

꽃 Preheat oven to 350°F. Use the tines of a fork to poke a few holes in each potato, wrap in foil, and place on a baking sheet in the middle of the oven. Bake until a knife easily passes through the potatoes indicating they are done, 45 minutes to 1 hour. Cool until they are temperate enough to handle; but you'll get best results if you proceed with warm potatoes, so don't allow to cool completely.

꽃 Once you can handle the potatoes, use a clean dry towel to rub the skins off, and pass them through a potato ricer, tamis, or fine-mesh strainer into a 4-quart mixing bowl so that they resemble light fallen snow. Add 1 teaspoon of the salt, and ¼ cup of the flour, and begin mixing with a wooden spoon. Once the flour is incorporated, add another ¼ cup and continue mixing. When the mixture becomes too stiff for the spoon, knead with your hands. Continue kneading in another ¼ cup of the flour, and then another, until the dough can form a smooth ball that is slightly tacky but holds its shape well. Depending on the size and moisture of your potatoes, this will require 1 cup of flour total, or a bit more. Cover the dough with plastic wrap, and allow to rest 20 minutes before using.

꽃 While the potatoes are baking, begin the greens. Wash them carefully in a clean sink to remove any grit or dirt. Gently pull them apart into 2- to 3-inch pieces, but don't shake dry because the water left on the greens will help steam them.

꽃 Place the greens in a 4-quart Dutch oven with a tight-fitting lid over medium-low heat, and top with the ham and onions. Cover the pot, and slowly and gently wilt the greens, removing the lid and turning the greens with long-handled tongs every 5 minutes until the greens are thoroughly wilted, 15 to 20 minutes. Increase heat to medium, and add the vinegar, chicken stock, the remaining 2 teaspoons of salt, and pepper. Return cover to pot, and bring to a low boil. Reduce heat to a simmer, and simmer gently for 30 to 45 minutes, until the largest stems are thoroughly tender.

✤ Take tablespoon-size scoops of the potato dough, and roll them between the palms of your hands into little balls that look like perfectly formed tiny snowballs. One by one, drop them into the pot with the turnip greens until all the dough is used up. The dumplings won't be completely submerged—they will steam during cooking. Stir gently to make sure the dumplings aren't sticking to one another, put the lid back on the pot, increase the heat to medium, and return to a boil. Cook at a low boil until the dumplings are cooked through, 20 to 25 minutes. You can test by slicing open with a knife—the dumplings will be very soft. When they're cooked, there will be a uniform consistency all the way through. If the center is still doughy, resume cooking. Transfer to a serving bowl, arranging the greens and dumplings around one another, and pour the cooking broth over. Serve at once.

Pan-Fried Ham with Redeye Gravy

Redeye gravy hasn't been on any of our regular menus for some time, but it pops up often on special-event menus and on regular specials at lunch or dinner, almost always with ham. Surely originating as a way to make use of leftover coffee lest it go to waste, traditional redeye gravy was made with the pan drippings that remain after frying ham. Beyond that, coffee is involved, but recipes vary greatly from there.

The simplest preparations would call for coffee to deglaze the pan, and the resulting liquid was served with the ham and whatever accompaniments were on hand—be they biscuits, cornbread, grits, or mush. Some folks would add a little flour and cook a roux in the drippings before adding the coffee, which I think is an improvement, especially if the roux is cooked a nice, toasty brown. Being a junkie for nuanced, layered flavors even when they are as bold as a coffee-based gravy, I've added trinity, a little stock, and Worcestershire.

A must with fried ham, I do prefer this with cornbread over biscuits, but both are good. If you're super adventurous, serve your fried ham over toasted rye and soak it all in this gravy. You'll be glad you did.

PREP TIME: 30 minutes
EQUIPMENT NEEDED: 10-inch cast-iron skillet, clip-on thermometer, long-handled tongs, wooden spoon
SERVES: 4 to 6

3 tablespoons bacon grease, lard, or leftover pan drippings
4 to 6 slices smoked ham, ½ inch thick and 4 to 6 ounces each
2 tablespoons all-purpose flour
¼ cup minced yellow onion
2 tablespoons celery, minced
2 tablespoons green bell pepper, minced
½ cup strong coffee
¾ cup chicken, pork, or ham stock
1 teaspoon freshly ground black pepper
1 tablespoon Worcestershire sauce
Kosher salt, to taste, if needed, depending how salty your ham is

☙ Melt the bacon fat, lard, or pan drippings in a 10-inch cast-iron skillet over medium-high heat until a little bit of ham dropped into the skillet sizzles vigorously, 350°F on a clip-on thermometer. Add the ham steaks (you will probably need to cook them in two to three batches depending on the size) in a single layer, and cook quickly until the first side browns well, 2 to 3 minutes, then turn gently with long-handled tongs. Brown the other side, another 1 to 2 minutes, and transfer to a serving platter. Cook remaining ham in a similar manner. When all ham is cooked, you must work quickly to make the gravy.
☙ While the skillet is still hot and the pan drippings remain, add the flour, stirring vigorously with a wooden spoon to begin the roux, and keep stirring as the flour begins to brown. Cook the roux to the color of peanut butter, 3 to 4 minutes. Working quickly with the heat still on, add the onion, celery, and bell pepper, and cook to sweat the vegetables until they soften, 3 to 4 minutes. Not skipping a beat, stir in the coffee, which will quickly turn the contents of the skillet into a paste—which is fine, just keep stirring. Add the stock, pepper, and Worcestershire sauce, and bring to a boil, 1 to 2 minutes. If the gravy is too thin for your taste, boil it to reduce and thicken until it coats a spoon thickly. Taste for seasoning and salt if needed, or add more pepper if desired. Pour over the ham steaks and serve.

Buttermilk Pie

I first came across this most delicious pie in Henrietta Dull's *Southern Cooking*, published in Atlanta in 1928, although buttermilk was already making its mark in Southern sweets by the last half of the nineteenth century with receipts for buttermilk pudding in *Mrs. Hill's New Cook Book* (1867) and buttermilk ice cream in *Housekeeping in Old Virginia* (1879). It turned out to be one of the most brilliant custard pies I've ever made, improved even from Mrs. Dull's recipe with the addition of orange zest, which lightens the pie beautifully.

Buttermilk contributes such a wonderful richness but also that tangy acidity that keeps the pie honest without becoming cloying. Properly made and baked just right, the curd you get in the center of the pie is exquisitely sticky so it coats your palate, with the acid of the buttermilk and aromatic fruitiness of the orange zest making the tongue and nose dance in unison.

One of summer's most refreshing desserts if served chilled, or winter's most rich and comforting if served warm, I love this tangy sweet pie for its versatility. I tend to prefer it during summer with macerated fresh fruit, especially raspberries, but I'll also make it during winter to enjoy warm out of the oven with some preserved quince and whipped cream. Of course, it's delicious by itself—no need for accompaniments simple or fancy, though a little whipped cream is always a treat for which you need no excuse.

PREP TIME: 2 hours including pie crust and baking
EQUIPMENT NEEDED: 9-inch pie pan, stand mixer with wire whip attachment,
    box grater or citrus zester, 1-quart mixing bowl
MAKES: one 9-inch pie

1 prepared 9-inch pie shell, well chilled
½ cup (1 stick) unsalted butter, cut into bits and softened
1½ cups granulated sugar
1 tablespoon all-purpose flour
2 teaspoons cornstarch
½ teaspoon kosher salt

1 tablespoon finely grated orange zest
5 large eggs
1¼ cups lowfat buttermilk, divided
3 tablespoons sour cream

❦ Preheat oven to 325°F. Prepare one 9-inch pie shell, and refrigerate thoroughly before filling.

❦ In a stand mixer with the wire whip attachment, cream the butter and sugar until light and fluffy, 5 to 6 minutes. Beat in the flour, cornstarch, salt, and orange zest until smooth. Break the eggs into a 1-quart bowl, then beat into the creamed butter and sugar mixture one at a time, incorporating each egg thoroughly before adding the next, until smooth. Beat in the buttermilk and sour cream in thirds, being sure to incorporate after each addition. Pour into prepared pie crust, and bake on the lower rack of the oven until lightly browned on top and the center is set, 50 to 60 minutes. The center will jiggle as one mass rather than ripple like water when shaken gently. Cool on a wire rack before cutting or covering and refrigerating. Excellent either warm or cold, but don't try to slice while hot—the filling won't hold up. You can test by cutting a slice and starting to lift it out. If it pulls away cleanly from the rest of the pie, it's cooled enough to slice. If the filling runs back together, let it cool awhile longer. Serve with macerated fresh fruit.

Jelly Roll Cake

Seeing a recipe for a jelly roll in *The Taste of Country Cooking* by Edna Lewis was one of my personal development's defining moments, and will always be special to me because I came to truly understand what was happening to American food culture. A classic case of industry making a home-cooked staple into an industrially produced snack.

Many nineteenth- and early twentieth-century cookbooks offer recipes for jelly rolls while few modern cookbooks do, a rather peculiar disappearing act for something that was in the repertoire of many a home cook in the early twentieth century. In the meantime, one place that jelly roll cakes have continued to appear is the processed snack-cake rack in convenience stores and supermarkets. While I can't say so authoritatively, it would seem that jelly rolls have been co-opted by the industrial bakeries and have for now been relegated to the status of junk food.

Jelly rolls offer many opportunities for dramatic presentation, and you also have seemingly endless options as far as jelly flavors or even custard or cream fillings go. You can serve these with ice cream, whipped cream, or on their own.

PREP TIME: 1 hour

EQUIPMENT NEEDED: jelly roll pan or 12-by-18-inch sheet pan with edges, baking parchment, pie pan, stand mixer with wire whip, sifter, large rubber spatula

MAKES: one 12-inch roll cake, serves 8 to 12

2 tablespoons (¼ stick) unsalted butter, softened and divided

¾ cup granulated sugar

4 large eggs

2 teaspoons ice water

2 teaspoons vanilla extract

¾ cup all-purpose flour, sifted before measuring and resifted

½ teaspoon kosher salt

1 cup jelly of choice, full flavored tart jellies such as currant jelly work best

Powdered sugar, for dusting

☙ Preheat oven to 375°F.

☙ Line a jelly roll pan, or 12-by-18-inch sheet pan with edges, with baking parchment by first buttering it with 1 tablespoon of the butter and then pressing the parchment into the bottom of the pan, using the butter as a kind of mortar. Leave a little excess parchment on the ends of the pan to make lifting the finished cake out of the pan easier. Butter the top of the parchment well and also the sides of the pan with the remaining tablespoon of butter.

☙ Place sugar in the hot oven in a pie pan to heat for 5 minutes. Break the eggs in the bowl of a stand mixer with the wire whip, and begin whipping on high speed until frothy, 1 to 2 minutes. Continue beating and add the ice water, then the hot sugar a couple tablespoons at a time until incorporated. Add the vanilla and salt and continue whipping until thick and foamy, another 6 to 8 minutes.

🌱 Remove the bowl from the stand mixer, and fold in the flour in thirds, sifting the flour over the foamy egg mixture to prevent lumps. Turn the batter into your parchment-lined baking sheet. Use a spatula to carefully spread the batter evenly over the pan, all the way to the corners. Bake in the preheated oven until set and golden brown, 18 to 20 minutes.

🌱 Allow the cake to cool 10 minutes before turning out, but try to work with the cake when still warm to the touch, as it will be easier to separate from the parchment. Roll out enough fresh parchment to cover the cake and spread out over the top of the cake. Very carefully lift the cake out by handling the parchment from underneath—not touching the cake, which is delicate and thin. Turn the cake over onto the unbaked piece of parchment and gently lay on a work surface. The cake should now be upside down. Very gently, pulling from the corners, peel the baked parchment off of the cake.

🌱 Stir the jelly well to soften it before spreading over the cake. With a clean rubber spatula, gently spread jelly over the cake, leaving 1 inch around the edges clean. Working from the parchment underlayment rather than the cake, gently but firmly roll the cake, tucking one edge under and then pulling one end of the parchment over the top to roll it up. Wrap the roll in parchment and pull tight. Wrap again in plastic wrap and refrigerate at least 6 hours before serving.

🌱 To serve, cut into 1-inch slices, dust with powdered sugar, and serve with whipped cream or your favorite ice cream.

Salty Sorghum Taffy

During hard times, small farmers in the mountains often wouldn't have cash on hand to buy candy, or at least would have better uses for what money they did have. Getting to the general store to buy candy was just as big an issue for some—in the more remote parts of the mountains, traveling to the nearest general store and back might take the better part of a day, and such trips were made only when they had to be. Sorghum candy is tasty and easy to make, and a fun way to involve kids, as an extra set of hands is always needed to help pull the taffy.

Don't try to make this without a friend around to help pull the taffy. Cellophane wrap can be found at craft stores and cut to size if you want to wrap the candy for presentation, or simply place the taffy in single layers separated by wax paper in a tin box in a cool dry spot, where it will keep for days.

PREP TIME: 45 minutes

EQUIPMENT NEEDED: jelly roll pan or 9-by-13-inch cake pan, 2-quart heavy-bottomed stainless-steel or enamel saucepan, clip-on candy thermometer, long-handled wooden spoon, rolling pin, kitchen shears, cellophane or wax paper for wrapping

MAKES: 1 pound

¼ cup (½ stick) plus 1 tablespoon unsalted butter, chilled and cut into tablespoon-size bits, divided
1 cup granulated sugar
1 cup sorghum molasses or regular molasses
2 teaspoons kosher salt
¼ cup water
½ teaspoon baking soda

⚜ Use 1 tablespoon of the butter to grease a jelly roll pan or 9-by-13-inch cake pan and reserve.

⚜ Place the sugar, sorghum molasses, salt, and water in a 2-quart heavy-bottomed stainless-steel or enamel saucepan over medium-high heat with a clip-on candy thermometer. Stir constantly with a long-handled wooden spoon as the syrup cooks to make sure it heats evenly and to keep it from boiling over the sides of the pan. Keep a close eye on the pot, as the syrup will burn easily if not stirred. Cook to the low range of the hard ball stage of sugar cooking, 252°F. Remove from heat at once, stir in the remaining ¼ cup butter, and then finally the baking soda. The mixture will foam. Pour out into the buttered pan, and cool until it is as hot as you can handle without burning yourself, 6 to 10 minutes. The hotter you can handle the candy, the creamier your finished taffy will be—but be careful!

⚜ Gather the hot candy into a ball and begin pulling it—having a friend to help makes it easier. Working quickly, stretch it out 2 to 3 feet, fold, stretch, fold, stretch, and repeat until the candy loses its gloss and turns opaque. After 8 to 10 minutes, it will be cool and start becoming too stiff to stretch easily. Set it back on the buttered cookie sheet, and press it out into a square with your hands, ½ inch thick if possible. Use a rolling pin to flatten the square until it is ¼ inch evenly across the sheet of candy. Cover with plastic wrap, and allow to set for 1 hour. Cut into ½-by-1-inch pieces with kitchen shears or a clean scissors. Wrap in cellophane or store in a tin lined with waxed paper between each layer.

Kentuckiana

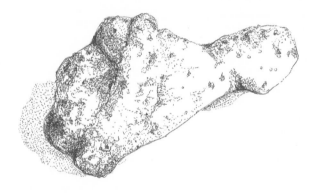

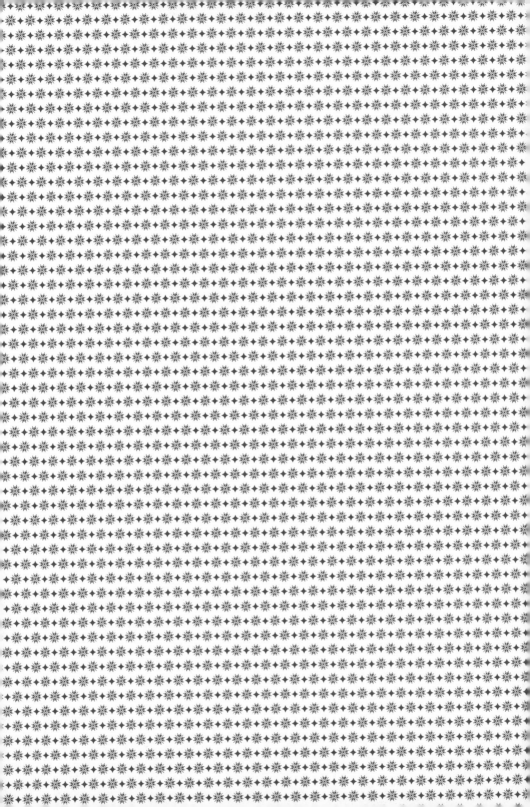

Friends from virtually every other part of the country are always somewhat bemused when I refer to my home country as "Kentuckiana," as if I'm alluding to some far-off land they've never heard of, or even a place that doesn't really exist. It's a term I grew up with but didn't really take to until I was an adult and realized the cultural (and topographical) similarities between the lands on both sides of the Ohio River.

When I became interested in learning more about the cooking of my own ancestry, my detective work led me to research not only where my family came from but also how they got to that little farm I remember from my youth. The path was interesting, and common in the early eighteenth century for European immigrants to the lower Midwest. They'd take the Wagon Road south from Philadelphia to the Cumberland Gap to enter Kentucky and eventually catch the Buffalo Trace, the trail blazed by migrating buffalo that crossed the Falls of the Ohio near present-day Louisville, and headed west through southern Indiana to Vincennes and across the Wabash River through Illinois to the mighty Mississippi.

As land was surveyed, offered, and settled along these various trails, the Virginia and Carolina Piedmont was settled, followed by eastern Kentucky, and folks eventually followed the available land to my part of southern Indiana. My great-great-great-great-great-grandparents took a plot of sixty acres on one of the branches of the Buffalo Trace. Southern Indiana and northern Kentucky around the Buffalo Trace were settled by the same ethnic groups—German, Ulster, and English mostly—as settled Appalachia, and the cooking styles maintain many similarities to this day. I began to sense why I grew up with fried chicken and biscuits as celebration foods when everyone said they were "Southern."

What is distinct about Kentuckiana's history to the present is the whiskey industry. Prior to the Civil War, there were distilleries on both sides of the Ohio River (William Henry Harrison even operated one for a short time), so whiskey and whiskey barrels were ingrained in the life of the people in the area. During the Civil War, the distilleries in Indiana and Ohio lost their major market in New Orleans as it was a risky proposition to get the product past Vicksburg and Natchez. They all suffered greatly, and the industry all but disappeared in Indiana and Ohio, giving way for Kentucky to cement its dominance in what would become known as the bourbon industry.

Whiskey traveled down the river, and oftentimes oysters would come back up the river once steamboats could navigate against the current, particularly in winter months when the oysters were thought to be tastier and the cold would help them make the trip and arrive in Louisville in good condition. Special tax incentives for wool production led to a peculiar (and delicious) type of barbecue in the western part of Kentucky around Owensboro, with mutton as the meat and sorghum molasses as the baste. Kitchen gardens were kept by most every family with land, and given the particular ethnic makeup of the area—German, Scotch, and Irish—vegetables such as cabbages, kohlrabi, turnips, and cucumbers were major crops for home kitchen processing. Repurposed whiskey barrels were used to ferment sauerkraut, hold pickles, and make beer, cider, and wild cherry wine for the family cellar.

It's believed that the practice of frying chicken in fat was brought to America by the Scots, so naturally the practice took hold in Kentuckiana. In my hometown there was scarcely a major family event such as a wedding, jubilee, graduation, or confirmation party without an ample amount of fried chicken accompanied by relishes, potatoes, and whatever vegetables were at hand.

Hunting and foraging have always been revered pastimes here, and the most astute foragers still know where to find the most reliable pawpaw patch, persimmon trees, and the best places to look for morels in spring and hen of the woods in fall. Duck, rabbit, deer, and squirrel were favored game meats, and I enjoyed many a squirrel supper while growing up.

Every family farm had a smokehouse in those days, and hog butchering was done in the yard as it was in most of the country. Dairy was to eventually emerge as a minor industry in the area, so veal often made an appearance, and by the mid-twentieth century, beef was making inroads as well.

The culinary traditions of Kentuckiana are rich and celebrated, owing much to the bourbon industry and the cosmopolitan city of Louisville, the de facto capital of the region. One of my favorite means of reliving the arts of the old homestead of Kentuckiana is Lettice Bryans's *The Kentucky Housewife*, published in 1839. I often try to reproduce these recipes true to her narrative in the book, but just as often adapt them to modern tastes, including my own. One foot in history, one foot in the future.

Chicken and Dumplings, ca. 1920

Chicken and dumplings was a tough dish to put on the menu, because it's one for which almost everyone has a reference point, and expectations can often be unrealistic, since the chicken and dumplings on which you grew up may bear no resemblance at all to the one I knew.

Where I grew up, chicken and dumplings was a simple, brothy dish with thick-cut egg noodles added to the pot with the broth after the chicken meat had been cleaned from the bones. In many households, there was only chicken, noodles, broth, salt, and pepper—no garlic, herbs, onions, or other vegetables—yet if cooked just right, it was the most soul-satisfying bowl of goodness you could imagine. Other versions of chicken and dumplings might have fluffy biscuit-like dumplings and a panoply of vegetables floating in a thick cream gravy. Not my cup of tea, but to others, it's a precious food memory.

This is different from how my mom made it—she would roll out and cut the dumplings, whereas we plop them into the hot broth for a thicker, chewier dumpling like knefles, a rustic German farm dumpling my mom would use in bean dishes. You can add any vegetables you want to the pot, just be mindful that some take longer to cook than others. Personally, I feel like just a little onion is all that's required.

PREP TIME: 2 hours

EQUIPMENT NEEDED: 4-quart stock pot, 2-quart mixing bowl, table fork, 2-quart or larger baking dish, colander, tablespoon, long-handled wooden spoon, 2-quart pot

SERVES: 6 to 8

1 medium fryer chicken, 3 to 3½ pounds, quartered
2 quarts cold water
2 bay leaves
2 large eggs
1 tablespoon plus 1 teaspoon kosher salt, divided
¾ cup plus 2 tablespoons whole milk
2½ cups all-purpose flour

½ teaspoon baking powder

2 cups yellow onion, finely diced

2 teaspoons coarsely ground black pepper

✿ Place the whole chicken in a 4-quart stock pot, cover with 2 quarts cold water, and add the bay leaves. Place over medium-high heat and bring to a boil, then reduce heat to a low boil. Skim off any foam or scum that rises to the top.

✿ While the chicken is boiling, make the dumplings. Crack the eggs into a 2-quart mixing bowl and beat well with a fork. Add 1 teaspoon kosher salt and the milk, and beat thoroughly to combine. Then add all the flour and baking powder at once, and stir vigorously with a wooden spoon until the dough comes together into a sticky, firm dough. No need to knead or over-mix. Once the dough has come together and is free of lumps, cover and refrigerate until needed.

✿ Cook the chicken at a low boil for 1½ hours, until chicken is just beginning to fall from the bones. Remove from heat. Carefully remove the chicken from the pot, and place in a 2-quart or larger baking dish to cool. Strain the stock through the colander into a separate 2-quart pot, and reserve, discarding the bay leaves and any other bits left in the colander.

✿ Add the stock back to the 4-quart stock pot, and bring to a low boil over medium heat, then lower heat to maintain a high simmer. Add the onions and a tablespoon of salt; you can add more later to your taste if you desire.

✿ While the stock and onions come to a boil, pick the chicken meat from the bones, discarding the skin and bones, and add the meat to the pot in the largest pieces you can pick from the bones. Using a tablespoon, dip the spoon into the hot stock, then quickly spoon up a tablespoon-size bit of dough and drop it into the steaming pot by knocking it on the rim. Working quickly, repeat until all dough is used up. Stir gently from the bottom with a wooden spoon to make sure the dumplings aren't sticking.

✿ Turn heat to medium high and bring to a boil, then cover and reduce to a simmer. Cook another 10 minutes, until dumplings are puffy and cooked through. Taste and add more salt if desired. Stir in pepper and serve straight from the pot.

Sweet Tea–Brined Pork Loin

Brining pork in sweet tea was the genius notion of one of our better chefs over the years, Corey Fuller. One of pork's most alluring qualities is that it pairs well with many different flavors and can take up the flavor of anything it's cooked with. Sweet tea lends it a toasty bitterness in addition to the sweetness from some added sugar, making a finished pork loin roast that tickles every single taste bud.

We've served this with many seasonal accoutrements over the years and still make one seasonal change every year for sweet corn season, but this dish is usually served with sweet potato hash and baked bean puree partly because it was always the most popular combination, and also because it's just kind of awesome—the meat is toothsome; the baked bean puree, creamy, smoky, and a little sweet. Sweet potatoes are classic with pork, and a little crispy bacon in the hash adds a nice salty crunch. During our short sweet corn season in Chicago, we'll take a break from sweet potato hash and serve it with succotash (page 110), one of my favorite ways to celebrate sweet corn season.

PREP TIME: 30 minutes to prepare the brine, 8 hours brining, 20 minutes for cooking

EQUIPMENT NEEDED: 4-quart heat-proof mixing bowl, fine-mesh strainer, several feet butcher twine cut into 10-inch lengths, 10-inch cast-iron skillet, long-handled tongs, 2-quart Tupperware or dish with tight-fitting lid

SERVES: 4 to 6

3 tablespoons black tea, such as English breakfast
2 whole pieces star anise
1 bay leaf
4 allspice berries
4 whole cloves
1 teaspoon crushed red pepper
½ cup packed dark brown sugar
1 tablespoon kosher salt
2 cups boiling water

Enough ice to bring strained tea up to 1 quart total volume
2 pounds boneless pork loin roast, cut into 4 to 6 steaks of 5 to 8
    ounces each, depending on how many you want
1 to 2 tablespoons clarified bacon grease or lard for pan-frying

❦ Place the tea, anise, bay leaf, allspice, cloves, red pepper, sugar, and salt in a heat-proof 4-quart mixing bowl. Pour boiling water over and stir gently to combine. Let stand for 1 hour, then strain through a fine-mesh strainer, discarding the spices. Measure, then add enough ice to make 1 quart brine. Cover and refrigerate while you prepare the loins and butcher twine.
❦ Cut one 10-inch-length butcher twine for each portion of loin. Cut loin into 1¼-inch steaks, and tie each around with a length of twine, tying snugly but not too tightly. Place the tied pork loin steaks into the brine (it's OK if there's still ice in the brine—in fact, colder is better), and allow to soak for 6 to 8 hours. Do not over-soak or the texture of your finished loins will suffer. Remove loins from brine, pat them dry with clean towels, and refrigerate in a tightly covered container until needed, up to 7 days.
❦ Preheat oven to 425°F. Melt enough lard or bacon fat to just cover the bottom of a 10-inch cast-iron skillet thinly. Place over high heat just until smoking, then reduce heat to medium and add the pork loins, pressing down on the steak to make sure the bottom sears well against the pan. Press for 10 to 15 seconds. Brown well on the first side, 2 to 3 minutes, then turn with long-handled tongs and place in the preheated oven to finish cooking, allowing 4 minutes for a nice pink or 8 minutes for well done. After removing from oven, rest for a few minutes before cutting. Serve with any bean dish and sweet potato hash (page 183) or succotash (page 110).

Fried Chicken

It's kind of funny that I've become known for fried chicken, since it's something I resisted for a long time. Not because I don't like fried chicken; in fact, it's one of my life essentials. Growing up where I did in southern Indiana, no special occasion was ever allowed to pass—be it a wedding, an eightieth jubilee, a twenty-fifth anniversary party, a graduation, you name it—without a chafing dish or pot of fried chicken on offer. In fact, it was usually the main event at these types of gatherings. I am made of fried chicken.

My reticence had more to do with fried chicken's iconic status in Southern cooking. I felt like it was too expected, too predictable, and would likely crowd out other dishes that might allow us to tell more of the South's story.

We initially started fried chicken as a promotion on Tuesday nights, and within months it was on the front page of the *Chicago Tribune* dining section in a Kevin Pang piece called "Fry Masters" and soon after in the pages of *Bon Appétit* as one of the top fried chickens north of the Mason-Dixon Line. More press continued to follow, and putting the genie back in the bottle was never an option. In the meantime, I realized that if fried chicken is such an integral part of my own personal story and my family's history, and if I'm good at making it, what's the problem?

As much as I worried about fried chicken crowding out other Southern dishes, fried chicken sells, and folks enjoy it. It's a moneymaker for us, so without it we probably wouldn't be able to tell as many other interesting stories as we do.

My "signature" cinnamon pork chops

I made my first dredge when I was seven years old, and without my mom's permission. I'd asked earlier in the afternoon what was for dinner, and she said it would be pork chops, which we usually fried in a breading just like chicken, in a cast-iron skillet with lard. I don't know what gave me the notion that pork chops would be good with cinnamon and clove, but while my mom was downstairs doing laundry, I got out a cast-iron skillet, some lard, and fired it up. I filled a shallow dish with flour, salt, and pepper, and then took the cap off the cinnamon and just let it pour in—the whole bottle. I followed suit with the cloves, dipped some pork chops in milk, and then dredged them, oblivious to the would-be clue that I was off track as the dredge was brown with spices. Within a minute of those chops hitting the lard, the overwhelming scent of cinnamon shrouded the house; my mom came running up from the laundry room in a panic, kicked me off the stove, and did her best to save dinner. Fortunately that was all the mayhem that ensued, since I suppose it could have been worse—at least I didn't burn the house down! I did learn a big, fat lesson in seasoning—

use restraint, because you can always add more and re-season, but once it's in there, you're not getting it out.

So, my first grand culinary experiment as an over-ambitious seven-year-old was a failure, the pork chops were terrible; but since our family wasn't made of money in those days, we went ahead and ate them. My mom, dad, or any one of my brothers or sisters can still get the biggest laugh when we all get together just by bringing up my "signature" cinnamon pork chops.

Fortunately, I learned much in subsequent years and have a dredge and some frying techniques that'll yield you some fried chicken to impress any company. The dredge at this point is the result of my own experimentation going all the way back to that fateful cinnamon-tastic day. A few years ago, I updated my soaking and frying techniques from Edna Lewis's inspiration, brining in a mild vinegar solution and frying with a hint of butter and salt pork. Her elegant technique threw my own chicken over the top. That's why I attribute my fried chicken and my whole way of cooking to Edna Lewis—her cooking could be as confident as it was because her technique, while based in African American country cooking, was always impeccable. And so we have this fried chicken, which I have no doubt you will enjoy.

PREP TIME: 10 minutes to prepare the brine, 8 hours or overnight for brining, 45 minutes for frying

EQUIPMENT NEEDED: two 4-quart mixing bowls with tight-fitting lids, 2-gallon heavy-bottomed cast-iron or enamel Dutch oven or countertop fryer, digital clip-on thermometer, large shallow pan, long-handled tongs, meat thermometer, wire rack or serving platter with clean towels for draining

SERVES: 2 to 4

FOR THE BRINE
2 quarts iced water
1 tablespoon plus 1 teaspoon kosher salt
1 teaspoon freshly ground black pepper
1 tablespoon granulated onion
2 tablespoons distilled white vinegar
2 bay leaves
3 to 4 sprigs fresh thyme, or 1 teaspoon dried

1 small frying chicken about 3 pounds, cut at the joints—leg, thigh, breast, wing, plus the lower back (my favorite when I was a kid because it's all crispy skin!)

☙ Put water, salt, pepper, onion, vinegar, bay, and thyme in a 4-quart bowl with a tight-fitting lid, and stir gently to disperse the seasonings—this will take as long as 5 minutes to dissolve the salt because the liquid is iced. Gently add the chicken pieces, cover tightly, and refrigerate at least 8 hours or overnight before using within 3 days.

FOR THE DREDGE
4 cups all-purpose white flour, sifted
1 cup fine-grind cornmeal, white preferred but may substitute yellow
1⅛ teaspoons baking powder
1 tablespoon freshly ground black pepper
¼ cup kosher salt
1 teaspoon dried thyme
2 teaspoons ground sage
1 tablespoon Spanish paprika
1 teaspoon dried basil
1 teaspoon dried oregano
1 teaspoon ground coriander
½ teaspoon ground cloves
½ teaspoon ground nutmeg

☙ Place the flour and cornmeal in a 4-quart mixing bowl, then one by one sprinkle the other seasonings over the flour while stirring to combine thoroughly. This will take more stirring than you think—dry ingredients don't disperse like wet ingredients. Once combined, cover tightly and set aside until needed.

TO FRY
3 quarts lard or vegetable oil
1 cup clarified butter
3 to 4 strips bacon or 1 thick slice smoked ham

☙ Place 3 quarts fresh lard or your favorite vegetable frying oil, the clarified butter, and a thick slice of ham or 3 to 4 strips of uncooked bacon into a 2-gallon heavy-bottomed cast-iron or enamel Dutch oven, and heat the oil to 375°F over medium-high heat. Use a clip-on thermometer to monitor your heat. During cooking the bacon or ham will darken and brown—just remove it once it's nice and crispy, but before it burns.

☙ In the meantime, place your dredge in a large shallow pan and take your chicken, still dripping wet from the brine, and lay it in the dredge, turning gently to coat, and make sure all the chicken pieces are thoroughly coated with dredge. Leave chicken in the dredge a few minutes to soak up more flour. Once the oil reaches 375°F, remove the breasts from the dredge and, using long-handled tongs, gently lay skin-side down in the hot oil. Cook the breasts for 3 minutes before adding the thighs. Gently add the thighs skin-side down also. One minute later, add the legs and wings. Use a clip-on thermometer to maintain the temperature at 325°F, lower than the temperature you started with—watch the oil temperature carefully as it will heat back up pretty quickly after you add the chicken. Seven to eight minutes after adding the legs and wings, use long-handled tongs to gently turn the chicken over. The skin should be crispy and golden brown. Continue cooking another 6 to 8 minutes, until the thickest part of the breast registers 155°F internally on a meat thermometer. Total cooking time from adding the breasts will be 18 to 20 minutes. Drain on a wire rack or towel, and serve at once or refrigerate to serve cold.

Duet of Duck
with Bourbon Giblet Jus

When I was coming up in the industry, it was still most common to see duck in fine restaurants one of two ways: a whole roasted half, or a seared and sliced breast. Serving a seared and sliced breast with a leg and thigh confit was cutting edge. How times change.

If I'm going to eat an animal, duck is probably my absolute favorite. I love the richness of the meat, how succulent it is when prepared well, and its signature gamey funk that pairs so marvelously with the earthy flavors of fall and winter. A particular challenge where duck is concerned is reaching the fullest expression of its many parts. I like the breast cured, seared, and roasted to a nice juicy medium. (I differ with many connois-

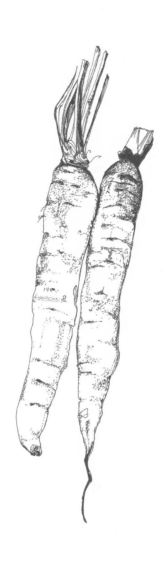

seurs here, but at medium you have the optimal ratio of juice rendered in liquid form in the meat, yet not cooked out; it's the juiciest temp.) The leg and thigh are best as confit, and while I do enjoy duck liver pâté, if I'm representing the whole duck, there are a few ways I can use the giblets; but the home cook in me wants to go for a giblet gravy, which in the interest of keeping the dish gluten free, comes in the form of a jus rather than a thick roux-based gravy. Finally, there has to be crispy skin.

How to achieve all this? First, we cut out the neck fat, season it, place it between two sheet pans, and weight it to press the skin and fat flat, then render it in the oven until golden brown and crispy. This also yields a bit more duck fat, always a bonus. We've already potted the duck limbs, so we can slice that and pan-fry it in the rendered duck fat. We cure and sear the breast, then finish it in the oven, and finally the carcass is roasted until golden brown and made into a stock with the giblets; then the stock is reduced to a jus, the giblets are minced and returned to the sauce, it's seasoned with bourbon and Worcestershire, and mounted with a little butter to finish. These various components can then be served together with some tasty seasonal sides.

Good choices for side dishes are sweet potato hash, charred Brussels sprouts, and rutabaga confit—but my absolute favorite is creamed Brewster oat groats because the earthy flavors of the oats and mushrooms plus the sweetness of the parsnip just make for the happiest of plates.

PREP TIME: Once all items are prepped, 30 minutes to cook final dish; for the various preparations, allow 2 days

EQUIPMENT NEEDED: two 10-inch or 12-inch cast-iron skillets, digital food thermometer, metal spatula, wire rack or plate with paper towels for draining, spice or coffee grinder, wire rack and drip tray or pan, shallow pan, two 12-by-18-inch sheet pans with edges, large stainless-steel baking dish or braising pan, 4-quart stainless-steel or enamel stock pot, small ladle, colander, 2-quart saucepan, fine-mesh strainer

SERVES: 4 to 8

2 4-pound Pekin ducklings
3 tablespoons rendered duck fat, divided
4 duck breasts, cured overnight (recipe follows)
4 1-inch slices potted duck, refrigerated (page 146)

Crispy duck crackling (recipe follows)
Bourbon giblet jus (recipe follows)

☙ Purchase two 4-pound Pekin ducklings for this recipe, and prepare the legs, thighs, and drumettes into potted duck (page 146). Save the wing tips and second joints for the jus. Cut the breasts for curing, and save the neck skin and fat for crackling. Trim the remaining excess skin and fat from the back and organ cavity, and use for potted duck. The carcass, giblets, and wing tips should be free of excess skin and fat for the jus.

☙ Preheat oven to 325°F.

☙ In a 10-inch or 12-inch cast-iron skillet, melt 1 tablespoon duck fat over medium-low heat, and place the duck breasts skin-side down and listen for a little sizzle—you want a little, not a lot to render the fat underneath the skin. As the breasts begin giving up their fat after 4 to 5 minutes (you'll see it adding to the pool of fat in the pan), increase heat a bit at a time until the burner is at medium high and the breasts are at a full sizzle. Cook the skins to a light brown, turn them over, and transfer the whole pan to the preheated oven and cook for 3 minutes, when the internal temperature should read 135°F. Rest 6 to 8 minutes before slicing.

☙ In the meantime, melt the remaining duck fat in another large cast-iron skillet that is big enough to hold the potted duck slices, and heat the duck fat just to the point of smoking over medium-high heat. Carefully add the potted duck slices, and reduce heat to medium. Cook until the first side is well browned and crispy. The potted duck will tend to stick to the pan at first but in a while will release itself once crispy, after which you can very carefully use a metal spatula to scrape them up from the pan and carefully turn them over. No need to brown heavily on the second side, just cook until lightly crispy and pulling away from the bottom of the pan. Remove and drain on paper towels or a wire rack for a few minutes before serving.

☙ Arrange the sliced breast around the potted duck cakes and ladle the giblet jus around. Crumble crispy duck crackling over all. Serve with Brewster oat groats (page 149) and rutabaga confit (page 148).

TO CURE THE DUCK BREASTS
4 skin-on duck breasts
4 whole stars anise
1 tablespoon whole allspice berries

1 tablespoon whole cloves
1 tablespoon whole black pepper
1 tablespoon kosher salt

❦ Trim the duck breasts of their tenderloins and excess skin and fat, to make each breast a clean rectangle. Add trimmings to the confit pot with the legs and thighs. Place spices in a spice or coffee grinder, and pulse to coarsely crush the spices. Arrange breasts flesh-side up in a shallow pan, and sprinkle with half the spice mixture, and then half the salt. Turn the breasts over and sprinkle with the remaining spices and salt. Place skin-side up on a wire rack or perforated pan to drain over a drip tray, and place in the refrigerator, uncovered, where nothing will drip on them. Refrigerate overnight, then rinse under cold running water, pat dry, and place in a covered dish in the refrigerator until ready to use.

CRISPY DUCK CRACKLING
1 tablespoon rendered duck fat
Neck fat and skin from two ducklings, each saved in one large piece, if
    possible, any meat or glands trimmed from the skin and fat
2 teaspoons kosher salt
1 teaspoon freshly cracked black pepper

❦ Preheat oven to 325°F.
❦ Use the rendered duck fat to oil well two identical 12-by-18-inch baking pans that fit inside one another when stacked. (You'll want a pan with sides of at least ¾ inch so the rendering fat will stay in the pan and not drip in the oven—restaurant half-size sheet pans are ideal and inexpensive.) Oil one well on the inside, and the other well on the bottom, where it will contact the duck skin from above. Spread the duck skin in a single layer over the sheet pan oiled on the inside, and evenly distribute salt and pepper over all. Place second sheet pan on top, weight down with a cast-iron skillet, and place in the preheated oven. Bake until rendered, golden brown, and crispy, about 1 hour. Carefully drain off excess fat, and cool the crispy treats on paper towels. Store at room temperature in an airtight container for up to 1 week.

BOURBON GIBLET JUS   MAKES: 1½ cups
Carcasses and wing tips from two ducklings
Necks and giblets from two ducklings

2 cups yellow onion, coarsely chopped

1 cup carrot, peeled and coarsely chopped

1 rib celery, coarsely chopped

4 cloves garlic, mashed

2 bay leaves

4 sprigs fresh thyme

4 sprigs fresh marjoram

1 tablespoon whole black peppercorns

¼ cup best bourbon

2 tablespoons dark brown sugar

2 teaspoons Worcestershire sauce

1 teaspoon kosher salt, or more to taste

¼ cup (½ stick) cold butter

⚜ Preheat oven to 425°F.

⚜ Place the duck carcasses, wing tips, necks, and giblets in a large stainless-steel or enamel baking dish or braising pan, and set on the top rack of the preheated oven. Cook until the carcass is nicely browned but not too dark, 25 to 30 minutes. Remove from oven and carefully transfer the cooked duck parts to a 4-quart stainless-steel or enamel stock pot. Add the onion, carrot, celery, garlic, bay leaves, thyme, marjoram, and peppercorns. Set the baking dish over a burner, add an inch of cold water, turn on the burner, and begin scraping off any brown bits from the pan with a sturdy metal spatula while the water heats and comes to a boil. Once you're satisfied you've gotten all the tasty brown bits up, add the water to the stock pot with the duck parts and fill the remainder with cold water to cover. Set over medium-low heat, and slowly bring to a boil, regularly skimming any foam or scum that rises to the top with a small ladle. Reduce heat to maintain a very low boil, or more ideally, a very high simmer at 200°F for 4 hours. Carefully strain stock through a colander into a 2-quart saucepan and return to a boil, this time maintaining an even, low boil. Retain the gizzards, livers, and hearts, but discard remaining strained solids.

⚜ Reduce the stock to approximately 1 quart, which will take an hour or so (but keep an eye on the pot every 5 minutes, since humidity and altitude can affect these things), then strain through a fine-mesh strainer and return to the saucepan. Continue reducing until it is thick and syrupy and coats a spoon. Mince the giblets and add them to the reduced stock, then add the bourbon, sugar, Worcestershire, and salt; continue reducing until very syrupy and thick as corn syrup. There will be between 1 and 1½ cups of liquid now, which is expected. Remove from heat and add the chilled butter, stirring it in until melted and creamy. Taste for seasoning and add more salt, sugar, or Worcestershire if desired. Serve at once.

Potted Duck

Potting, or confit, is one of the oldest means of preserving all manner of foods, but especially fish and fowl. It's a process of long, slow cooking of a fish or animal in its own juices, possibly with some introduced liquids in moderation for seasoning, the idea being to cook the animal down until it is fully rendered, the meat and (optionally) bones and gelatin-rich juices falling to the bottom, with the fats rising to the top to effectively form an airtight seal, or cap, on the pot.

Before the invention of modern canning in France in 1806 by Nicolas Appert and even for some time after, as it took time for the technology to spread, this was how food was preserved for later use. As a consequence of the long, slow cooking process that formerly served to cook out all bacteria and other microorganisms and render fats to form an airtight cap, a lot of really cool things happen to make the meat uniquely delicious: gelatin is rendered from joints and bones, which makes it sticky and palate coating in addition to being more nutritious; the meat becomes so tender it can virtually melt on your tongue; and with the gelatin and fat fully rendered, it coats your palate and is unquestionably the richest form that any fowl or game preparation can take.

In the old days, this process was often done in a single pot that could then be sequestered in the cellar until later use—it is remarkably efficient and was surely ingenious for the time. For ease of use during storage and service, most of us chefs have updated this technique to something that is done in a braising pan before cleaning the meat to store separately. Done right, it's great enjoyed cold as a pâté or cold cut, or pan-fried as a hot dish.

PREP TIME: 12 hours, plus overnight for setting
EQUIPMENT NEEDED: four 8-ounce canning jars, 4-quart mixing bowl, long-handled wooden spoon, large drip-proof pan with fitting perforated

drain pan (restaurant hotel pans work perfectly and are inexpensive at restaurant and kitchen supply stores), 4-quart casserole with tight-fitting lid

MAKES: 1½ to 2 pounds, or three to four 8-ounce Ball jars

2 large ducklings, 4 to 5 pounds each (this is perfect in tandem with the duet of duck, page 140)
1 tablespoon plus 1 teaspoon kosher salt
1 teaspoon freshly cracked black pepper
¼ cup brown sugar
A few sprigs fresh thyme
A few bay leaves
6 cloves garlic, smashed
2 cups duck fat or lard, melted but not hot

❧ Clean your ducks under cold running water. Remove the legs, thighs, wings, neck fat, and cavity fat. Clean bones of all skin and fat to make stock. Save skin and fat to line the potting pan. Keep breasts, skin-on, to cook separately.

❧ Separate the legs from the thighs at the joint. Place legs, thighs, and wings in a 4-quart mixing bowl, and toss with the salt, pepper, and brown sugar. Place in a single layer on a perforated draining pan over a drip-proof pan, cover loosely with plastic wrap, and refrigerate overnight to cure.

❧ The following day, in a heavy 4-quart casserole with a tight-fitting lid, lay out the duck's back and cavity fat on the bottom of the casserole, and arrange the legs, thighs, and wings, skin-side up, in layers with the thyme, bay leaves, and garlic. Cover with any remaining fatty trim from the breasts and tail, and pour over the melted duck fat or lard.

❧ Cover tightly and cook in a 275°F oven for 8 hours—overnight works well. Remove from oven and check consistency of the thigh meat. It should easily fall off the bone. Allow to cool enough to handle, then carefully remove the legs, thighs, and wings; clean them of all rendered skin; and pick the meat from the bones, discarding the bones and rendered skin pieces. Drain off the rendered fat and save for culinary uses—it's fantastic for making vegetable confits, biscuits, or general pan-frying.

❧ Taste the meat for seasoning, and add salt or pepper if desired. You can store as loose shreds tightly covered in the refrigerator for up to 1 week. Alternatively, you can knead and mash the meat in a 4-quart mixing bowl with the back of a long-handled wooden spoon until it will form a ball (this may require the addition of a tablespoon or two of leftover duck fat), and pack it tightly into 8-ounce Ball jars. Cover tightly and refrigerate for up to 2 weeks. This is something we do often for its compact and novel presentation. To unmold for slicing, dip the jar into a warm water bath for 15 to 20 seconds, until the meat slides out in one congealed mass. Slice and enjoy either cold or pan-fry in lard or the rendered fat you saved from the braise.

Rutabaga Confit

A guest once asked me a hypothetical question—if I were to start a fan club for underappreciated vegetables, which one would be its poster child? Brushing aside what an odd question it was, I thought about it for a second and there was no question the answer is the rutabaga. In spite of its appearance on menus in some of the best restaurants each winter, it continues to languish in obscurity relative to the other winter roots—turnips, beets, carrots, even salsify and parsnips.

I grew up in a German American farming family, and we always had turnips in the garden, so they are an obsession of mine and I often eat them out of hand like an apple. On the other hand, turnips don't cook up as delectably as rutabagas—storage turnips especially lack the dense, creamy texture when cooked that rutabagas have in spades. So, while I'll use turnips in salads and slaws, when I'm cooking I reach for rutabagas, and I personally eat a bushel or so a year besides what we use on our menus.

This is how we prepare rutabagas for our favorite fall duck dish, served with Brewster oat groats. The rutabagas' creamy texture and earthy flavor complement the dish perfectly. This preparation is also delicious with venison and all manner of roasts.

PREP TIME: 4 hours
EQUIPMENT NEEDED: 2-quart or larger casserole with tight-fitting lid
SERVES: 4 to 6

1½ pounds rutabagas, peeled and diced into ½-inch cubes
1 quart rendered duck fat, lard, or vegetable oil
1 tablespoon kosher salt

⅛ teaspoon cayenne pepper
1 bay leaf

❦ Preheat oven to 225°F.
❦ Place the peeled and diced rutabagas in a 2-quart or larger casserole. Melt the duck fat or lard, but do not heat any more than necessary to liquefy it. Pour over the rutabagas, then sprinkle in the salt, cayenne, and bay leaf. Cover the casserole tightly and place in preheated oven for 4 hours, until rutabagas are tender when lanced with a fork. Carefully strain the fat off, saving it for later use frying or sautéing. Serve rutabagas at once.

Creamed Brewster Oat Groats with Parsnips and Hen of the Woods

I say it often, but many times the most inspiring moments in my kitchen occur when a new Anson Mills product shows up for the first time. A few seasons back they came out with Brewster oat groats, so-called because they are a millennium-old landrace oat dating to the times Brewster's held a monopoly on seeds, cultivation, barms (yeast), and all manner of related subjects. Anson Mills uses an ancient British Isles peelcorn oat for these groats, peelcorn oats being a special strain that ripens without a hull if you pick it at the right time, saving a lot of processing time if you can manage all the variables—obviously a useful trait before mechanized grain processing.

When I opened our first sack of Brewster oat groats and took a big whiff, I was immediately transported back to my childhood, after a long day baling hay at my Aunt Rita and Uncle Lee's farm, resting on a bale of hay in a freshly loaded hayloft, orangeade in hand, the sun setting, and a cool breeze wafting in, carrying the unmistakable sent of freshly cured hay to my head—its sweet, grassy smell of summer making everything perfect after a hard day's work. It was one of those moments that are hard to describe, but it filled me with the joy of the seasons, of my youth well spent, and a compulsion to translate those feelings into a meaningful way to feed people.

It also made me think of fall, of the beginning of the end of the cycle of life, old age, and the beginning of decay, which sometimes in food can be a beautiful thing. It reminded me of well-hung game and that particularly delicious funk of duck aged just so. Parsnips dance nicely with the sweeter carbohydrates in the oats and also the earthier elements, giving root to the stalk; and hen of the woods mushrooms, at their best in early fall, add umami and the delicious taste of decay reborn as a new organism.

There's a reason I like to make creamed dishes with vegetable purees during the fall and winter: the cream isn't as rich because the fodder in the pasture thins in fall and is gone during winter; vegetables such as parsnips can fill in so beautifully, with their creamy texture when pureed, natural sweetness, and earthy flavors. You can use less cream and actually come out way ahead in flavor and lower in fat.

This dish is also delicious as a light lunch or with poultry (especially turkey) and all manner of game. You can of course use any oat groats, but this is one grain that is especially worth procuring from Anson Mills. There's nothing else quite like it.

PREP TIME: 1 hour for parsnip puree and oats, 20 minutes to finish
EQUIPMENT NEEDED: 2-quart saucepan, fine-mesh strainer, 12-inch cast-iron
    skillet, 1-quart saucepan with tight-fitting lid, long-handled wooden
    spoon, food processor with feeding tube
SERVES: 4 to 6

    1 cup Brewster oat groats, or substitute regular oat groats or farro
    1 quart cold water
    2 teaspoons kosher salt, divided
    ¼ cup (½ stick) unsalted butter, cut into small bits and chilled, divided
    ½ cup shallots, minced
    4 cloves garlic, mashed and minced
    1 cup hen of the woods mushrooms (may substitute shiitakes caps),
        pulled apart into ears, the stems sliced into ½-inch strips
    ½ cup heavy whipping cream
    1 cup parsnip puree (recipe follows)
    1 teaspoon Worcestershire sauce
    1 teaspoon freshly ground black pepper

❦ Place the oat groats in a 2-quart saucepan, cover with the cold water, and add 1 teaspoon salt. Gradually bring to a full simmer, but do not boil, over medium heat. Maintain a simmer to slowly cook the oats until they are al dente—they will pop a bit when you bite into them but give way to a creamy, not starchy interior. This will take an hour at a full simmer, and most of the water will have been absorbed into the oats, leaving little in the pan. Once cooked, remove from heat and rinse under cold running water to stop the cooking, and strain through a fine-mesh strainer.

⚜ Melt 2 tablespoons butter in a 12-inch cast-iron skillet over medium-high heat until foaming but not brown. Add the shallots, garlic, and mushrooms, and sauté to sweat well; just begin to brown the butter a bit, 4 to 5 minutes, stirring constantly with a wooden spoon. Add the heavy cream and parsnip puree, bring to a boil, and add the oat groats. Stirring constantly, return to a boil and cook until as thick as risotto or coarse-ground grits. Add remaining teaspoon of salt, the remaining 2 tablespoons of cold butter, the Worcestershire, and pepper. Stir well, taste for seasoning and add more salt if desired, and serve at once.

PARSNIP PUREE

In addition to using in our Creamed Brewster Oat Groats, this puree is delicious with grilled or fried fish, seafood, poultry, and green vegetables.

MAKES: 1 cup

> ½ pound parsnips, peeled and sliced into ½-inch thick coins
> Whole milk to cover, approximately 1 cup
> ¼ teaspoon kosher salt
> A few grains cayenne pepper
> 1 tablespoon unsalted butter

⚜ Place peeled and sliced parsnips in a 1-quart saucepan with a tight-fitting lid, arrange and pack into the bottom of the pot as tightly as you can, and pour in enough whole milk to just cover the parsnips. Cover tightly and bring to a boil over medium-low heat. Occasionally remove the lid, stir to prevent scorching, and check the tenderness of the parsnips. Simmer until the parsnips are a bit beyond fork tender and are easily broken up with a spoon, 25 to 30 minutes. Drain off the milk and reserve.

⚜ Place the parsnips, salt, and cayenne pepper in the bowl of your food processor. Puree until smooth, adding the reserved milk bit by bit though the feeder tube (which will also vent the steam) to make a creamy puree that has the consistency of a milk shake. To finish the puree, add the butter while pureeing on high speed until thoroughly incorporated. Transfer to a small bowl and use right away or refrigerate for up to 1 week.

Braised Sausages with Sauerkraut and Parsnips

One of my absolute favorite meals on a cold winter night, this simple braise of sausages and kraut hits the spot every time, especially with a dollop of creamy mashed potatoes to mix with the braising juices. In seasonal German American farmhouse cooking, this would always be something to look forward to come winter, when the cured and smoked sausages were ready and hanging in the smokehouse and the season's sauerkraut was made and waiting, in the whiskey barrel in which it was fermented, on the back porch.

You can use any of your favorite sausages for this dish, but I typically like to use both smoked and unsmoked sausages for the textural and flavor contrasts they offer. For unsmoked sausages, look for Thuringers or knackwurst if you can find them, although a good-quality bratwurst or even hot dog by your local butcher works well, too. For smoked sausage, you can use andouille or any good, firm smoked pork sausage such as Polish, which is similar to many old farmhouse sausages of previous generations.

Look in the refrigerated section of your market for a quality fresh sauerkraut, which will usually be found in jars or vacuum bags. In a pinch, you can use canned sauerkraut from the dry goods section of your market. The results will still be good, just not quite the same.

There's no salt in this recipe, as the sausages and sauerkraut will contribute much on their own. If you like a little more of a salty taste, serve salt on the side at the table.

PREP TIME: 3 hours

EQUIPMENT NEEDED: 4-quart cast-iron or enamel Dutch oven with tight-fitting lid, long-handled wooden spoon, long-handled slotted spoon, small bowl, tongs

SERVES: 4 to 6

2 tablespoons lard or pan drippings

4 strips bacon, cut into ½-inch strips

1 pound Thuringer or knackwurst, cut into 1-inch thick slices

1 pound smoked Polish sausage, cut into 1-inch thick slices

1 quart sauerkraut, drained

½ pound parsnips, peeled and chopped into ½-inch pieces

2 tablespoons Creole or other brown mustard

2 cups Pilsner beer, Hefeweizen, or pale lager, nothing heavily hopped

1 teaspoon freshly ground black pepper

ѱ Preheat oven to 325°F.

ѱ In a 4-quart cast-iron or enamel Dutch oven with a tight-fitting lid, melt the lard over medium heat and add the bacon. As soon as the bacon begins to sizzle, maintain heat to cook the bacon just until crisp and golden brown, stirring regularly with a wooden spoon to separate the pieces of bacon, which will have a tendency to stick together, and also to help them brown evenly. Once browned to your taste, remove the bacon with a slotted spoon and transfer to a small bowl to hold while you cook the sausages.

ѱ Add the cut sausages to the pan, maintaining heat at a sizzle, and brown the sausages well on all sides, moving them around with a pair of tongs to brown evenly. Once browned, drain off all but 2 tablespoons of the rendered fat from the bottom of the pan. Add the sauerkraut, parsnips, mustard, beer, pepper, and reserved crisped bacon to the pot, and stir gently to distribute everything evenly. Place the lid on the pan, and set in the center of the top rack of the oven.

ѱ While the braise is cooking, check the pot periodically to make sure the juices are maintaining and not evaporating. In the unlikely event that the braise dries out, simply add a little more beer to keep it nice and steamy. Cook for 2 hours, until the parsnips are tender and the sausages are plump from being steamed by the beer. Allow the braise to rest for 15 minutes, covered, before serving. Serve with mashed potatoes or boiled potatoes with butter.

Mashed Potatoes

Since half of my family is German and the other half is mostly Appalachian Ulster with some Black Dutch, potatoes have always loomed large at the table whether for breakfast, lunch, or dinner. Among potato preparations, mashed potatoes are the ultimate. Use medium- or "B"-size potatoes for the optimal skin-to-flesh ratio, and look for thin-skinned varieties for the same reason. Potatoes with a good middle ground between waxy and starchy flesh are best—look for Désirées, Yukon golds, red skins, Kennebecs, or red Norlands among others. That said, I've never met a mashed potato I didn't like, so use what you can find from your favorite farmer or local farmers' market. Your farmer will usually be able to tell you which potatoes are best for mashing.

PREP TIME: 1 hour

EQUIPMENT NEEDED: 2-quart saucepan, 1-quart saucepan, wooden spoon,
   colander, stand mixer with flat beater attachment, long-handled rubber
   spatula

SERVES: 4 to 6

1 pound skin-on potatoes, whole
¼ cup (½ stick) unsalted butter
6 garlic cloves, smashed and minced
½ teaspoon cayenne pepper
¼ cup sour cream
¼ cup buttermilk
2 teaspoons kosher salt

✺ Place the potatoes in a 2-quart saucepan, and cover with 1 inch of cold water; there is no need to salt the water. Bring to a boil over medium-high heat, then reduce heat to a low boil. Boil until the potatoes are fork tender—how long will depend on the size of the potatoes, but for medium Yukon gold potatoes, count on 30 minutes. Once your potatoes are cooked, set aside but leave in the hot water while you infuse the garlic butter.

✺ Melt the butter over medium heat in a 1-quart saucepan. Once the butter is melted, add the mashed garlic and cayenne, and cook for 5 minutes, stirring gently with a wooden spoon every minute or so. Your kitchen will smell like garlic butter heaven by the time 5 minutes is up.

✺ Drain the potatoes in a colander, and immediately place in the bowl of a stand mixer with the flat beater attachment. Mash at low speed to your desired consistency and then mash in the garlic butter. Using a rubber spatula, fold in the sour cream, then the buttermilk and salt. Serve hot at once, or may hold for 20 to 30 minutes in a low oven.

Charred Brussels Sprouts with Shallots and Pecans

One of the top reasons to look forward to fall is this simple dish. I'm a junkie for any member of the cabbage family, and Brussels sprouts are one of my favorites. This particular recipe is especially good if you're successful getting a nice char on some of the leaves and a very gentle wilt on the rest, so there's plenty of texture to each bite. We serve this as a side for the table, but this goes especially well with game fowl and fish, though personally I'd eat it with just about anything.

In late fall and early winter when Brussels sprouts are at their absolute best, I've been known to eat a whole plate of these for dinner and then for lunch again the next day.

PREP TIME: 30 minutes
EQUIPMENT NEEDED: 4-quart mixing bowl, 10-inch or 12-inch cast-iron skillet, long-handled large metal basting spoon
SERVES: 4 to 6

2 pounds Brussels sprouts

1 tablespoon vegetable oil, for sautéing

3 to 4 large sprigs fresh thyme

½ cup thinly sliced shallots

½ cup chopped raw pecans

2 tablespoons (¼ stick) butter, chilled and cut into bits

2 teaspoons freshly squeezed lemon juice

½ teaspoon freshly ground black pepper

1 teaspoon kosher salt, or more to taste

♦ Prepare the Brussels sprouts by cutting a circle around the root stem with a paring knife, then separating the leaves from the stem. Once you get to the tightly bound yellow center, simply slice it very thinly—⅛ inch is perfect. Toss the leaves and sliced parts together until evenly distributed, and hold in a 4-quart bowl until you're ready to cook.

♦ Heat a 10-inch or 12-inch cast-iron skillet over high heat to the point of smoking. Working quickly, add the vegetable oil. As soon as it smokes, which will be almost instantly, add the Brussels sprouts, which will sizzle. Evenly distribute the thyme, shallots, and pecans over the top of the Brussels sprouts. Use a long-handled metal basting spoon to turn and check the sprouts on the bottom—as soon as they have a nice char on them, they are ready to turn. Turn and toss the sprouts with the spoon to be sure the shallots aren't all sitting on the bottom—they will burn quickly—then tilt the skillet toward you slightly, holding the skillet's handle with an oven mitt or dry towel, as it will be hot. Turn the heat off. Place the butter in the raised back side of the pan. It will start to melt and brown almost instantly, and run down the pan toward you. Toss the sprouts briefly with the basting spoon, being careful to scoop up some of the accumulating butter to dress the sprouts as you turn them. Once sprouts are gently wilted, 3 to 4 minutes, turn off the heat, allow the pan to sit level again, and sprinkle lemon juice, pepper, and salt over. Toss once more, remove the thyme sprigs, and serve immediately.

Black Walnut Sorghum Pie

I came up with this as an alternative to pecan pie many years ago. While I know fans of pecan pie are many, for me it was always too syrupy sweet. Substituting sorghum for corn syrup is one way to get more flavor into the pie, and black walnuts have a natural bitterness that keeps the sticky rich base honest. I always try to use black walnuts in abundance every fall and winter because they take me home more than almost any other ingredient: autumn days spent in the woods, the smell of fallen leaves and decaying wood beneath my feet, the unmistakable pungent aroma of the black walnuts' fleshy hulls as they turned black—the ultimate sign they were ready to be harvested and cleaned.

Cleaning black walnuts for eating was a bit of a chore better described as a ritual. The fleshy, aromatic hull, green when live and black when ripe and ready, had to be rubbed off, a tedious and messy process that left anyone without gloves with badly stained hands for days—a worthwhile price to pay for these joys of the wild woods. Then the nuts, still in their shell, needed to be soaked and scrubbed to remove the remainder of the hull, after which they would need to dry and cure for a few weeks before cracking and picking out the precious meats.

This pie always takes me back to those innocent and carefree days of boyhood, for the unmistakable flavor of the wild woods in those nuts, and the dark, withered taste of winter in the sorghum. As the years keep flying by, when I want to freeze time if only for a moment, I make this simple pie.

PREP TIME: 2 hours, including time to prepare crust
EQUIPMENT NEEDED: 9-inch pie pan or 10-inch tart pan, pie weight or dried
    beans with aluminum foil, wire cooling rack, 4-quart mixing bowl,
    electric hand mixer with whisk attachments, rubber spatula
MAKES: one 9-inch pie

1 uncooked prepared pie shell, well chilled (recipe follows)
2 cups uncooked dry beans of any kind, to use as a pie weight
¼ cup (½ stick) unsalted butter, cut into small bits and softened
½ cup granulated sugar
1 teaspoon kosher salt

3 large eggs
1 cup sorghum molasses
2 cups black walnut meats or pecan pieces
2 tablespoons good Kentucky bourbon or vanilla extract

✿ Preheat oven to 350°F.

✿ Prepare and thoroughly chill crust in a 9-inch pie or 10-inch tart pan. Prick chilled crust with the tines of a fork, and line with foil and pie weights (or dried beans), then bake for 25 minutes, until the edges are just beginning to brown. Remove weights and cool on a wire rack before removing foil.

✿ In a 4-quart mixing bowl with a hand mixer, cream the butter, sugar, and salt very well until creamy and fluffy, 5 to 6 minutes. Add the eggs one at a time, beating well after each addition. Cream until light and fluffy, another 3 to 4 minutes. Reduce the speed to low, and add the sorghum, beating to combine thoroughly. Fold in the walnuts and whiskey or vanilla with a rubber spatula. Pour into the pie shell, and bake at 350°F for 45 to 50 minutes, until a toothpick comes out clean. Serve hot or cold with ice cream or lots of whipped cream.

Short Crust for Sweet Pies

Pie crust that is easy to handle while rolling and shaping, yet flakes easily with a fork after baking, was one of the secrets that mystified me for years in the kitchen. I always believed lard was the key, but even with lard sometimes the crust wouldn't turn out just like I wanted. I will give three major secrets I learned. First hint: it isn't to minimize water in the recipe. While you don't want to overuse water because it's true that with all-purpose flour you'll get a crust that more closely resembles hard tack than pastry if you use too much water, that's not necessarily the key. If you use a soft-enough flour, you can add a little more water, which makes the crust easier to handle.

Use pastry flour, made from soft wheat that's lower in gluten, the protein that makes crusts tough—although I've found White Lily's regular all-purpose flour is soft enough to make a fine pie crust. Alternatively, you can use all-purpose but substitute a portion of it for rice flour, which doesn't have any gluten and will get its starchy grains between the gluten strands and soften it up. For this recipe, I would use 1¾ cups all-purpose and ¼ cup rice flour.

Don't overwork the dough or knead it too much. Just work it enough to come together. Even pastry flour has some gluten and can toughen if worked too much. Finally, flatten the dough into a thin disk, crimping the edges in to be free of cracks or irregularities, wrap in plastic, and chill thoroughly before rolling out. It will roll smoothly and cleanly.

PREP TIME: 20 minutes

EQUIPMENT NEEDED: 4-quart mixing bowl, French rolling pin, 9-inch pie pan

MAKES: one 9-inch pie shell. To make enough for a top crust if you want a double-crusted pie, make the recipe times one and a half.

- 2 cups sifted pastry flour, or White Lily all-purpose flour
- 2 tablespoons granulated sugar
- ½ teaspoon kosher salt
- ½ cup plus 2 tablespoons lard or unsalted butter, chilled and cut into small bits
- 7 to 8 tablespoons ice water

☙ In a 4-quart mixing bowl, combine the flour, sugar, and salt; then work the lard or butter into the flour with your hands, rubbing gently between your fingertips and palms. You want to just barely work the two together for a flaky crust, but make sure there are no clumps of lard or butter and that the mixture is soft and still a little bit lumpy. Add the water a few tablespoons at a time until the dough comes together. As you add the water, press the dough together to incorporate the water until the dough forms a ball. You don't want to overwork the dough or it will be tough. Coarser is better as long as it holds together. Shape into a thin disc 6 inches in diameter, press the edges to eliminate any cracks, and gently roll out on a well-floured surface. Roll the dough up around your rolling pin, and gently unroll it into your pie pan. Cut excess away from edges, and shape the edges by crimping or decorating with the tines of a fork. Chill thoroughly before filling.

Chocolate Pecan Tart

Many old Kentucky cookbooks offer recipes for this decadent dessert. Even though chocolate and pecans aren't strictly seasonal in their availability, I prefer pecans during the late fall and early winter when I have new crop pecans, hickories, or black walnuts. New crop nutmeats have a slight tenderness to go along with the crunch, and they always taste sweeter, at least to me. Of course, nuts and chocolate are available and fantastic any time of year. Warmed until hot and sticky, and paired with caramel or chocolate sauce and Sea Island benne ice cream, who cares what the weather is outside?

You shouldn't worry too much about the specific cocoa content of your chocolate as long as you're using bittersweet, but if your chocolate—and I encourage you to seek out fair-trade, slavery-free chocolate—lists its cocoa content, look for around 70 percent.

PREP TIME: 2 hours, including time to prepare crust

EQUIPMENT NEEDED: 10-inch tart pan, pie weight or 3 cups dried beans and aluminum foil, wire cooling rack, 2-quart saucepan, long-handled wooden spoon, 4-quart mixing bowl, wire whisk, 8- to 12-ounce bowl, pastry brush

MAKES: one 10-inch tart

1 uncooked prepared 10-inch tart shell, well chilled
12 ounces bittersweet chocolate, either chips or coarsely chopped bars
6 tablespoons (¾ stick) unsalted butter, cut into tablespoon-size pieces
4 large eggs, divided
¼ cup granulated sugar
2 tablespoons sorghum molasses
2 tablespoons espresso or strong coffee
½ teaspoon kosher salt
2 tablespoons bourbon
1 cup chopped pecans

♛ Prepare and thoroughly chill a pie crust in a 10-inch tart pan with removable bottom.

❧ Preheat oven to 350°F.

❧ Prick chilled crust with the tines of a fork, and line with foil and pie weights (or dried beans), then bake for 20 minutes, until the edges are just beginning to brown. Remove weights or beans, and return to the oven for 10 minutes, when the bottom will be just barely cooked through but not browned. Cool on a wire rack before filling.

❧ In a 2-quart saucepan over very low heat, melt chocolate and butter, stirring regularly with a wooden spoon until smooth and glossy. In a 4-quart bowl, beat three of the eggs well with a wire whisk. Add the sugar, sorghum, espresso, salt, and bourbon to the eggs, and whisk vigorously until thoroughly combined. Whisk in butter and chocolate mixture, beating vigorously until smooth, thick, and creamy. Stir in the nuts with a wooden spoon.

❧ Beat the remaining egg in a separate 8- to 12-ounce bowl, and use a pastry brush to brush the inside of the prepared crust with egg. Pour in the chocolate and smooth the top. Bake on the bottom rack of the oven for 20 to 30 minutes at 375°F, or until center is set. Cool on a wire rack and serve warm if possible, with whipped cream or caramel ice cream.

Pawpaw Panna Cotta

Since I grew up in the sticks of southern Indiana, it was inevitable that sooner or later, I'd fall into a love affair with pawpaws. The largest true fruit native to the continental United States, it is also fabulously elusive, appearing on exotic-looking trees near creek beds and shady springs throughout eastern North America. They are extremely perishable, offering virtually no shelf life and therefore unavailable for transport, meaning you gather and eat them locally. On top of that, in even a good year the season lasts three weeks tops.

The pawpaw doesn't cooperate with modern designs on fruits and vegetables as commodity products made to package and ship thousands of miles before staying for weeks in wholesalers' and then retailers' coolers before reaching your kitchen. Once a pawpaw is ripe, you have to pick it, handle it with kid gloves, and even then you have maybe two days to use it before you have a rotten mess on your hands. It challenges us to cook fresh, so very, very fresh, and it will only cooperate if we handle it with the greatest of care.

For years, long before Big Jones, each year as pawpaw season came and went, I imagined that when I opened my own restaurant, I would do something hardly anyone does: serve pawpaws. But how to do that, when they are so tender and spoil so quickly? I needed to work with three important characteristics: texture (custard-like and creamy), aroma (floral, tropical), and taste (floral, tropical, strawberries). Panna cotta fit the bill for its creamy texture and ability to carry flavors and let them sing.

This is a very quick and easy recipe that you can also pull off with bananas, mangoes, or a combination. Be careful with papayas or pineapple—they contain an enzyme that will digest the gelatin and leave you with a blasé mess. The pawpaw flavor is best left to sing on its own, but for accompaniments, you might serve a simple late-season raspberry puree or coconut macaroons.

To find pawpaws, you either need to know someone with some bottomland woods, or find just the right farmer at your local farmers' market to befriend. More and more farmers with the right kind of land are learning that they can market these due to the growing interest in foraged foods. Look for them to pop up at the farmers' market in the last month before your expected first frost date.

PREP TIME: 45 minutes prep, 6 hours chilling time
EQUIPMENT NEEDED: 6 soufflé molds or round-bottom teacups, cookie sheet, 2-quart saucepan, wire whisk, fine-mesh strainer, thin spatula
MAKES: four 1-cup molds or six 6-ounce molds

1½ cups heavy cream, refrigerated
2 envelopes unflavored gelatin
½ cup granulated sugar
½ teaspoon salt
1 teaspoon vanilla extract
3 cups fresh pawpaw pulp (6 to 10 pawpaws), strained through a fine-mesh strainer

❦ First, set your molds in the refrigerator to chill—rounded-bottom teacups are ideal, or use soufflé cups or even small Jell-O ring molds. Teacups are usually 6 ounces and will make six portions. One cup–size molds will make four to five; or for ten portions, use ½ cup–size cups or ramekins. Set the molds on a perfectly level cookie sheet for easy transport.

🌿 Place the heavy cream in a 2-quart saucepan, and whisk in the gelatin. Allow to soak for 20 minutes before heating. After soaking, whisk in the sugar, salt, and vanilla. Bring to a boil over medium heat, stirring occasionally with a wire whisk. Boil for 1 minute exactly, remove from heat, whisk in the pawpaw pulp, and quickly transfer to the chilled molds. Allow to cool for 10 to 15 minutes before placing in the refrigerator, uncovered, in a spot where nothing will drip on them. They will set in 4 to 6 hours depending on the size of your molds. After setting, cover individual molds with plastic wrap and refrigerate until needed, up to 1 week. To unmold, quickly dip the mold in and out of hot water for 15 seconds, run a thin spatula around the edges, and invert until the panna cotta slips out. Serve with cookies and raspberries or blackberries that have been macerated in a little sugar.

Persimmon Pudding Pie

Wild persimmons are one of the more obscure seasonal foraged foods of the eastern deciduous forests of North America, not limited strictly to the South. Their fussiness is often cited for their lack of popularity, because they're only tasty after a good deep frost—which also happens to rupture the flesh into a mushy pulp, not to mention their seed-ridden interior, requiring a laborious sieving process. On the contrary, I'd attribute their lack of popularity as much to the misguided and heavy-handed recipes that are often foisted upon this elegant fruit, drowning its subtle flavors of citrus peel, spice box, autumn decay, and resinous herbs in a thick paste of molasses, brown sugar, and often even evaporated milk, making a brick that has a texture more reminiscent of fudge than pudding, but called pudding nonetheless.

I never liked persimmon pudding much because it seemed like a bad substitute for pumpkin pie (my life's true obsession) with its virtually identical treatment ingredient-wise, in spite of their very different flavor profiles. I always did enjoy snacking on a little fresh persimmon picked straight from the ground, fallen after frost, and they are especially tasty when there is a nip in the air and the pulp is well chilled.

In my mind, the best expression for this fruit is a pudding that's light and pulpy, with bright citrusy and spice-box flavors that allow the fruit's natural characteristics to shine. We season the pudding simply with a little orange peel, allspice, Ceylon cinnamon (important as it's warmer and more subtle than common cassia), and coriander. Sorghum molasses is better used as an accoutrement, whereby it can provide delightful fruity esters to the plate that blend seamlessly with the persimmons, and the sorghum molasses' dark, brooding, caramel and mineral flavors are better layered, creating a dance of flavors—rather than the bear hug you get when regular molasses is added to the pudding recipe, smothering the persimmon.

PREP TIME: 1 hour

EQUIPMENT NEEDED: 10-inch pie pan, pie weight or dried beans, wire cooling rack, 4-quart mixing bowl, wire whisk

MAKES: one 10-inch tart

  1 uncooked prepared pie shell, well chilled
  4 eggs
  1 cup granulated sugar
  1 teaspoon kosher salt
  ½ teaspoon ground cinnamon, Ceylon preferred
  ½ teaspoon ground allspice
  1 teaspoon ground coriander
  ½ teaspoon freshly ground black pepper
  1 pint strained wild persimmon pulp
  1 cup heavy whipping cream

❦ Prepare and thoroughly chill a 10-inch pie crust in a tart pan.
❦ Preheat oven to 375°F.
❦ Prick chilled crust with the tines of a fork, and line with foil and pie weights

(or dried beans) then bake for 25 minutes, until the edges are just beginning to brown. Remove weights and cool on a wire rack before removing foil.

❦ Reduce oven heat to 325°F. In a 4-quart mixing bowl, beat the eggs with a wire whisk until frothy, then beat in the sugar. Add the remaining ingredients and whisk until evenly combined. Pour into your prepared 10-inch pie crust, and bake on the top rack of the oven until lightly browned on top and the center is set, approximately 30 minutes. It will jiggle as one mass when shaken when it is done. If the center is liquid or wavy when shaken, continue baking. Cool on a wire rack for an hour before serving. May be covered and refrigerated up to 1 week.

❦ Drizzle with sorghum molasses and serve with vanilla ice cream or fresh whipped cream.

Salty Sorghum Ice Cream

Good sorghum molasses is replete with rich caramel flavors, and I love salted caramel, so this ice cream came very naturally to me. As an added bonus, good sorghum has wonderful fruity undertones and even a bit of vanilla as well, so this particular ice cream has a more interesting and broader flavor profile than a simple caramel ice cream.

I especially enjoy serving this ice cream with black walnut pie or even a good lemon tart or buttermilk pie: the contrast of the caramel flavors of the sorghum with the citrus of those pies is pretty magical. Of course, this is also delicious with bread pudding or on its own with a little extra sorghum drizzled on top or a sprinkling of pecans or roasted peanuts.

PREP TIME: 20 minutes for custard base, 20 to 30 minutes
    for freezing
EQUIPMENT NEEDED: 2-quart or larger saucepan, wooden
    spoon, 4-quart or larger mixing bowl, wire whisk,
    fine-mesh strainer, 2-quart or larger ice cream
    freezer
MAKES: 1½ quarts ice cream

½ cup granulated sugar

½ cup plus 2 tablespoons sorghum molasses

2 cups heavy cream

2 cups skim milk

2 teaspoons kosher salt

6 large egg yolks

❦ Place the sugar, sorghum molasses, cream, milk, and salt in a 2-quart or larger saucepan, and bring to a boil, stirring often with a wooden spoon. Reduce heat to maintain a low boil while you prepare the eggs.

❦ Separate the six egg yolks into a 4-quart or larger mixing bowl, and whisk until smooth. While whisking, add a tablespoon of the hot milk mixture to temper the eggs, whisking constantly to incorporate, then add a bit more. Add the remaining hot milk mixture in a thin steady stream, whisking constantly. Whisk periodically while cooling for 30 minutes. Strain through a fine-mesh strainer. Cover tightly and refrigerate for at least 6 hours or overnight before freezing according to your ice cream freezer's manufacturer's instructions.

The
Delta and
the *Deep*
South

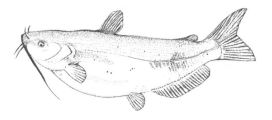

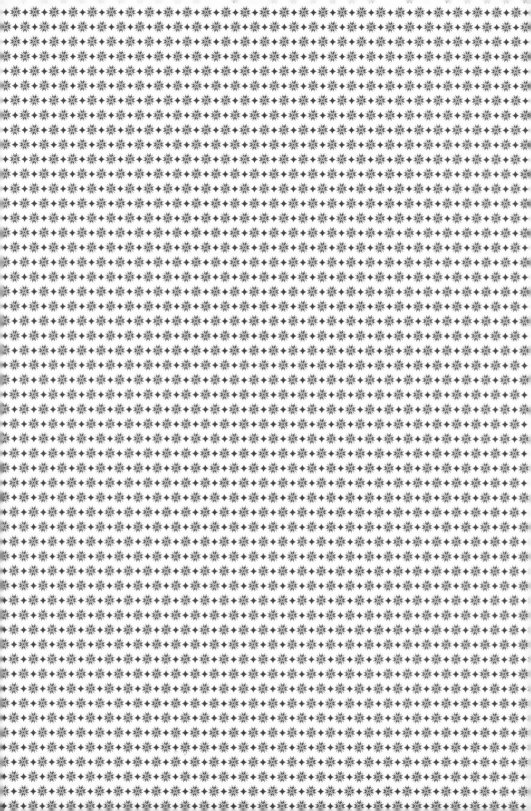

The Mississippi Delta was described by author James C. Cobb as "the most Southern place on Earth," and it's hard to disagree, but for our purposes in this book we will include it with the Deep South—the Southern climes of Mississippi, Alabama, and Georgia—for their many similarities, even if the Delta is the most elegant example of what makes the South *Southern*.

Encompassing the land in northwest Mississippi between the Mississippi and Yazoo Rivers, the Delta is a mind-melting place, flat almost beyond belief, with some of the richest soil in the United States. The vast alluvial plain was borne from the rivers' deposit of thousands of years' worth of rich silt and loam that would provide the perfect foundation for cotton, rice, sugarcane, and indigo in its plantation days, which has evolved to include corn, soybeans, and sweet potatoes.

Perhaps the Delta and the Deep South are so Southern because much of the area came into its own during the antebellum period, with plantations driving the economy and establishing a wide wealth gap that would persist for generations into the future. Fabulous wealth in the hands of the planters while slaves and even many white working-class folks subsisted in wretched poverty was a situation that got no better during reconstruction and early twentieth century, and even today many of the counties in this area remain among the poorest in the United States.

The aftermath of the Civil War gave rise to a culture of tenant and sharecropper farming, which gave little more to the hands working the fields than the same penniless existence they had as slaves, and persistent low crop prices during the late nineteenth and early twentieth century caused many small-time farmers, both black and white, to lose their farms in a mammoth consolidation that once again left much of the land in the hands of a few wealthy landowners. It was during this time of strife and heartbreak that blues music was born, and then rock and roll, two enduring contributions that African Americans have made to American culture.

The most substantial contribution to the cuisine of the Deep South that can be attributed to Native Americans is the hot tamale, a peculiar and wickedly delicious hand-held treat that differs from Mexican tamales in that they are smaller and the dough is made from cornmeal rather than masa, or ground, cooked hominy. In many ways it's surprising that Native American cooking isn't more ingrained, since in the early settlement of the Deep South, the Delta particularly, Native Americans were enslaved on the plantations until the African slave trade took hold during the antebellum decades.

Most of the foodways here are rooted in poor folks' cooking, although the plantation past still casts a mark on the Delta table. Perhaps more than anywhere else in the South, the sweet potato reigns supreme, catching catfish from the many rivers and lakes is a rite, and cornbread here is often little more than fried mush you have to eat straight out of the skillet, drizzled with cane syrup or honey and, maybe if times are good, slathered with a little butter. The African staples of okra, crowder peas, and collard greens are perennial on tables here; oysters often make their appearance from the Gulf; and rice graces the table far more often than wheat-based bread.

At Big Jones we have a special affinity for the Delta, because of its connection to Chicago via the Great Migration, when tens of thousands of poor African Americans left for the northern cities, especially Chicago, giving rise to a unique signature soul food here and, perhaps more importantly, Chicago blues and eventually Chicago soul. Consequently, you'll often find such delicacies from these parts on our menus, whether it's smothered okra, fried catfish, or hoppin' john made with crowder peas and rice. This cooking is tailor-made for sweet tea and lemonade, although in a tip of the hat to bluesman Robert Johnson, we're just as wont to enjoy it with whiskey.

Cheese Straws

We were only able to offer these on the regular menu for a short while before demand overwhelmed what we were able to produce in our small kitchen, but during the time they were on the menu, the recipe requests were daily. We still offer them on special occasions as accoutrements to a larger menu and will do so as long as we're open.

Cheese straws are an icon of Southern hospitality and for good reason. This recipe is easy to make, and the ingredients aren't hard to come by. It just takes a little time and dedication. Some folks use a cookie press with the star-shaped cutter rather than rolling these out by hand. That works mighty well, but I found that the hand-rolling method gives more control over the thickness and weight of the straws.

PREP TIME: 90 minutes
EQUIPMENT NEEDED: box grater, stand mixer with flat beater attachment, rolling pin, pizza cutter, two 12-by-18-inch sheet pans with raised edges
MAKES: forty 6-inch straws

10 ounces sharp cheddar cheese, shredded on the large side of a box grater

2 ounces best blue cheese, crumbled

1¾ cups all-purpose flour

½ teaspoon baking powder

10 tablespoons (1¼ sticks) butter, at room temperature

4 egg yolks

1 teaspoon cayenne pepper

1 tablespoon paprika

2 teaspoons kosher salt, plus more for sprinkling

❀ Preheat oven to 325°F.

❀ Place the cheeses, flour, and baking powder in the bowl of a stand mixer with the flat beater attachment. Mix on low speed to work the cheeses into the flour until the mixture resembles a coarse meal, like uncooked grits, 6 to 8 minutes. Add the butter and continue mixing on low until the whole looks like it wants to come together into a coarse dough, another 4 to 6 minutes. With the mixer running on low speed, add the egg yolks one at a time, incorporating each before adding the next. Continue mixing until the dough forms a cohesive mass and begins to form a smooth ball, another 4 to 6 minutes. Add the spices and salt, and mix just to integrate, 2 minutes.

❀ On a well-floured surface, roll out dough a ¼ inch thick, and sprinkle lightly with kosher salt. Using a pizza-cutting wheel, cut into ¼-inch-wide strips, 5 inches long. Carefully twist each straw from the ends into a spiral, gently twisting the two ends in opposite directions. Transfer to a lightly greased baking sheet with edges to prevent rendering butter from running over. Bake on the top oven rack until lightly browned and crispy, 15 to 20 minutes. Store in a tightly covered container. Will improve for several days, but be sure to enjoy within 1 month.

Boiled Peanuts

When we first opened Big Jones, we didn't offer bread service, instead presenting each table that sat down to dinner a plate of fresh, hot boiled peanuts. As you might imagine, the reactions were all over the map—folks from the South, often prone to be homesick, might literally shriek with joy at the sight and dig right in, while many Yankees with no sense of context would not be shy about declaring their outrage. That was a battle we didn't want to fight, and we acquiesced, not long after devising the cornbread recipe (page 4) that has become so beloved.

If you haven't tried boiled peanuts, you have to—they are one of the most supremely addictive snacks that exists, and far healthier as a salty bite than all the starchy, processed, transfat-laden crap you'll find in the snack aisle of your grocery. Not only are they all natural, but if you like peanuts, they are the most delicious salty snack you can have.

These days, we make a few batches of boiled peanuts during the peak of peanut season in August and keep them around as long as they last. You can make this recipe with dried or cured "green" peanuts (cured but unroasted), which are available in most supermarkets nationwide. But to truly experience them, you must make them with raw freshly dug peanuts, which you can find in season at Hardy Farms Peanuts (hardyfarmspeanuts .com) if your local produce market doesn't stock them.

PREP TIME: 5 to 7 hours
EQUIPMENT NEEDED: 4-gallon stock pot, long-handled spider skimmer
MAKES: 5 pounds boiled peanuts

   5 pounds raw green peanuts
   6 quarts water
   1 cup kosher salt
   2 tablespoons cayenne pepper
   6 bay leaves

℘ Place all ingredients in a 4-gallon stock pot, and bring to a rolling boil. Reduce heat to a low boil and cook, stirring every half hour or so, by using a long-handled spider skimmer to turn the peanuts on the bottom over the top to ensure even cooking. Maintain a low boil while cooking. Boil for 4 hours. Dried, or cured, peanuts will take 8 hours. You can strain the peanuts and eat right away, hot out of the pot (a great idea for parties), or store them in their liquid to reheat as needed. Will keep in the refrigerator for 7 to 10 days.

Fried Green Tomatoes

One of our most anticipated seasonal dishes of the year, fried green tomatoes appear sometime in May when the hothouse growers show up with them at our local farmers' markets, with field-grown green tomatoes following sometime in June and lasting up until frost in September or October.

Prepared correctly, fried green tomatoes are crispy on the outside and toothsome yet tender but not the least bit mushy on the inside, and you'd never suspect they were cooked in oil. Southern purists insist that they be cooked in a cornmeal dredge, though more than a few households like them in wheat flour. I use a cornmeal dredge and cut it with cornstarch. It ensures a more even crust and fries up with the finest texture you can imagine.

PREP TIME: 15 minutes preparing the soak, 1 hour to soak, 30 minutes to cook
EQUIPMENT NEEDED: 2-quart mixing bowl, wooden spoon, pie pan, 12-inch
    cast-iron skillet, digital clip-on thermometer, long-handled tongs,
    serving plate lined with paper towels
MAKES: 16 to 20 slices, serves 6 to 8

> 4 large green slicing tomatoes, about 3 pounds, sliced ⅜ inch thick
> 2 cups lowfat buttermilk
> 2 tablespoons Louisiana-style hot sauce
> 1 cup fine-grind white cornmeal
> 1 cup cornstarch
> 2 teaspoons kosher salt
> ½ teaspoon cayenne pepper
> 2 cups lard or vegetable oil

☙ When slicing green tomatoes, slice off the very top and bottom of the tomatoes, to expose the flesh on the ends. Set the top and bottom slices aside to use for piccalilli or chutney. Soak the tomatoes by layering the slices in a 2-quart mixing bowl. Cover with the buttermilk, add the hot sauce, and move the tomato slices around a bit with a wooden spoon to make sure the buttermilk and hot sauce are dispersed around all the slices. Cover with plastic wrap and refrigerate for 1 hour before frying.

❦ In a pie pan, mix the cornmeal, cornstarch, salt, and pepper with a fork until evenly combined, and taste for seasoning. In a 12-inch cast-iron skillet, heat the lard or vegetable oil over medium-high heat, to 350°F on a digital clip-on thermometer. Piece by piece, remove the tomato slices from the buttermilk and hold sideways over the bowl for a moment to run off excess buttermilk, but don't shake—you want to maintain an even layer of buttermilk on both sides of the tomato. Lay each tomato slice in the dredge, and turn some dredge over the top of each slice to coat, then gently press into the dredge with your fingers; then turn over and press the other side. Turn sideways and gently tap one edge of the slice to shake off excess dredge.

❦ Gently lay the slices in the hot oil in a single layer, leaving a little space between each. You will need to fry two to three batches to cook all the tomatoes. Fry 3 to 4 minutes on the first side, just until the cornmeal is beginning to brown—we're not looking for a dark or even golden brown here, or the tomatoes will turn mushy. Gently turn and cook 2 to 3 minutes on the second side, just until crispy. Place cooked tomatoes on a serving plate covered with a clean dry towel to drain, and hold in a low oven while you cook the remaining batches.

Goat Cheese and Potato Croquettes

When I think of croquettes, I think of Southern tearooms and elegant ladies' lunches. Prepared correctly, croquettes are one way to sneak a little crispy fried goodness into otherwise proper meals or snack times.

We have served these delectable morsels on and off since the day we opened, making them a Big Jones classic. We've served them with any number of sauces: green goddess has always been the most well received, but most mayonnaise-based sauces also work well with them, especially those incorporating a lot of fresh herbs. While not ostensibly a salad course, laying these upon a bed of your favorite lettuce lends a different texture and adds enough fresh green flavor to keep them light, since they can be very rich.

PREP TIME: 20 minutes for the potato filling, 1 hour to chill the filling, 1 hour for breading and deep frying

EQUIPMENT NEEDED: two 2-quart mixing bowls, wooden spoon, small ice cream scoop, cookie sheet, pie pan, countertop deep fryer or 8-quart cast-iron Dutch oven for deep frying, digital clip-on thermometer, long-handled tongs, slotted spoon, serving plate lined with paper towels

MAKES: 12 to 16 croquettes, serves 6 to 8

1 cup leftover mashed potatoes, refrigerated
1 cup shredded baked potato, refrigerated
2 teaspoons fresh thyme leaves
1 tablespoon finely chopped chives
1 large egg plus 1 yolk
1 teaspoon kosher salt
1 teaspoon freshly ground black pepper
¾ cup fresh goat cheese, coarsely crumbled

♛ Place both the mashed and shredded potatoes in a 2-quart mixing bowl. Make sure your hands are clean, and work potatoes together with your fingers until the shredded and mashed potatoes stick together and look like coarse, dry mashed potatoes. Sprinkle the thyme and chives over the potatoes, and knead well to combine. Press a well in the center of the potatoes, and add the eggs, placing them in the well in the center. Use a table fork to scramble the eggs, and then mix them into the potatoes, which will soften the potato mixture considerably and turn it somewhat sticky. Add the salt and pepper, then the goat cheese. Mix gently with a wooden spoon, being careful to avoid breaking up the bits of goat cheese too much. Cover tightly with plastic wrap, and chill 1 hour or overnight before proceeding to bread and fry the croquettes.

TO BREAD AND FRY
3 large eggs
¾ cup water
4 cups French bread crumbs, or Japanese panko bread crumbs
2 to 3 quarts vegetable oil for deep frying

꘎ Preheat oven to 250°F.

꘎ Use a small ice cream scoop to shape the potatoes into small balls of about 3 tablespoons (1½ ounces) each. Roll between the palms of your hands to smooth on all sides, and place on a cookie sheet with plenty of space between each ball. In a 2-quart mixing bowl, whisk the eggs until frothy and then whisk in the water.

꘎ Place the bread crumbs in a large pie pan. Roll each potato ball first in bread crumbs, then roll gently between your fingers again to work in the bread crumbs. Then roll each ball in the egg wash, wetting all sides, and roll in the bread crumbs once again, this time looking to coat the ball well so that you can't see any of the potato mixture through the bread crumb coating. Roll (gently!) between the palms of your hands again to finalize the shape of the croquette. Return breaded croquettes to the cookie sheet, and refrigerate until you are ready to fry them.

꘎ Use a countertop deep fryer or 8-quart cast-iron Dutch oven with a clip-on thermometer for frying. Fill with 3 inches of cooking oil. Over medium-high heat, heat oil to 325°F on a digital clip-on thermometer. Gently drop croquettes into the hot oil five to six at a time at a time (you will need to fry in two to three batches), making sure there is plenty of space between each ball—don't overcrowd or they may not brown evenly. Turn every 2 minutes with long-handled tongs while cooking. Fry 5 to 6 minutes, until a deep rich golden-brown color. Remove with a slotted spoon, and drain on a serving plate lined with paper towels. Keep in a low oven while you fry remaining batches. Serve hot with basic mayonnaise or green goddess (page 216).

Pecan Chicken Salad

Chicken salad is one of the dishes that really helped my thinking evolve regarding what type of restaurant I wanted Big Jones to be. For the first couple of years we were open, it was one of those classic, yet stodgy dishes I had no interest in serving, even though there is a storied history of chicken salad and ladies' teas and lunches throughout the twentieth century, especially in the Deep South, where the summers are long and hot.

My reticence to serve chicken salad stemmed primarily from the modern state of the dish—it's sold almost exclusively in diners, cafeterias, bad delis, and supermarket ready-to-eat sections, and is invariably a wretched abomination made from bland, dry, even stale-tasting chicken breast dressed in some congealed, drab industrial mayonnaise with scarcely enough seasoning to distinguish itself from cold pap. If it's seen primarily as a "light" or diet food, it's only because chicken salad as we know it today will surely destroy any healthy appetite.

Of course, as the restaurant evolved, I realized we really should serve chicken salad, at least at lunch, because we could do it right and rectify the wrong being perpetrated by the purveyors of the white, sticky, flavorless lumps sold in between bread or in containers in bad restaurants and markets everywhere. When done right, chicken salad is really delicious, filling, and also refreshing on a hot summer day when you need a hearty lunch without feeling the heat.

Start with a whole chicken—period. There's flavor in every bit, but most of it is in the legs and thighs. If it fits your liking, also boil the giblets with the chicken and mince them very fine to add to your chicken salad. This will make your chicken salad taste more like, well, chicken. Second, use homemade mayonnaise from good farm-fresh (I mean real farm, not supermarket-advertising "farm") eggs. After that, you have many options, but I'd say mustard, and lots of it, is key. You can add nuts, dried fruits, other vegetables—you name it. But use just enough dressing to make your salad feel juicy on your tongue. Any more than that, you may as well put a bowl of mayonnaise on the table with a ladle in it. This recipe already has 1½ cups in it, and it's mostly chicken! Why use more?

All that said, here's my favorite recipe. It's not a "creative" chicken salad, and I didn't mean it to be. When something hits the spot, why reinvent the wheel? I like to serve this with home-baked rye bread (page 21) and lots of fresh fruit from the farmers' market.

PREP TIME: 2 hours

EQUIPMENT NEEDED: 4-quart stock pot, digital food thermometer, casserole dish, 2-quart mixing bowl, wooden spoon, 4-quart mixing bowl

MAKES: 4 pounds, serves 8 to 12

1 whole 3-pound fryer chicken with optional giblets

1½ cups mayonnaise

¼ cup plus 2 tablespoons whole-grain mustard such as Creole, Dusseldorfer, or Pommery

3 tablespoons freshly squeezed lemon juice

3 tablespoons honey
1 cup coarsely cracked pecan halves
1 cup celery, finely diced
1 cup yellow onion, finely diced
1 cup golden raisins
2 teaspoons kosher salt
2 teaspoons freshly ground black pepper

꽃 Place the chicken and optional giblets in a 4-quart stock pot and cover with cold water. Place over medium-high heat and bring to a boil, then reduce to a simmer and cook until chicken registers 155°F on a digital food thermometer, checking both the breast/wing and thigh/back joints. This will take 20 to 25 minutes. Remove from heat and strain off the bouillon, reserving for later use in stocks or soups. It freezes perfectly.

꽃 Place the chicken and giblets in a shallow casserole dish to cool for 30 minutes, when it will be cool enough to handle. Pull the chicken apart at the joints, remove and discard the skin, pick the meat into bite-size pieces, and return the meat to the casserole; cover tightly with plastic wrap, and refrigerate until thoroughly chilled, at least an hour. Discard the bones. This part can be done the day before or an hour before you want to make your chicken salad—just make sure it's well chilled before you proceed.

꽃 Place the mayonnaise, mustard, lemon juice, honey, pecans, celery, onion, raisins, salt, and pepper in a 2-quart mixing bowl, and stir well with a wooden spoon to combine and make the dressing. Place pulled chicken meat in a 4-quart mixing bowl, and add the mayonnaise mixture. Toss well with a wooden spoon until everything is thoroughly combined. Cover tightly with plastic wrap, and refrigerate 1 hour before serving. Will keep up to 1 week in the refrigerator.

Crispy Catfish à la Big Jones

I first dreamed up a variation of this dish for a sustainable seafood reception that Supreme Lobster, one of Chicago's top fish houses, was throwing for industry people at the Columbia Yacht Club. Supreme had selected some of Chicago's top chefs to showcase what delicious things you could serve while also making sustainable choices when purchasing seafood.

I was charged with serving walleye, perhaps my favorite freshwater fish after bluegill. As I am often wont to do, I came up with an exceedingly ambitious dish (for a tasting-station party, at least) consisting of pan-fried walleye with creamy grits, buttered baby lima beans, tasso beurre monté, and piccalilli. It was kind of absurd as well as kind of awesome. There we were at this tiny station on a yacht with a dredging pan, frying pans, saucepans, and a big ol' pot of grits, four portable butane burners going constantly. But even as we made a huge mess, it was such a hit I had to bring it home and make it a regular offering.

Walleye is not always available, and I am also keen to work with American farm-raised catfish, as it's endorsed as a sustainable model of aquaculture by the Marine Stewardship Council, the Shedd Aquarium, and the Monterey Bay Aquarium. Fortunately, catfish works equally well with this recipe.

One way to make me swoon is to serve me lima beans, butterbeans, or field peas in a creamy gravy with coarse-ground grits. It's like common folks' version of Oysters and Pearls, the famed dish of Thomas Keller's French Laundry, which was a celebration of textures and aquatic flavors. Grits and peas or beans are a celebration of textures and earthy flavors. In a way, catfish is even better than walleye for this dish because of the deep earthy flavor you get from catfish.

Beurre monté is another preparation made famous by the French Laundry, and we use variations of it often. It is an emulsion of butter in a liquid base. You heat any water-based liquid to a boil and swirl in butter off the heat, beating vigorously, to melt it into the base liquid. If you want a thick emulsion, use a small amount of liquid (a minimum of a tablespoon is strongly advised) relative to the amount of butter you intend to mount. Whatever you do, don't boil it or let it get hotter than 190°F, or it will break and is lost. It also needs to be maintained over 120°F or so for optimal texture. For this dish, we flavor it with shallots and tasso for sweetness, umami, and smokiness. The piccalilli refreshes everything with its bright acidity, important because there are a lot of rich flavors here.

We regularly offer this as a special when we have catfish in the house, and it's always a hit. With a little planning, it's easy to make at home too.

PREP TIME: 1 hour for the grits, butterbeans, and beurre monté; 30 minutes to fry the fish

EQUIPMENT NEEDED: two 1-quart saucepans with tight-fitting lids, wooden spoon, small wooden spoon, 12-inch cast-iron skillet, digital clip-on thermometer, 2 pie pans, long-handled tongs, serving plate lined with paper towels

SERVES: 4 to 6

Prepare one recipe of creamy grits (page 38), and hold in a low oven, covered tightly.

BUTTERED LIMA BEANS

2 cups frozen baby lima beans, defrosted
½ cup cold water
½ teaspoon kosher salt, or more to taste
Pinch of cayenne pepper
¼ cup (½ stick) unsalted butter, chilled and cut into teaspoon-size bits

⚜ Place lima beans in a 1-quart saucepan, add the water, and cover with a tight-fitting lid. Place on burner over high heat and bring to a boil, 5 to 7 minutes. Reduce heat and maintain a low boil until beans are tender, another 5 to 7 minutes. Add salt and cayenne once the beans are tender, and return to high heat and boil to reduce the water until only a couple of tablespoons remain in the bottom of the pan under the lima beans, a few minutes longer.
⚜ Keep stirring regularly.
⚜ Remove from heat and swirl in the butter, moving the pan in circles to swirl everything in the pan. Add the butter a bit at a time, continuing to swirl the pan and adding each new bit of butter as the previous one melts into the sauce that is coming together. Once all the butter is melted in, you should have a creamy, delicious pot of beans. If you like them creamier, use the back of a wooden spoon to mash a few against the sides of the pan and stir the mashed beans in. Continue until you have the texture you want. Taste and re-season if desired. Set in a warm place, but not too hot—over 190°F and your butter sauce will break. It's best to cover the beans and set them on a back burner that is off while you prepare the rest of the dish.

TASSO BEURRE MONTÉ

6 tablespoons (¾ stick) unsalted butter, chilled and cut into teaspoon-size bits, divided
3 tablespoons tasso, finely minced

3 tablespoons shallots, finely minced

1 tablespoon Worcestershire sauce

1 tablespoon cold water

¼ teaspoon salt

☙ In a 1-quart saucepan, heat 1 tablespoon butter over medium heat until foaming but not brown. Add the minced tasso and shallots, and increase heat to sauté, stirring with a small wooden spoon. Cook until the tasso and shallots are well sweated and taking on some nice caramel color. The butter will be browning also—take care not to get the pan too hot; if it seems to be approaching a burning temperature, remove from the heat and stir the pot to cool it off a bit. Once well sweated and lightly browned, add the Worcestershire and water, and bring to a boil, which should only take a moment. Remove from heat, and swirl the pan while you add the remaining chilled butter bit by bit, swirling the pan constantly and melting each addition before adding the next. Once all the butter is melted, add the salt, swirl for a minute more, and set in a warm place next to the lima beans while you prepare the catfish.

FRIED CATFISH

2 cups lard or vegetable oil

2 cups lowfat buttermilk

1½ cups Carolina Gold rice flour, or your favorite rice flour

1½ cups white or yellow corn flour

2 teaspoons kosher salt

1 teaspoon freshly ground black pepper

4 catfish filets, 5 to 8 ounces each, depending on what's available and your appetite

4 stalks green onion, thinly sliced, to garnish

☙ Place the lard or vegetable oil in a 12-inch cast-iron skillet with a clip-on thermometer, and heat to 350°F over medium heat. Place the buttermilk in one pie pan, and in a second pie pan place the rice and corn flours, salt, and pepper; mix the dry ingredients with a fork until thoroughly combined.

☙ Once the lard or oil reaches 350°F, dip the catfish filets one by one in the buttermilk, turning to coat evenly, then turn into the flour, turning several times to coat evenly, and lay gently into the oil. Once your filets are well browned on the first side, 3 to 4 minutes, gently turn with long-handled tongs and finish the other side, another 2 minutes. Watch your thermometer closely and maintain oil at or just above 350°F.

⚜ Once both sides are well browned, remove to a serving plate lined with paper towels to drain for a few minutes, and hold in a low oven until ready to serve. Garnish with sliced green onion, and serve with grits and buttered lima beans as side dishes and tasso beurre monté and piccalilli (page 222) as condiments.

Crowder Peas

We have a short field pea season in Chicago. Crowder peas don't show up at market until August, and they're usually done by the end of the month. Fortunately, they freeze well, so we always buy enough to last into winter. Purple hulls are the easiest to find at our farmers' markets here in Chicago, but if you can find silver hulls (sometimes called Mississippi silver peas) where you're located, those are my absolute favorites. That said, lady peas, pink eyes, whippoorwills . . . I've never met a field pea I don't just adore. They're especially good cooked as fresh shell peas, so look for them at your local farmers' market at the peak of summer, and if you can't find them, ask a farmer to grow them. If you must, you can buy them dried and soak them in cold water overnight before preparing this recipe.

These are traditionally served with rice, but if you cook them long, low, and slow until they start to fall apart and make their own gravy, they are also fantastic with grits. As far as proteins go, I like them best with roasts, smoked pork dishes, and fried fish. At Big Jones we sometimes serve them with pork loin brined in sweet tea (page 135), garnished with pickled peaches (page 230). Talk about good eating.

PREP TIME: 50 minutes

EQUIPMENT NEEDED: 2-quart saucepan, long-handled wooden spoon, long-handled slotted spoon

SERVES: 4 to 6

4 ounces smoked skin-on hog jowl or bacon, cut into thin strips

2 cups yellow onion, finely diced

½ cup celery, finely diced

½ cup green bell pepper, finely diced

2 cloves garlic, mashed and minced

1 small jalapeno, seeded and minced

2 cups shelled crowder peas, or other fresh field pea or bean

1½ cups chicken stock, or more as needed to cover peas

1 bay leaf

2 teaspoons fresh thyme leaves

2 teaspoons salt, or more to taste

2 teaspoons Worcestershire sauce

In a 2-quart saucepan, heat the smoked jowl or bacon over medium-low heat, and slowly cook and render, stirring often with a wooden spoon. Cook until jowl bacon is crisp, 6 to 8 minutes. Remove bacon with a slotted spoon and set aside, leaving the rendered fat behind in the saucepan. Increase heat to medium high, and add the onion, celery, bell pepper, garlic, and jalapeno. Sauté 6 to 8 minutes, stirring constantly, until vegetables sweat and just begin to brown, 5 to 6 minutes. Add the peas, stock to cover, bay leaf, and thyme, and bring to a low boil. Reduce heat to medium low, and simmer until peas are tender in the center, creamy and not starchy to the bite, 10 to 30 minutes, depending on how early or late the peas are in the season—so keep a close eye on the peas. Later peas typically require more cooking. Add salt, reserved bacon, and Worcestershire. Taste for seasoning, and serve at once over steamed rice or creamy grits (page 38).

Sweet Potato Hash

Perhaps our most popular vegetable side of all time, this is one of only a few dishes served year-round. This isn't all that far off from established Southern eating, since in the old days even before cold storage was available, families would build sweet potato mounds in which they could bury their harvest and eat it right up to the next year's crop. I think this hash hooks folks on the perfect balance of sweet, salty, creamy, chewy, and crunchy. Sweet potato hash is tasty with pork, barbecue, and game dishes, especially duck and goose.

PREP TIME: 1 hour
EQUIPMENT NEEDED: 4-quart mixing bowl, wooden spoon, 9-by-13-inch ceramic casserole, 12-inch cast-iron skillet, long-handled tongs
SERVES: 4 to 6

1½ pounds sweet potatoes, peeled and diced into ½-inch pieces
1 tablespoon vegetable oil
1 teaspoon kosher salt, divided
3 strips thick-cut bacon
1 tablespoon unsalted butter
¼ cup yellow onion, finely diced
½ teaspoon freshly ground black pepper
¼ cup cane syrup or maple syrup
1 teaspoon Worcestershire sauce
4 stalks green onion, very thinly sliced, to garnish

♛ Preheat oven to 350°F. Place the diced sweet potatoes in a 4-quart mixing bowl, sprinkle the vegetable oil over the potatoes and ½ teaspoon kosher salt, and toss with a wooden spoon to ensure all sweet potato pieces are lightly coated with vegetable oil. Transfer to a 9-by-13-inch ceramic casserole dish, and bake on the bottom rack of the oven until barely fork tender but still with a little bite, 12 to 15 minutes. They should have very little, if any, browning. Remove and cool completely to room temperature before making the hash.
♛ Place the bacon strips in a 12-inch cast-iron skillet, and cook over medium heat as you always would bacon, to render the fat and cook the bacon crisp on both sides, turning with tongs, 5 to 6 minutes. Remove the bacon, pat dry with paper towels, cut into small dice, and reserve. Keep the rendered bacon grease in the pan for the next step.
♛ Place the butter in the skillet with the leftover bacon fat, and heat over medium-high heat until the butter is foaming but not browning. Add the onions and sweet potatoes, and sauté, stirring and tossing often with a wooden spoon, until the onions and sweet potatoes are taking on a little toasty brown color, 4 to 6 minutes. Drain off excess fat, season with the remaining half teaspoon of salt and the pepper, and add the reserved bacon, cane or maple syrup, and Worcestershire. Toss for a moment over heat to

reduce the syrup into a glaze and coat the potatoes, using the wooden spoon to scoop up the syrup over the potatoes. Transfer to a serving dish, and garnish with sliced green onion.

Mississippi Mud Pie

My Aunt Patsy Dunkel used to make a version of mud pie (though I think hers was a little denser and she called it mud cake) that is still one of the most unforgettable treats from our family gatherings. When we were planning Big Jones's opening dessert menu, for better or worse I planned it around a rich chocolate mud pie. I've since removed this from the menu because some of the mass-market processed foods that are part and parcel of the recipe don't fit into the way we've come to cook. For more than three years after I took it off the menu, however, we would still get requests to bring it back. While we're unlikely to do that, I can share the recipe; it's easy to make.

PREP TIME: 90 minutes
EQUIPMENT NEEDED: food processor, 9-inch pie pan, 4-quart mixing bowl,
    2-quart saucepan, 2 wire whisks, 1-quart mixing bowl
MAKES: one 9-inch pie

TO PREPARE THE CHOCOLATE COOKIE CRUST
2½ cups Oreo (or your favorite chocolate cookie) crumbs, crushed in
    the food processor into a coarse meal
5 tablespoons unsalted butter, softened to room temperature

❦ Pulse the cookie crumbs and butter together in the food processor until mixture just holds its shape when pressed into the sides of a pie pan, 2 to 3 minutes. There is no need to butter the pie pan—press the crust into a 9-inch pie pan, being careful to distribute evenly and cover the inside and edges of the pan thoroughly. Refrigerate until needed.

TO PREPARE THE FILLING AND BAKE
½ cup (1 stick) unsalted butter
4 ounces bittersweet chocolate

2 tablespoons unsweetened cocoa powder
¼ cup sorghum molasses or dark corn syrup
1 cup granulated sugar
1 tablespoon vanilla extract
¼ cup bourbon
1 teaspoon kosher salt
3 large eggs plus 1 yolk
1 cup chopped raw pecans
3 cups miniature marshmallows

❧ Preheat oven to 325°F.

❧ Place the butter, chocolate, cocoa, sorghum or corn syrup, sugar, vanilla, bourbon, and salt in a 4-quart mixing bowl. Set up a double boiler with a 2-quart saucepan filled with 1 inch of water set over medium heat until simmering. Set the mixing bowl with the butter, chocolate, and other ingredients over the simmering water, and use a wire whisk to stir occasionally as the ingredients melt. After 15 to 20 minutes, you will have a warm, glistening bowl of melted chocolate. Beat well with a whisk until smooth and glossy, 2 to 3 minutes. Remove from heat.

❧ In a 1-quart mixing bowl, beat the eggs with a whisk until frothy, then slowly whisk into the chocolate, pouring in a slow, steady steam while whisking. Stir in the pecans. Pour the filling into the prepared crust, spread marshmallows evenly over the top, resisting the temptation to pile them on—just make one even layer. Bake on the lower rack of the oven until internal temperature reaches 185°F, which will take 40 to 45 minutes. Cool at least 15 to 20 minutes before cutting and serving. This is delicious warm and gooey or straight from the refrigerator.

Red Velvet Cake

In the months leading up to our opening, when friends and acquaintances learned we were planning to open a Southern restaurant, one of the inevitable questions (and commands) was, "Are you going to have red velvet cake? You have to have red velvet cake!" I was never a big fan of this cake, however, so it wasn't high on my list of things to do.

My intentions changed significantly when I crossed two recipes in a short period of time: one for red velvet cake in *The Lee Bros. Southern Cookbook*, which had a hefty quantity of cocoa and vanilla in addition to some orange zest to give forth a cake with real flavor and character; the other was a recipe for chocolate beet cake in an old "road food" cookbook spotlighting a roadside diner in North Dakota. (I apologize because the name of the book and restaurant have escaped me ever since, but the influence stuck.) The earthy flavor of beets with the bitter cocoa and aromatic vanilla and orange was a no-brainer, and we could coax a red color out of the beets to boot. Perfectly natural and delicious.

Of course with the addition of beets with its much more natural rust color as opposed to bright red food dye, this became a highly divisive menu item from the early days. Some folks loved it; others hated it. A year or so after opening, the cake had developed a cult following of obsessed devotees, yet we'd still meet the occasional dissenter. All else aside, it did become so popular that I felt it was consuming our mission, which is to tell the story of Southern food as we know it, and that involves a lot more than one cake. We sell a lot of desserts, but not so many that it's ever made sense to offer more than one cake on the menu at any given time. If I was going to serve any other cakes, red velvet would have to step aside. We still offer it occasionally.

You can roast your beets up to a week before making the cake—just store them whole with the skin on, and peel and chop them before proceeding with the recipe. If you really want to use food color, use it sparingly, but I'd suggest buying red beets (if you can find the bull's blood variety, it has the richest color) at your farmers' market during fall or winter for this recipe. You'll get the best color and flavor. Supermarket beets don't usually perform as well.

Red velvet cake is another one of those foods associated with the South that is wildly popular, yet with origins cloaked in mystery. It's likely that older forms of cocoa powder, before alkali processing became the norm, would turn a rusty red color in the presence of the baking soda during baking. Once alkali processing of cocoa was standard, red food color was introduced to achieve the red color when desired. This theory is consistent with the appearance of recipes for "red devil's food cake" in early twentieth-century cookbooks.

Many folks insist on cream cheese icing with their red velvet cake, and it's truly a modern tradition. I urge you to try roux icing (page 49). It's probably more traditional to the origins of red velvet cake; but either way, it is more velveteen than cream cheese icing and doesn't overwhelm the delicate flavors of the cake so everything shines.

PREP TIME: 1 hour mixing and baking, 30 minutes frosting
EQUIPMENT NEEDED: three 9-inch cake pans, sifter, 4-quart mixing bowl, food
    processor, rubber spatula, stand mixer with flat beater attachment,
    2-quart mixing bowl, wire whisk, wire cooling rack
MAKES: one 9-inch three-layer cake

> 1 cup (2 sticks) unsalted butter, softened to room temperature, plus a
>   bit more for buttering pans
> 3 cups cake flour
> 1½ teaspoons baking powder
> ½ teaspoon baking soda
> ½ teaspoon kosher salt
> Zest and juice of 1 orange
> ¼ cup cocoa powder, plus a bit more for dusting cake pans
> 1 cup roasted red beets, peeled and diced into ½-inch pieces
> 1 tablespoon red food color (optional)
> 2 teaspoons vanilla extract
> 2 tablespoons corn oil
> 2 tablespoons honey
> 2 cups granulated sugar
> 4 large eggs
> 1 cup lowfat buttermilk

꽃 Preheat oven to 325°F.
꽃 Butter three 9-inch cake pans, dust with cocoa powder, and reserve.
Sift the flour before measuring. Combine the flour with the baking powder, baking soda, and salt in a 4-quart mixing bowl and resift together to mix evenly.
꽃 Zest the orange, and place in the bowl of the food processor, then use a hand juicer or fork to juice the orange into the food processor bowl with the zest, being careful to remove seeds. Add the cocoa powder, beets, optional food color, and vanilla extract. Puree for a minute or two until smooth. Add the oil and honey, then turn off the food processor and use a rubber spatula to scrape the sides down. Puree until smooth and creamy as a milk shake, another minute or two.

❦ In the bowl of a stand mixer with flat beater attachment, cream the softened butter and sugar together first on low speed, increasing speed to high
after the sugar and butter are incorporated, 3 to 4 minutes. Beat until light
and fluffy, another 3 to 4 minutes. Crack the eggs into a 2-quart mixing bowl
and remove any bits of broken shell. Add the eggs one at a time, beating
each into the butter mixture well before adding the next. After all the eggs
have been added, continue to beat until doubled in bulk, creamy, and lemon-
colored, another 4 to 5 minutes. Reduce speed to low and mix in the beet
mixture until incorporated and the mixture is a smooth, even pink color.

❦ Sift a third of the flour mixture over the butter mixture, then fold in by
turning the egg mix over the flour gently using a rubber spatula until incorporated, then add one-third of the buttermilk, and fold in gently. Repeat until
all flour and buttermilk are incorporated and you have a smooth, lump-free
batter.

❦ Divide the batter into three floured cake pans, and place on the center
rack of the oven until they pass the toothpick test, 35 to 40 minutes. Cool on
wire racks 10 minutes before turning the cakes out. Refrigerate thoroughly
or freeze before icing with roux icing.

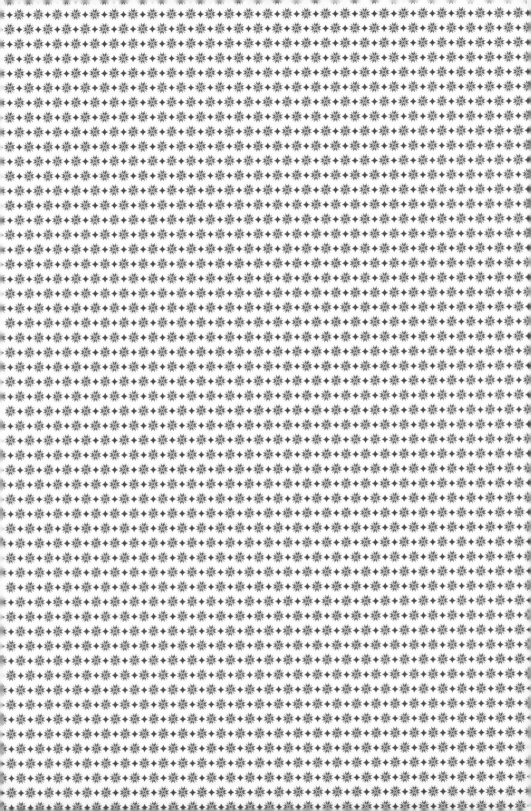

The *Bar*

As a chef, I love to drink. As a German American/Appalachian Ulster and Black Dutch mutt, I love to drink. As someone who was raised in the Ohio River Valley along the old Buffalo Trace, I love to drink bourbon. My naturally curious nature has led to studies of many of the world's great alcoholic beverages, which as you might imagine can oftentimes be very hard work. Count among my other favorites champagne, gin in its many forms, Scotch whiskey, the white wines of Germany, red wines of the Rhône, Piedmont, and Dundee Hills, the fortified wines of Madeira and Italy, the ancient liqueurs and elixirs of Europe, absinthe, and even a great vodka. Still, I usually come back to bourbon or rye whiskey from the great distilleries of Kentucky.

Every restaurant is a manifestation of someone's vision, and the most successful spots are deeply personal in some way, the heart and soul of a creator. As the chef and co-owner of Big Jones, I have always had responsibilities far beyond what constitutes our beverage menu, though by necessity it's always been a reflection of my own personal tastes and preferences when I hit the bottle. As such, you can always find over one hundred American whiskeys on offer, and modest but smart selections of beer and wine. Any proper bar in this day and age, in my opinion, stocks dozens of mixers from house-made bitters to various absinthes, maraschino liqueur to amaros and cinotto. If you sit at my bar and have your own favorite cocktail in your mind, we should be able to make it for you. If you want to peruse our offerings, we have many house specialties featuring local and artisanal spirits and house-made infusions from shrubs to bounces and bitters.

There's a wide rift in the bar arts today, and it's seldom talked about, perhaps because it is best considered a matter of personal taste, and when enjoying a stiff drink it seems an inappropriate time to be dogmatic. The question is, of course, shaken or stirred. James Bond perhaps did the most damage when he requested his martini "shaken, not stirred," and additionally he demonstrated a predilection toward "dry" martinis. As big of a franchise as the Bond movies are, these preferences became synonymous with the classy, tasteful, even masculine way to drink. We beg to differ. Not to slight Mr. Bond's personal taste, we will always make any drink to any guest's specifications. Where we do differ is our personal tastes, which reflect our default methodology for mixing drinks at Big Jones.

With reference to a martini shaken as opposed to stirred, in my opinion shaking dilutes the alcohol too much to be thoroughly savored, especially when you're talking about vodka. If I'm having a vodka martini, I want to taste the vodka (this would be a great time to take a shot at pretentious barkeeps who trash-talk vodka because "it has no flavor," but I digress), and the best way to achieve this is by stirring. It's also the best way to preserve the perfectly clear jewel-like presentation of the drink, especially with gin, which can often cloud slightly when shaken due to the many botanical oils suspended in gin. Our feelings are much the same with Manhattans and Sazeracs, which when properly mixed should be mighty stiff and as crystalline as a gemstone.

More dilute cocktails are appropriate for shaking, especially those containing fruit juice or more than a dram of heavy liqueurs or simple syrup, as shaking will help suspend the heavier mixers in the lighter alcohol. Obviously, when mixing egg to get the desired foaming, a long, vigorous shake is called for. Of course, if you like your daiquiris stirred or your Manhattans shaken until there are shards of ice floating in your glass, that's your preference—and, really, the only right way to mix a drink is the one that gives you a drink you enjoy.

Many of these concoctions are quick and easy to make, and others are what can only be described as labors of love. What we try to bring forth in each drink besides a shot in the arm is a story, whether it is a spirit, an ingredient, or method of preparation. Sometimes, the stories are even about people. One of the aspects of Southern food that hooked me is the rich tapestry of stories that make up its history. The same can be true of a great drink, and the bar is perhaps the best place of all to share stories— over a drink, of course.

Sazerac Cocktail, ca. 1940

Thought by many to be the original cocktail, the Sazerac dates to a time when alcoholic drinks were ostensibly made and consumed for therapeutic reasons. In spite of its "medicinal" roots, it remains one of the most perfect cocktails you can make with a brown liquor, offering the perfect balance of aroma, sweetness, alcoholic burn, and rich texture. Originally made with French brandy (cognac, specifically) and absinthe sometime in the 1830s, the Sazerac has been through three distinct phases leading to many variations extant today.

During the 1870s, the phylloxera epidemic in Europe destroyed the French brandy (and wine) industry temporarily, and rye whiskey, wildly popular and widely available at that time, became the favored spirit base and has remained so into the modern day, though many still make Sazeracs with brandy and some even prefer bourbon, which is too sweet and lacks the required spice in my opinion. Absinthe was banned in the United States in 1912, and one of the key ingredients was changed again, this time to anise-flavored liqueur instead of absinthe, pastis being the most famous of these. The invention of Herbsaint in 1934 brought about another major change, as it was somewhat closer to absinthe in its flavor profile and color than pastis. It gradually gained favor and today is still known by most bartenders as the key aromatic liqueur for Sazeracs.

Many brands of absinthe have been reintroduced in recent years as updates to FDA regulations have determined safe content levels for thujones, the allegedly psychoactive compound lent by wormwood, the herb used as a key flavoring in absinthe. Therefore, today you can enjoy a Sazerac many different ways, including one close to the original—just substitute a good cognac for the rye, a good absinthe for the Herbsaint, and a little loaf sugar for the cane syrup. Of course, this is my favorite version. The rye lends a spice and the cane syrup a depth of flavor that together balance everything beautifully.

MIXING TIME: 5 minutes
EQUIPMENT NEEDED: footed rocks glass, cocktail shaker, 2-ounce jigger, ½-ounce jigger, bar spoon, paring knife, vegetable peeler, cocktail strainer

2 ounces rye whiskey
2 dashes Peychaud's bitters
½ ounce cane syrup
1 bar spoon Herbsaint
Orange zest, for garnish

꽃 Chill a footed rocks glass. Place 1 cup of ice cubes in a cocktail shaker, and add the rye, bitters, and cane syrup. Stir gently with a bar spoon for 10 seconds, then allow to rest on the ice for a few moments while you cut a fresh orange peel garnish and rinse the glass. With a vegetable peeler, cut a section of orange peel ¾ inch in diameter for the garnish, avoiding the white pith as much as possible. Add Herbsaint to the chilled glass, give it a swirl, and pour off excess. Stir the whiskey mixture another 5 seconds more and strain into glass. Garnish with orange peel.

Chatham Artillery Punch

I first tasted Chatham Artillery Punch at a Southern Foodways Alliance Symposium, and the tub was mixed by the inimitable David Wondrich. After reading *The Happy Table of Eugene Walter*, a collection of many of Walter's recipes for entertaining, I came across his receipt for the same punch, which he received by way of a Savannah socialite named Henrietta Waring.

The origins of the punch are murky, but by the late nineteenth century it was quite famous, especially for being the very libation that knocked Admiral Dewey out cold during his 1890s visit to Savannah. Walter claims it was once said to have "the perfume and lightness of a meadow in spring," which is apt, yet only to disguise the potency of this concoction.

I made a few minor modifications to Walter's receipt: one to use añejo rum instead of dark rum, the other to use oleo-saccharum to impart citrus oils rather than steeping the whole juiced lemons in the mix. For the white wine, try to find a scuppernong or muscadine wine that is not too sweet—it will likely produce the most authentic result.

Be careful when serving this punch—it's potency is legendary, and it will live up to its reputation. That said, it is supremely aromatic, refreshing, and a pleasure to drink, a truly aristocratic libation worthy of your most esteemed guests who deserve nothing less than the Cadillac of punches.

PREP TIME: 20 minutes for the base, 1 week for aging, 30 minutes for the punch
EQUIPMENT NEEDED: citrus juicer, 2-quart pitcher for soaking tea, fine-mesh strainer, 5-gallon bucket, long-handled stainless-steel spoon, 50-gallon cedar tub or repurposed antique bathtub, punch ladle
MAKES: enough punch for 300 to 400

3 cups freshly squeezed orange juice

2 cups freshly squeezed lemon juice

4 ounces gunpowder green tea—steeped in 2 quarts cold water overnight, then strained

1 pound dark brown sugar

1 pound white sugar

3 bottles fruity, dry white wine

1 liter añejo rum

1 liter Christian Brothers VSOP brandy

1 liter best bourbon, such as Buffalo Trace or Larceny

1 liter London dry gin

2 cups oleo-saccharum (recipe follows)

12 bottles champagne, well chilled

♔ In a 5-gallon bucket, combine the juices, tea, and sugar. Stir with a long-
handled stainless-steel spoon to dissolve the sugar, then add remaining ingredients except for the champagne. Allow to stand for 1 week before finishing the punch, or store in an oak whiskey barrel, in which it will keep for
months. You can either finish the punch with the champagne and serve to a
large party, or pour single servings over ice and top with champagne to taste.
♔ To serve to a large party, the best vessel is a large cedar tub. Fill with
medium-small ice cubes if the punch will be drunk quickly, as it is strong
and you'll appreciate the dilution. If it's to be enjoyed over several hours, use
a few large blocks of ice, which will melt slowly yet keep the punch cold, together with some small or crushed ice cubes to get the punch chilled down
quickly. Serve with a punch ladle into champagne flutes or punch glasses.

Oleo-Saccharum

Translated from the Latin as "oil sugar," oleo-saccharum was an essential
preparation in the earliest days of mixology and also in the crackpot faux-
pharmacies of the nineteenth century. Most of us know that oil doesn't
like to mix with water, and we also know that sugar does mix easily with
water, and that oil mixes reasonably well with sugar. So, this preparation
is a great way to get citrus oils to dissolve in water, using sugar as a carrier.
Necessary for many punches (including our Chatham Artillery Punch)

and more than a few old-school cocktails, this is not hard to make and it stores well, so it's a great preparation to keep around in case you want to add a delightful citrus note to anything from iced tea to gin and tonics, or more ambitious cocktails and punches.

PREP TIME: 45 minutes prep, 1 week for infusing, 10 minutes for straining
EQUIPMENT NEEDED: vegetable peeler, 4-quart mixing bowl, bar muddler,
    1-quart glass jar with tight-fitting lid, fine-mesh strainer
MAKES: 2 cups after straining

Zest of 6 oranges
Zest of 12 lemons
5 cups granulated sugar

♏ Use a vegetable peeler to peel the oranges and lemons, avoiding as much of the white pith as you can. Whatever you do, be sure to get more of the zest than the white pith, and you're good. Place the zest in a 4-quart mixing bowl, and add sugar in bits as you accumulate more zest, until all the orange and lemon zest and sugar are in the bowl. Use a bar muddler to work the sugar into the peels and get the oils to purge and wet the sugar. Cover tightly with plastic wrap, and let stand overnight.

♏ Muddle the mix once again, and pour all into a 1-quart jar with a tight-fitting lid, cover tightly, and set in a cool, dark place (the basement or closets away from heating vents are ideal) for 1 week. Strain through a fine-mesh strainer, again using a bar muddler to coax all of the oils through the strainer back into the glass jar, seal, and refrigerate until needed. Will keep under refrigeration for 3 to 4 weeks. For longer-term storage, dissolve into an equal volume of white rum or vodka. This solution is shelf-stable indefinitely, though best within a couple of months. If you've preserved your oleo-saccharum in a rum or vodka solution, you will then need to double the dose in any recipe calling for oleo-saccharum.

The Consummation

One of the servers on our opening team was a darling lady named Laura, who moved to Austin some time ago after serving for four years. As much as we miss her, she makes it back to Chicago every so often to visit and we always try to plan an afternoon cocktailing date. One summer on such an occasion, we were sitting at the newly rebuilt bar at Big Jones and pondering our options. Laura, like myself, has quite a taste for champagne, and on this particular day she was thinking an afternoon of bubbles. I, on the other hand, was hoping to play out my recently developed obsession with Aviation cocktails, the gin-lemon-maraschino-violette elixir that dates to Prohibition. It's pretty much the perfect summer cocktail, at least as far as gin options go—it's herbaceous and flowery, like many a garden that time of year, with that citrusy tang that evokes the childhood lemonade stand (or for me, lemonade shake-ups at the county fair) with gin's trademark astringency to keep the palate fresh.

In hopes of a compromise, I made us a couple of Aviations and poured champagne over. No big surprise, it worked so beautifully that we had to take cabs home by the time we'd satiated ourselves. My friend and expert mixologist Wade Turnipseed once described the Aviation as "Like your grandparents' first kiss, when they were young and beautiful"—which I thought was beautifully poetic, and it just happened that both sets of my grandparents got married during Prohibition. Thus, the name the Consummation was born. This is an early summer cocktail, especially when freshly picked violet blossoms are to be had for a garnish. A perfect summer quencher with a bit of a punch.

MIXING TIME: 6 to 7 minutes
EQUIPMENT NEEDED: 10-ounce cocktail glass, cocktail shaker, 1½-ounce jigger, citrus juicer, ½-ounce jigger, bar spoon, cocktail strainer

1½ ounces London dry gin
½ ounce freshly squeezed lemon
½ ounce Luxardo maraschino liqueur
1 bar spoon crème de violette

3 to 4 ounces dry sparkling wine
Lemon twist or garnish

♕ Chill a 10-ounce cocktail glass. Place 1 cup of ice cubes in a cocktail shaker, and add the gin, lemon juice, maraschino liqueur, and crème de violette. Shake vigorously for 20 seconds, then strain into cocktail glass and top with sparkling wine. Garnish with lemon twist, maraschino cherry, or fresh strawberries if in season.

Sweet Leaf

The Sweet Leaf cocktail is a variation on the Clover Leaf, which is a variation on the classic pre-Prohibition Clover Club, so named for the old Philadelphia gentlemen's club of the same name. Harkening back to a time when men were men and not the least bit shy about imbibing a pink cocktail in public, this cocktail packs a punch that would, in the old slang, put a little hair on your chest.

Most old recipes for this drink call for grenadine, which in the old days was a potent pomegranate syrup (grenadine being French for pomegranate) rather than the innocuous red syrup of sugar, citric acid, and red food color we know it as today. A few of the old recipes do call for raspberry syrup, and given our great local fruit-growing region along the southeastern shores of Lake Michigan, we opted to go that route.

Often garnished with fresh mint, we made the call to use a few drops of tincture made from the slightly exotic Cherokee sweetmint to add a bright, woodsy scent to the cocktail, which sets off both the gin and the raspberry perfectly. The addition of egg white, true to the original, makes for a creamy and frothy texture that I especially love in late summer gin cocktails. As with any recipe calling for uncooked egg of any kind, use only the freshest eggs you can find from a good farmer who pastures the hens, or use a pasteurized egg substitute.

MIXING TIME: 5 minutes

EQUIPMENT NEEDED: 10-ounce cocktail glass, cocktail shaker, 1½-ounce jigger, citrus juicer, 1-ounce jigger, ¾-ounce jigger, ½-ounce jigger, cocktail strainer, eye dropper for applying tincture

1½ ounces London dry gin
1 ounce freshly squeezed lemon juice
¾ ounce raspberry syrup (recipe follows)
½ ounce dry vermouth
1 egg white
3 drops Cherokee sweetmint tincture (recipe follows)

Chill a 10-ounce cocktail glass. Place 1 cup of ice cubes in a cocktail shaker, and add the gin, lemon juice, raspberry syrup, vermouth, and egg white. Shake vigorously for 20 seconds, then strain into the chilled cocktail glass, wait a few moments for the froth to rise and cap the top, and dot with the sweetmint tincture.

RASPBERRY SYRUP

PREP TIME: 5 minutes plus 3 days to macerate

EQUIPMENT NEEDED: 1-quart glass jar with tight-fitting lid, fine-mesh strainer, pint glass jar with tight-fitting lid

MAKES: 2 cups

1 pint fresh raspberries
1½ cups granulated sugar

⚜ Place raspberries in a 1-quart glass jar with a tight-fitting lid, add the sugar, and turn gently to distribute the sugar evenly without breaking up the raspberries. Cover tightly and refrigerate for 3 days. Carefully decant the clear, sweet juice that has rendered, and gently strain the raspberries through a fine-mesh strainer without pressing the raspberries—just let the clear juice fall through. Discard the fruit or add to a batch of preserves. Transfer to a pint jar with a tight-fitting lid and refrigerate for up to 10 days, or freeze.

Cherokee sweetmint is an herb with an aroma that anyone who hikes regularly in the eastern deciduous forests of the United States will immediately recognize, but most others will find completely exotic. It grows wild in meadows and along trails, and it sports such a penetrating scent that merely brushing a plant as you walk by is likely to fill your head with the aroma. Woody, minty, and dominated by the unmistakable mark of menthol, it's refreshing as can be, but so potent it's best used in small doses. With this tincture, a quick infusion is a must lest it become so strong as to dominate any flavors and aromas it is mixed with. So, stick with the specified 2 days for the infusion. To find Cherokee sweetmint, talk to the herb specialist at your local farmers' market, or just ask around—many old-timers will know where to find it.

PREP TIME: 5 minutes plus 2 days for infusing
EQUIPMENT NEEDED: 1-pint glass jar with tight-fitting lid, fine-mesh strainer, eye dropper bottle

1 cup neutral grape spirit such as grape vodka, white brandy, or pisco
1 cup tightly packed Cherokee sweetmint leaves

⚘ Place the spirits and sweetmint leaves in a 1-pint glass jar with a tight-fitting lid, and store in a dark spot at room temperature for 48 hours. Strain through a fine-mesh strainer, return the infused spirit to the jar, and store in a dark spot at room temperature indefinitely. Keep in a small eye dropper bottle for use on the bar.

Blue Yodel No. 1

Named for country music pioneer Jimmie Rodgers and his immortal song "T for Texas," Blue Yodel No. 1 was created by our Bar Director and Captain Andrew Shay as a distinctively Southern spin on a Manhattan, with Tennessee rye as the base spirit and a Texas smoked whiskey rinse, lending a whiff of the barbecue pit to this very stiff drink. While we use George Dickel rye, you should feel free to use your favorite rye; and if you can't come by Balcones Brimstone whiskey, I recommend an Islay malt Scotch whiskey for the rinse. It won't be quite the same, but it will be delicious and just as stiff as the original.

MIXING TIME: 5 minutes
EQUIPMENT NEEDED: footed rocks glass, cocktail shaker, 2-ounce jigger, 1-ounce jigger, bar spoon, cocktail strainer

2 ounces George Dickel rye whiskey
1 ounces Dolin Rouge vermouth
2 dashes Angostura bitters
1 bar spoon Balcones Brimstone smoked whiskey or Islay malt Scotch
Maraschino cherry garnish

♛ Chill a footed rocks glass. Place 1 cup of ice cubes in a cocktail shaker, and add the rye, vermouth, and bitters. Stir gently for 5 seconds with a bar spoon, then allow to rest on the ice for a moment while you prepare the glass. Add the smoked whiskey to the chilled glass, and give it a swirl, but do not discard. Stir the cocktail 5 seconds more and strain into glass. Garnish with a maraschino cherry.

Bloody Mary Jones

From day one, I knew we needed to offer a badass Bloody Mary if our brunch plans were to succeed. It's one mixed drink you can get literally anywhere, and there are a lot of bad ones. There are some pretty good prefabricated mixes, at least if you're into the heavily spiced, bombastic style of Bloody. In keeping with the style of my cooking, I wanted our Bloody to be at once a mouthful, but also fresh, light, and ultimately refreshing in a way that would make folks want to keep drinking (responsibly of course).

I say this about gumbo and I'll repeat it about Bloody Marys—your Bloody is only as good as your Worcestershire sauce. Fortunately, there are a few good commercial Worcestershires on the market, Lea & Perrins chief among them. Even so, you'll like the result even better if you have some homemade Worcestershire (page 236) on hand. As far as the hot sauce goes, I just love Crystal—use it if you can find it, but you can use your favorite. I also like this recipe with Texas Pete or Louisiana Gold.

Use organic tomato juice if you can; the flavor is so much better. Regardless of the tomato juice, give it a taste before using—some commercial tomato juice is really salty, and you may want to adjust the celery salt in the recipe.

Finally, don't waste your hard-earned treasure on a designer vodka for this drink—save the fancy vodkas for martinis or drinking straight. You want a vodka that has a lot of flavor, and those usually aren't the most expensive. Look for Tito's Handmade, Luksusowa, Wyborowa, Snow Queen, Stolichnaya, or one from your local distillery.

MIXING TIME: 20 minutes, plus overnight or up to two days to chill
EQUIPMENT NEEDED: 2-quart glass serving pitcher, citrus juicer, bar spoon, microplane
MAKES: 1½ quarts of mix, serves 8 to 12

32 ounces organic tomato juice
¼ cup freshly squeezed lemon juice
¼ cup Crystal hot sauce
1 teaspoon celery salt
1 teaspoon black pepper
2 tablespoons Worcestershire sauce
Vodka
Fresh horseradish, for grating and seasoning to taste
Okra pickles for garnish
Cucumber pickles for garnish
Lime wedges for garnish

⚜ In a 2-quart serving pitcher, combine the tomato and lemon juices, hot sauce, celery salt, pepper, and Worcestershire. Stir with a bar spoon to combine well, and chill thoroughly. This step is best done the night before to give the mix time to infuse and harmonize. If refrigerating overnight, cover tightly with plastic wrap before placing in the refrigerator.
⚜ The following day, simply pour vodka over ice and top with Bloody Mary mix to taste. Use a microplane to grate horseradish over the top of each filled glass and garnish with pickles and lime wedges.

Death in the Afternoon

Being fans as we are of Hemingway at Big Jones, we've often found inspiration in his cultural savvy as well as his writing. While he's known as a heavy drinker, we've found great appreciation for his ability to sleuth out the best libations for any given part of the day, Death in the Afternoon being the perfect example. Hemingway's simple concoction consists of champagne with a dram of absinthe, a combination that will surely send you into an early slumber.

The drink is magnificently refreshing and sunshiny, but we did feel it was just a bit on the sweet side, so we pulled out some cherry bud bitters. Made from the unopened blossoms of cherry trees in early spring, the bitters are mightily astringent and woody, with just a hint of a new spring flower. A few drops soaked into a sugar cube lend just the right amount of tannic power to cut the sweetness and make the cocktail refreshingly dry while retaining the heft and body of the absinthe's sugar. A twist of lemon keeps it honest.

MIXING TIME: 5 minutes
EQUIPMENT NEEDED: champagne flute, bar spoon, eye dropper, zesting knife

    5 ounces of your favorite dry sparkling wine
    1 bar spoon (½ tablespoon) absinthe
    1 sugar cube
    4 drops cherry bud bitters (recipe follows)
    Lemon twist for garnish

⚜ Chill a champagne flute. Fill almost full with sparkling wine, and add the absinthe. Use a dropper to soak the sugar cube with the bitters, then drop into the wine. Use a zesting knife to cut a twist of lemon. Twist the lemon peel and rim the glass with oils that run to the surface of the peel, and drop the twist into the wine.

Cherry Bud Bitters

An excellent example of finding inspiration from ingredients, one spring when I was shopping at Green City Market at the very beginning of the season when there's not much new produce, Seedling's Peter Klein pulled up a lug of fine young tree shoots and asked if I'd be interested in some cherry blossoms. At that time, the buds were unopened, but Peter explained that we could put the branch cuttings in vases of water and we'd have sprays of cherry blossoms, which are very pretty not to mention fragrant. After tasting one, I had other ideas. The taste of cherry wood took the background behind a mammoth tannin punch and flavors of fresh tree sap with a hint of the flower-to-be. This was going to be bitters, and one day we'd find a cocktail fit for cherry bud bitters. It didn't take long as within weeks Death in the Afternoon was born.

PREP TIME: 30 minutes plus 1 month infusing time
EQUIPMENT NEEDED: 2-quart glass jar with tight-fitting lid, fine-mesh strainer, 1-quart glass jar with tight-fitting lid
MAKES: 3 cups

1 quart fresh unopened cherry blossom buds, completely removed
　　from branches
½ cup black peppercorns
12 bay leaves
2 cups neutral grape brandy, such as eau de vie or pisco
2 cups champagne vinegar

⚜ Place all ingredients in a 2-quart glass jar with a tight-fitting lid, cover tightly, and shake. Infuse in a cool, dark place for 1 month before using. Strain through a fine-mesh strainer, and return to a clean 1-quart glass jar with an airtight lid. Store in a cool, dark place for up to 1 year.

Rhubarb Julep

Rhubarb is one of the great joys of spring, and it's soon followed by mint's prime season, which is early summer. For us, that means infusions we make with rhubarb are ready to go at the precise moment that mint is bursting forth with its biggest growth spurt of the year, when summer temperatures finally arrive but aren't yet hot enough to dry the mint or turn it woody bitter.

Prime time for mint is when it is in the high 70s during the day and around 60°F at night. Here in Chicago we typically start seeing rhubarb at the end of April and the best mint toward the end of May, giving something like a rhubarb shrub a month to infuse before mint is ready.

The rhubarb julep actually happened by accident. When we first made rhubarb shrub, an old-time method of preserving fruit, we found it was ready at the same time we found ourselves at the market with beautiful mint all around us. Since we love mint juleps in early summer, this drink seemed perfectly natural. To make this drink properly, you'll want to invest in some proper julep cups—I wouldn't suggest pounding ice into a glass or ceramic mug! They are widely available online. This recipe fills an 8-ounce julep cup and is easier if you start with crushed ice, but you can use a bar mallet or muddler to break up the ice in the cup—just be sure to use a sturdy metal cup.

MIXING TIME: 6 to 7 minutes
EQUIPMENT NEEDED: 8-ounce julep cup, bar muddler, 2-ounce jigger, 1-ounce
    jigger, citrus juicer, ½-ounce jigger, bar spoon

    Handful of freshly picked mint leaves
    2 ounces best bourbon
    1 ounce rhubarb shrub (recipe follows)
    ½ ounce freshly squeezed lemon juice
    1 bar spoon Aperol

℣ Place 6 to 8 mint leaves in the bottom of a metal julep cup, fill the cup halfway with ice, and muddle to crush the mint and ice together. Add another few mint leaves, top off with ice to the rim, and muddle and crush the whole together. Add bourbon, rhubarb shrub, and lemon juice, and stir vigorously with a bar spoon until the cup frosts. Drizzle top with Aperol. Massage remaining mint leaves for a few seconds between the palms of your hands to release the oils, pile on top of the julep, and enjoy.

RHUBARB SHRUB

PREP TIME: 30 minutes plus 1 month to infuse
EQUIPMENT NEEDED: 4-quart mixing bowl, wooden spoon, 2-quart glass jar
    with tight-fitting lid, 1-quart glass jar with tight-fitting lid
MAKES: 4 cups

    1 pound rhubarb, washed and cut into ¼-inch slices
    2 cups sugar
    2 bay leaves
    1½ cups champagne vinegar

♔ Place the sliced rhubarb in a 4-quart mixing bowl, and use a wooden spoon to toss with the sugar to combine well, then transfer all to a 2-quart glass jar with a tight-fitting lid. Add the bay leaves and vinegar, shake to distribute everything, and place in a dark spot at room temperature for 1 month. Shake daily for the first week, then allow to settle for the remaining 3 weeks. Carefully decant the clear liquid that has rendered into a 1-quart glass jar with tight-fitting lid, by gently pouring off the clear liquid, allowing gravity to separate the rhubarb pulp at the bottom. Discard the rhubarb pulp, and refrigerate, tightly covered, for several weeks or longer.

Brandy Fix

Given our passion for the old arts of mixology as with cooking, a "fix" always seemed like a good idea because this nineteenth-century libation harkens back to a time when mixologists were pharmacists and vice versa. If you were feeling ill by any manner of symptoms, you might call for a fix to do the job. Of course, if you drank enough of any one of these "fixes," you'd surely be cured of any symptoms you were experiencing, at least until morning.

The brandy fix was perhaps the most common, and receipts from the nineteenth century vary widely, so we settled on the one we like best: brandy, pineapple syrup, lemon, and a green chartreuse float. We took the liberty of adding a tiny bit of Cynar, the exquisitely bitter artichoke liqueur, to temper some of the sweeter elements. As with all cocktails made with fruit juice, this one is shaken. The pineapple juice is made by macerating whole ripe pineapples on sugar and then drawing off the syrupy juice that is extracted by homeostasis. We'd love to see people drink more brandy as its value behind the bar seems to be lost to time—this cocktail is a great way to start.

MIXING TIME: 6 to 7 minutes
EQUIPMENT NEEDED: footed rocks glass, cocktail shaker, 2-ounce jigger, citrus juicer, ½-ounce jigger, bar spoon, cocktail strainer

2 ounces VSOP brandy
½ ounce freshly squeezed lemon juice
½ ounce pineapple syrup (recipe follows)
1 bar spoon Cynar
1 bar spoon green chartreuse

⚜ Chill a footed rocks glass. Place 1 cup of ice cubes in a cocktail shaker, and add the brandy, lemon juice, pineapple syrup, and Cynar. Shake vigorously for 20 seconds, then strain into the chilled footed rocks glass. Carefully float the chartreuse on top and serve.

PINEAPPLE SYRUP

PREP TIME: 30 minutes plus 3 days to macerate
EQUIPMENT NEEDED: 1-quart glass jar with tight-fitting lid, 1-pint glass jar with tight-fitting lid
MAKES: 2 cups

½ ripe fresh pineapple, peeled and diced into ½-inch cubes (about 2 cups)
1½ cups granulated sugar

⚜ Place diced pineapple in a 1-quart glass jar with a tight-fitting lid, add the sugar, cap tightly, and shake to distribute the sugar evenly with the pine-apple. Refrigerate for 3 days. Carefully decant the clear, sweet juice that has rendered, by slowly pouring the clear liquid off and allowing gravity to sepa-rate the pineapple pulp at the bottom. Discard the pineapple pulp or use for preserves. Transfer to a pint jar, and refrigerate for up to 10 days. Discard remaining fruit or use for preserves or chutney.

The *Pantry*

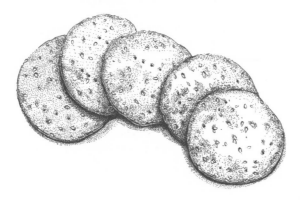

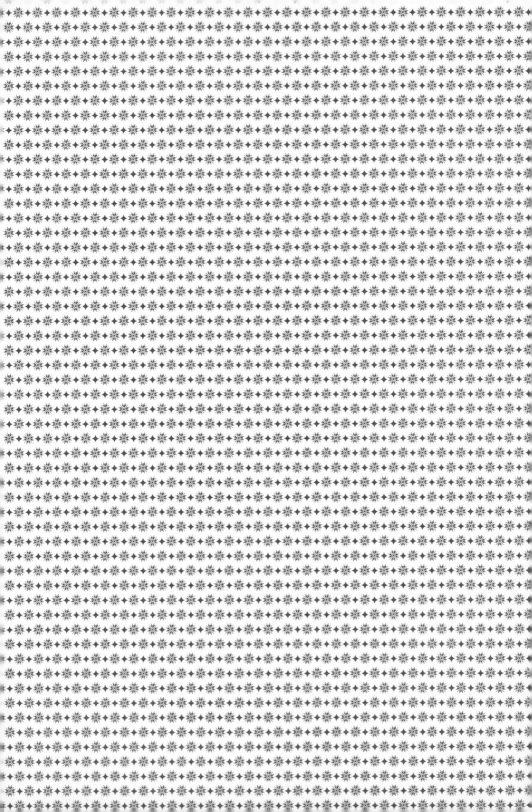

From the very beginning, I was committed to producing as much of our pantry from scratch with local ingredients when possible. I'd long been dissatisfied with the quality of basic condiments available in the food service and retail industries and saw it as a way to make a mark, because anything we make ourselves is an opportunity to serve something that isn't available anywhere else. After reading Edna Lewis, I realized it also offered a connection to the land and that is often lost in American food culture. We continue to work with and devise new pickle and preserves recipes utilizing any ingredients that can be preserved, looking toward all of today's available techniques while making sure the spirit of tradition is always present—taking the best homegrown produce we can find and preserving it with skill at its absolute peak.

Picking fruit for restaurants is a tricky business, so I have tons of respect for the farms from which I regularly buy fruit: Seedling, Mick Klug, Paul Friday, Oriana's Oriental Orchard, Spence Farm, Windy Knoll Farm, and many more. They have to pick something that's highly perishable and can attract (and bring into their customers' restaurants) pests, or might just rot within a day of getting it into my kitchen. Consequently, berries and stone fruits are usually picked within hours of being ripe, so they might be perfectly ripe when I get them to my kitchen. Sometimes, the weather doesn't deliver the sunlight, heat, or humidity needed to ripen fruit, and we wind up ripening it in a sealed brown paper bag for a day or two before we find the fruit perfectly ripe at midnight on a Saturday, and it's time to make peach pickles or preserves—no matter that we will need to serve hundreds of covers for brunch in the morning. This is the work of the old homesteads like my grandparents' and new homesteads like Big Jones and our family of small farmers.

I've risked speeding tickets to rush peppers from the Green City Market up Lake Shore Drive to Big Jones in order to get a particularly aromatic bunch of peppers into the pot for pepper jelly before they lose that scent. It's the smell not just of the pepper fruit itself, but of the whole plant, which you get in peppers that are really, really fresh and that scent dies within eight hours or so. When I buy the peppers, I don't know how long they've been off the plant, so I have to get them into the pot as soon as I possibly can. That is what preserves are all about.

My grandma had a pantry the size of most people's bedrooms and filled it every year with the produce of her garden and the nearby woods. I particularly enjoy making these many recipes because they are an inextricable link to our past food traditions and way of life, something I can share with our Big Jones family every day of the year.

Clarified Butter

PREP TIME: 1 hour
EQUIPMENT NEEDED: 2-quart saucepan, small ladle, fine-mesh strainer,
     cheesecloth

One of the essential pantry items of classical French cooking, and also Indian cooking, in which it is called ghee, *clarified butter is simply that—butter that has been "clarified," meaning the buttermilk and butter solids have been removed. This is most easily done by carefully heating the butter and boiling out the water while skimming off the solids that rise to the top and straining the remaining butterfat. You can make any quantity of this you want, but it's easiest to clarify a couple pounds at a time. Clarified butter will keep well in an airtight container in the refrigerator for a couple of months, so there's no need to be shy about making a little extra. No ingredient list here, just some simple instructions. This is easy, but stay near the stove and pay attention, otherwise you might wind up with browned butter (delicious but not what we're trying to make) or, worse, burned butter.*

🌱 Place 2 pounds of unsalted butter in a 2-quart saucepan over high heat. Melt the butter and gradually bring it to a boil, which will take 10 to 15 minutes. Reduce heat to medium to maintain a full, but not brisk, boil. As foam and scum begin to rise to the top, use a small ladle to skim it off. When you first begin this process of clarifying butter, if you use your ladle to move the foam to one side of the surface, the yellowish liquid below will have a milky appearance. That's a combination of butter solids and water bound by the lecithin naturally present in butter. As you cook it longer, the water will evaporate and the solids will separate. Some of the solids will float to the top to be skimmed off, while some will be drawn to the heat on the bottom and sides of the pan and stick. This is OK, but it's also why you don't want too much heat or the solids will burn.

⚜ After 30 minutes, depending on the size and shape of your saucepan and the heat of your burner, the butter underneath the boiling foam on the surface will begin to appear clear, like oil. Continue cooking and skimming until you can clearly see the bottom of the pan (which will have butter solids stuck to it) through the oil. The solids on the bottom of the pan may be browning somewhat, which is fine; simply stop cooking once the oil is clear. If you want brown butter, continue cooking gently to the desired color. Remove from heat and allow to cool for 15 minutes before straining through a fine-mesh strainer lined with cheesecloth; a coffee filter is a reasonable substitute. Transfer to an airtight container, and refrigerate up to 2 months or freeze for up to 6 months.

Basic Mayonnaise

We make a lot of mayonnaise-based sauces at Big Jones, from rémoulade and green goddess to our buttermilk-herb dressing and cayenne mayonnaise, plus a touch is called for in recipes such as pimiento cheese. Southern food aficionados are insistent on Duke's, while many other folks around the country like Hellman's, and there's no question that those are tasty mayos by canned standards. Try making your own sometime—it's easy, it doesn't take long, and will keep for a couple of weeks tightly capped in the refrigerator.

We make our own mayonnaise for the same reason you might like to— you can adjust it to your exact flavor preferences. In our case, we make a mayonnaise that's rich but somewhat neutral so it lends its body and creaminess to recipes rather than taking over in the flavor department.

Be sure to use really good, fresh eggs—it's good to know an egg farmer. You should also err on the side of adding the oil too slowly (not possible, really) rather than risking building it up too quickly. The idea is to make a really stiff emulsion and then cut it with water to your desired consistency.

PREP TIME: 20 minutes
EQUIPMENT NEEDED: 4-quart stainless-steel mixing bowl, balloon whisk, pint
    jar with tight-fitting lid
MAKES: 2 cups

3 large egg yolks

1½ teaspoons kosher salt

2 teaspoons dry mustard powder

2 teaspoons granulated garlic

½ teaspoon cayenne pepper

2 tablespoons distilled white vinegar

1½ cups neutral vegetable oil, such as sunflower or corn oil

2 tablespoons extra-virgin olive oil

¼ cup cold water

⚜ Place the egg yolks and dry ingredients in a 4-quart stainless-steel mixing bowl, and whisk until creamy, 2 to 3 minutes. While whisking, add the vinegar a few drops at a time, and continue beating until the eggs begin to thicken slightly. Continuing to whisk vigorously, add the vegetable oil very slowly, a teaspoon at a time at first, making sure to fully incorporate each addition and allow the emulsion that is forming to thicken a bit before adding the next addition. After ten additions by the teaspoon, increase each addition to tablespoons, careful that with each addition and further whisking the emulsion becomes thicker. By the time all of the vegetable oil has been added, the mayonnaise should be very thick and stand up in dollops when spooned up. Whisk in the olive oil, and beat until very stiff. Add water, a tablespoon at a time, until the mayonnaise reaches your desired consistency. It's not necessary to use all or even any of the water if you like a stiffer mayonnaise. Correct for seasoning if you like more salt, vinegar, or cayenne pepper. Refrigerate at once for up to 2 weeks in a tightly capped airtight container.

Green Goddess

A great all-around dipping sauce and fantastic salad dressing, green goddess is a very good thing to keep in your refrigerator. If you've been firing up the grill, it's great with grilled vegetables, but my favorite is to eat it with fried potatoes. One of our most requested recipes, many folks will be happy to see this in print.

Actually originating in San Francisco and long popular on the West Coast, green goddess couldn't possibly be more at home on a Southern food menu, with mayonnaise, buttermilk, and its many garden herbs.

PREP TIME: 30 minutes
EQUIPMENT NEEDED: blender, rubber spatula, 4-quart mixing bowl, wire whisk,
    pint jar with tight-fitting lid
MAKES: 5 cups

2 tablespoons flat leaf parsley leaves, tightly packed
2 tablespoons green onion, finely chopped
1 teaspoon fresh tarragon leaves, tightly packed
1 teaspoon fresh thyme leaves, tightly packed
¼ cup watercress leaves, tightly packed
1½ teaspoons anchovy paste
½ teaspoon freshly ground white pepper
1 clove fresh garlic, mashed
1½ teaspoons kosher salt
¾ cup buttermilk
1 cup mayonnaise
1½ teaspoons freshly squeezed lemon juice

🌱 Place the parsley, green onion, tarragon, thyme, watercress, anchovy paste, white pepper, garlic, and salt in the bowl of a blender, and wet with ½ cup buttermilk. Cover the blender tightly and work on low speed to grind the herbs, gradually increasing the speed to high. Stop the blender and scrape down the sides with a rubber spatula as needed, and add a little more buttermilk if needed to lubricate the puree. Puree to a smooth, fine, even bright green, 4 to 5 minutes. Transfer to a 4-quart mixing bowl, and whisk in the mayonnaise until smooth, then whisk in the remaining buttermilk a little at a time. Whisk in the lemon juice and taste for seasoning, adding more salt, pepper, or lemon juice as desired. Refrigerate for up to one week in a pint jar with a tight-fitting lid.

Standard Canning Instructions for Shelf-Stable Pickles and Preserves

This is the procedure you will need to use if you would like to prepare shelf-stable pickles and preserves for your cupboard, rather than storing them in your refrigerator. The process effectively pasteurizes the contents of the jar and helps put an extra-strong vacuum seal on the lid.

This is a basic canning procedure and should only be used for high-acid foods such as pickles and fruit preserves. If you wish to can low-acid foods such as basic vegetables in liquid without added vinegar or sugar, you absolutely must use the pressure-canning method, which is beyond the scope of this book.

YOU WILL NEED

- A deep stock pot with a footed screen that fits the bottom of the pot, to keep the jars off the bottom of the pot during canning, or a specialized "canner," a pot made for this purpose. The pot needs to be deep enough that the jars, when placed on the screen, will be completely submerged when the pot is filled with water.
- A jar lifter (a special set of tongs made to fit the neck of canning jars).
- Clean canning jars with lids that are in good shape—no cuts, tears, dents, or other damage.

BASIC INSTRUCTIONS

1. To sterilize your jars, wash them well in hot soapy water and rinse well.
2. Place the footed screen on the bottom of the stock pot, place your jars and lids in the pot, and cover with water.
3. Place pot on stove and bring to a boil. Boil 15 minutes.
4. Carefully remove the jars and lids with a jar lifter, and drain on a clean wire rack.
5. When the jars are cool enough to handle, fill with desired contents for canning and place lids on jars, twisting them to tighten snugly, but not too tight.
6. Place the filled and capped jars upright on the footed screen in the pot, and cover with water by at least ½ inch. During boiling, you will

need to make sure the jars stay submerged, as water boils off, by adding water as necessary.

7. Place over high heat and bring to a boil. Reduce heat if necessary to maintain a rolling, not hard boil.
8. Boil for 30 minutes for pint jars, 50 minutes for quart jars.
9. Turn off the heat and use a jar lifter to carefully remove jars, and place on a clean towel or pot holder to drain and cool.
10. As the jars cool, you should hear the lids "pop," which is when the contraction of the jar's contents due to their cooling creates a vacuum that causes the lids to buckle in and seal the jars.
11. As soon as the jars are cool enough to handle, you may label them and transfer to the cupboard.

Chow-Chow

A workhorse pickle relish of ours since day one, chow-chow is an essential thread in the fabric of Southern cuisine, and its preparation is as widely varied as the many regions of the South. The one universal as far as I can tell is the combination of cabbage, onions, and peppers (though the variations start right there as some prefer sweet and some hot), and then you'll find such eccentricities as the addition of green tomatoes, squash, or even eggplant; there are also many different schools of thought regarding the cut of the vegetables, ranging from thinly sliced to diced to minced or shredded.

We went with a julienne cut for no other reason than we like the presentation opportunities it gives us, with the long strips of green, white, and red. The essential purpose of the initial brining and soaking is to remove some of the more objectionable sulfur aromas present in cabbage and onions that can often concentrate and become unpleasant in a closed container like a jar. This allows you to better enjoy the flavors of both.

PREP TIME: 1 hour for stage one, overnight for brining, 1 hour for stage two
EQUIPMENT NEEDED: wooden spoon, two 4-quart non-reactive containers with tight-fitting lids, 4-quart colander, 4-quart non-reactive stock pot, cheesecloth, three 1-quart canning jars with lids, or six pint jars
MAKES: three 1-quart jars or six pint jars

½ cup kosher salt

3 quarts cold water

½ pound green bell pepper, finely julienned

1 pound red bell pepper, finely julienned

2 pounds green cabbage, very thinly sliced

½ pound yellow onion, finely julienned

꽃 In a 4-quart non-reactive container, use a long-handled wooden spoon to stir the salt into the water until dissolved. Place the vegetables in a clean 4-quart container, and cover with the salt water. Cover tightly, and refrigerate overnight or for up to 48 hours.

STAGE TWO

1½ quarts white vinegar

¾ cup cold water

2 teaspoons kosher salt

1 cup granulated sugar

6 whole allspice berries

1 teaspoon celery seed

1 Ceylon cinnamon stick

1 tablespoon whole coriander seed

1 tablespoon grated fresh ginger

1 teaspoon crushed red pepper

꽃 Clean and sanitize your kitchen sink, and place a 4-quart colander in it. Pour the soaked vegetables into the colander and drain, discarding the brine, while preparing the pickle. Place vinegar, water, salt, and sugar in a 4-quart or larger non-reactive stock pot, and bring to a boil. Bundle the spices into a sachet of cheesecloth and add to the pickle. Simmer for 15 minutes, then add the vegetables, pressing down to submerge all. Stirring with a wooden spoon occasionally, bring to a boil for 15 seconds and remove from heat at once. Discard the spice sachet. Carefully divide the vegetables and brine between sterilized canning jars and cap tightly. May be stored in the refrigerator for up to 2 months, or canned according to standard canning instructions.

Bread and Butter Pickles

Perhaps because I had both an appreciation for a good sour pucker and an insatiable sweet tooth as a youngster, when I first tasted bread and butter pickles from my grandma's pantry, I was startled. They were pickles, weren't they? Why were they sweet? Oh, the sour was there, but everything was flat out of whack, at least as far as my underdeveloped palate discerned. It would be years before I appreciated the added complexity of a dram of sweetness on my pickles, together with that acrid taste of turmeric adding both color and another layer of flavor, the bitter. I still like my sour pickles with some items like burgers, beef, and smoked pork preparations, but these sweeter pickles work so well with seafood, cheese, bread and butter (duh!) that I always keep them around.

PREP TIME: 1 hour
EQUIPMENT NEEDED: two 4-quart non-reactive stock pots, fine-mesh strainer, four 1-quart canning jars with lids or eight pint jars, long-handled ladle
MAKES: four 1-quart jars or eight pints

4 pounds medium (3- to 4-inch) pickling cucumbers
½ cup plus 1 tablespoon kosher salt
4½ cups distilled white vinegar
1½ cups cold water
3 cups granulated white sugar
2 tablespoons ground turmeric
¼ cup fresh ginger, peeled and thinly sliced
1 teaspoon celery seed
1 teaspoon yellow mustard seed
2 teaspoons crushed red pepper
8 whole allspice berries
8 whole cloves
2 bay leaves
2 tablespoons whole coriander seed
2 cloves garlic, smashed

꩜ Slice cucumbers ¼ inch thick, and rinse in cold water. While prepping the cucumbers, bring the remaining ingredients to a rolling boil in a 4-quart non-reactive stock pot. Reduce heat and simmer for 30 minutes to infuse. Divide cucumbers evenly between four 1-quart canning jars. Carefully strain the hot brine into another stock pot or saucepan, and discard the spices. Gently and carefully ladle the hot brine over the cucumbers into the jars while still as hot as possible. Place tight-fitting lids on jars, and cool on the counter overnight. They are ready to store in the refrigerator for up to 2 months, or can according to regular canning instructions.

Piccalilli

Piccalilli is one of the early exotics that resulted from the expansion of the spice trade in the eighteenth century, giving expression to turmeric in addition to cinnamon, cloves, and ginger in many receipts. It's one of the most versatile pickles we know of; its perfect balance of sweet, sour, tart, bitter, and spicy plus a broad range of aromatics make it pair well with anything. Over the course of the year, we'll serve it with fish, fowl, beef, cheese, and vegetables; in salads; and with roasts, grills, and gravy dishes. It keeps well too, making a great basic relish to have around the kitchen.

PREP TIME: 90 minutes
EQUIPMENT NEEDED: 4-quart non-reactive stock pot, long-handled wooden
    spoon, 4-quart colander, 4-quart mixing bowl, long-handled ladle, three
    1-quart canning jars with lids or six pint jars
MAKES: three 1-quart jars or six pint jars

STAGE ONE
2 tablespoons vegetable oil
6 cups green tomatoes, finely chopped
1 cup yellow onion, finely diced
2 cups green bell peppers, finely diced
2 cups red bell peppers, finely diced
2 cups distilled white vinegar

꩜ Place all ingredients in a 4-quart non-reactive stock pot, and slowly bring to a boil, stirring occasionally with a wooden spoon. Reduce to a low boil, and cook for 30 minutes, uncovered, stirring frequently. Strain in a 4-quart colander and discard liquid. Allow vegetables to drain in a well-ventilated spot for 30 minutes before continuing with stage two.

STAGE TWO
1 cup distilled white vinegar
¼ cup kosher salt
2 cups granulated white sugar
1 teaspoon ground allspice
2 teaspoons celery seed
¼ cup yellow mustard seed
3 to 6 sticks Ceylon cinnamon
6 to 12 bay leaves

⚜ Place the drained vegetables in a 4-quart mixing bowl, and add the vinegar, salt, sugar, allspice, celery seed, and mustard seed. Ladle into canning jars, and stuff one cinnamon stick and two bay leaves into the center of each, Place tight-fitting lids on jars, and store in the refrigerator for up to 2 months, or can according to standard canning instructions.

Five-Pepper Jelly

Of all the seasonal preserves we make, this is the one that is most missed when we run out, usually sometime during late winter—guests will still be asking for it months later, and once summer rolls around, we often get the question: "Is the pepper jelly ready yet?" I often wonder if we should make it year-round, but that would crowd out other preserves we like to make, which allow us more seasonal nuance and also show off our farms more ably. Additionally, there's no escaping that this recipe is only justified with the best peppers I can muster since they are the reason for making this jelly.

I use a blend of five peppers: these are widely available peppers you can likely find at your farmers' market during peak pepper season. In practice, we're most likely to raid the weekly pepper offerings of Leaning Shed Farm, Genesis Growers, Green Acres, and Stewards of the Land, and make a vintage jelly of that week's best peppers. Besides the ones listed in this recipe, we also often use Hungarian wax, Padrón, Romanian hot orange, pimiento, Brazilian birds, poblano, habanero, serrano, cherry bomb, and Hidalgo peppers.

Use any peppers you want—but if you'd like a mildly hot jelly, try to match the heat of your peppers with these varieties. Make the bulk from sweet pepper varieties, plus a smaller quantity of mildly hot, and whatever proportion of hot peppers meets your taste—for most people, one cayenne will do, with two to three cayennes or one to two habaneros making a pretty hot jelly. You can even make a jelly of one kind of pepper, though we like using a mix of sweet, herbaceous, and fruity peppers for a complex pepper flavor.

PREP TIME: 90 minutes
EQUIPMENT NEEDED: 4-quart non-reactive saucepan, 2-quart mixing bowl, sifter, long-handled ladle
MAKES: two 1-quart jars

> 1½ cups ripe red bell pepper, seeded and finely minced
> 1½ cups yellow bell pepper, seeded and finely minced
> ½ cup Anaheim or wax peppers, seeded and finely minced
> ½ cup jalapeno peppers, seeded and finely minced
> 1 fresh ripe cayenne pepper, seeded and finely minced
> 2¼ cups white vinegar
> 2 teaspoons kosher salt
> 5½ cups granulated white sugar
> 1¾ ounces dry high-methoxyl pectin, such as Sure-Jell pink box

In a 4-quart non-reactive stock pot, combine the peppers, vinegar, and salt. Slowly bring to a low boil, and cook for 30 minutes at a low boil to render the peppers. Remove from heat and set aside. In a 2-quart mixing bowl, combine the sugar and pectin, and sift together to combine thoroughly. While constantly whisking the vinegar and peppers, pour in the sugar and pectin mixture a little at a time, whisking constantly to make sure it's incorporated well and to prevent lumps. Slowly bring to a boil, stirring often and skimming any foam off the top with a small ladle. At the boil, raise heat to a rolling boil, and time the boiling for exactly 1 minute. After 1 minute, stir well, and remove from heat. Wear heat-resistant gloves while carefully ladling the hot liquid into two sterilized 1-quart canning jars and seal tightly. Cool to room temperature before refrigerating up to 6 months, or can according to standard canning instructions.

❦ The peppers will have a tendency to rise to the top of the jar as the jelly cools and sets, which is fine—you can just stir them in when you open the jar. Or to set the peppers throughout the jelly, gently turn the jar upside down every 3 to 4 hours when cooling and setting, which takes a full day.

Okra Pickles

Big Jones might very well have gotten nowhere were it not for these tasty pickles. They are a standby with our gumbo, Pickle Tasting, Boucherie Board, and Bloody Marys, and occasionally we bread and fry them. Whatever you might like to do with them, it's a good idea to put up as many as you can during late summer when you can find okra at the market. Look for young okra pods less than 3 inches long, as older, longer pods are usually tough and stringy.

PREP TIME: 30 minutes

EQUIPMENT NEEDED: 4 pint jars, two 2-quart non-reactive saucepan, two
    4-quart non-reactive stock pots, fine-mesh strainer, long-handled ladle

MAKES: four 1-pint jars

    3 generous pints whole okra pods
    1 small yellow onion, peeled and quartered lengthwise
    5 tablespoons kosher salt
    2 cups cold water
    1 quart distilled white vinegar
    ½ cup white sugar
    2 cloves garlic, smashed
    1 tablespoon whole black peppercorns
    1 teaspoon crushed red pepper
    1 teaspoon whole yellow mustard seeds
    1 teaspoon whole brown mustard seeds
    12 whole cloves
    2 bay leaves

❦ Wash the okra well under cold running water, and dry on paper towels or wire racks. Divide the onion and okra between four 1-pint canning jars—place a quarter of the onion in the bottom of each, and fill in the jars with the okra. Place remaining ingredients in a 2-quart non-reactive saucepan, and bring to a boil, stirring occasionally. Cook at a low boil for 30 minutes to infuse the spices. Remove from heat, and strain though a fine-mesh strainer into a heat-proof bowl or another saucepan. Discard the spices. Carefully, using a ladle, spoon brine into the jars, covering the okra. The okra will try to float: that's OK—it will fall back into the brine as the pickle takes hold. Cap the jars firmly with sealing lids while the brine is still piping hot. An occasional gentle shake of the jar is helpful to settle the okra under the brine. They should all be under brine within 24 hours. Can according to standard canning instructions, or refrigerate for up to 2 months.

Raspberry Preserves

We make more than 15 gallons of raspberry preserves every summer. My favorite time to make them is midsummer, with the first tart crop of berries. As summer rolls along, the berries become sweeter and your finished preserves will be good, but will lose some of that mouthwatering acidity you get in early fruit. One other variable you should take into account—raspberry season is fairly long, so watch the weather and try to buy your berries after a dry spell—they'll be more concentrated and your finished preserves will have a more intense flavor.

PREP TIME: 2 hours
EQUIPMENT NEEDED: 4-quart non-reactive stock pot, long-handled wooden spoon, 2-quart mixing bowl, sifter, ladle, three 1-quart or six 1-pint canning jars with lids
MAKES: three 1-quart jars or six 1-pint jars

2 quarts ripe red raspberries
½ cup hot water
Juice of 2 lemons
5 cups granulated white sugar, divided

½ teaspoon fresh cracked black pepper

1¾ ounces dry high-methoxyl pectin, such as Sure-Jell pink box

❦ Place the raspberries in a 4-quart non-reactive stock pot, pour the hot water over them (the hottest water from your tap is fine) along with the lemon juice. Pour 4 cups of the sugar over the berries (no need to stir yet). Cook slowly to start over medium-low heat. Gradually over an hour, the berries will render their juice, and you'll see red raspberry juice bubbling up over the sugar. Now begin to occasionally stir with a wooden spoon from the bottom of the pot to prevent sticking or scorching, but keep in mind that the more you stir, the more you break the berries. Be gentle. In the meantime, combine the remaining cup sugar, black pepper, and pectin in a 2-quart mixing bowl, and sift together to combine thoroughly.

❦ Once the berries have rendered fully and are making a thick syrupy stew with the sugar, increase heat to medium and stir occasionally while slowly bringing to a boil, another 30 minutes. At the boil, remove from heat and gently sift in the remaining sugar and pectin mixture, stirring constantly while adding to prevent lumps. Return to heat and bring to a boil over medium-high heat, 8 to 10 minutes, occasionally stirring gently from the bottom. Boil for exactly 1 minute, stir gently, and remove from heat. Carefully ladle into 1-quart or 1-pint canning jars and seal tightly. Cool to room temperature before refrigerating up to 6 months, or can according to standard canning instructions.

❦ The berries will have a tendency to float to the top during cooling and setting of the jelly, which is fine—you can just stir them in when you open the jar. Or to set the berries throughout the jelly, gently turn the jar upside down every 3 to 4 hours when cooling and setting, which takes a full day.

Elderberry Jelly

I got into working with elderberries during the summer of 2012, when a late spring frost devastated the stone fruit crop in the Great Lakes. Looking for anything I could buy from our local fruit growers, I figured out a few recipes to make with these tasty, brambly little berries. They are a little finicky to work with, but their flavor is distinctive and rich if you know how to coax it out. I love them because they sport a distinctive dark berry flavor with an intense streak of brambles—that woody, spicy, leafy flavor every shrub berry has to some degree. Elderberries are in my opinion the best expression of pure bramble flavor, followed by huckleberries and blackberries, both of which work with this recipe as well.

Ripe elderberries are somewhat sweet and lacking in acidity, so I add a couple of fruit acids, citric and malic. Citric acid is what it sounds like—*citrus* acid, or vitamin C. It's sour, like lemons. You could liken malic acid to green apples or green grapes—it's tart. I like to use a blend of both when elevating the acidity of fruit preserves. You can always use lemon juice to taste for citric acid and tart green apple juice or verjuice for malic acid, respectively, if you want to use whole fruit sources for the acids. I like the clean acid contribution of the pure acids in this recipe since it allows the elderberries to sing. Both citric and malic acids can be found in their pure state in natural food stores.

PREP TIME: 90 minutes
EQUIPMENT NEEDED: 4-quart non-reactive stock pot, fine-mesh strainer or jelly bag, heat-resistant 4-quart container, wire whisk, 2-quart mixing bowl, sifter, small ladle, five 1-pint canning jars with lids
MAKES: four to five 1-pint jars

    2 quarts fresh elderberries, stemmed and washed
    1 teaspoon cracked black pepper
    2 bay leaves
    7 cups granulated sugar
    1 tablespoon citric acid
    1 teaspoon malic acid
    ½ teaspoon kosher salt
    1¾ ounces dry high-methoxyl pectin, such as Sure-Jell pink box

❦ Stem and wash berries, and place in a 4-quart non-reactive stock pot. Add enough cold water to cover, plus the pepper and bay leaves. Slowly bring to a boil over medium heat, 12 to 15 minutes, then reduce heat to a low boil, and cook 5 minutes. Strain through a fine-mesh strainer or jelly bag into a heat-resistant 4-quart container; gently shake berries to coax out as much juice as possible, but do not force or press juice from the berries or it will cloud your jelly. Discard berries and seeds.

❦ Measure 5 cups of the juice, and return to the stock pot with 6 cups of the sugar, the acids, and salt. Slowly bring to a boil, stirring regularly with a wire whisk. In the meantime, combine the remaining cup of sugar and pectin in a 2-quart mixing bowl, and sift together to combine thoroughly. Sprinkle the sugar mixture bit by bit into the juice, whisking constantly. Bring back to a boil, skimming off any foam that rises with a small ladle. Once the jelly boils, increase heat to a rolling boil and time it for 1 minute. Remove from heat at once—longer boiling can make your jelly stiff. Transfer to sterilized pint jars with tight-fitting lids and cover. Can according to standard canning instructions, or cool to room temperature for a few hours before refrigerating. Will keep for several months under refrigeration. Freeze extra juice to start the next batch.

Apple Butter

Apple butter could be considered one of the signature potted or canned preserves of Appalachia, certainly the Blue Ridge Mountain region, in addition to my home country of southern Indiana. This is a home run with freshly baked cheddar biscuits and is also good with pork, duck, or to use in a stack cake—the quintessentially Appalachian cake composed of many thin layers of cake slicked with apple butter or compote between each.

A good cooking apple works best for this, especially one with a bit of tartness, such as Northern Spy, Gravenstein, Arkansas Blacks, Granny Smith, Esopus Spitzenberg, Empire, or Cox's Orange Pippin; but feel free to use your favorite apple.

PREP TIME: 5 hours
EQUIPMENT NEEDED: 4-quart non-reactive kettle, wooden spoon, blender, fine-mesh strainer, two 1-quart canning jars with lids
MAKES: two 1-quart jars or four 1-pint jars

5 pounds apples, peeled, cored, and coarsely chopped
1 pound dark brown sugar
2 sticks cinnamon
2 thick slices fresh ginger
2 bay leaves

½ teaspoon cayenne pepper
1 teaspoon kosher salt
2 cups fresh apple cider
Juice of 2 lemons

❦ Place all ingredients in a 4-quart non-reactive kettle, and begin cooking over medium-low heat. As apples give up their juice and soften, gradually increase heat to medium. Stir often with a wooden spoon to prevent sticking or scorching. Cook, uncovered, until apples are disintegrating and break apart easily when stirred, 50 to 60 minutes. Remove from heat and take out the cinnamon sticks, ginger, and bay leaves. Puree smooth in a blender, pass through a fine-mesh strainer, and return to a clean kettle. Set your oven to 250°F, and place the kettle, uncovered, on the lower rack. Stir every 15 to 20 minutes with a wooden spoon. Cook until the apples have reduced and thickened and coat a spoon heavily, 2 to 3 hours. Remove kettle from the oven, and pass the apple butter through a fine-mesh strainer into jars. You can store apple butter for a few months in the refrigerator if covered with a ¼-inch layer of melted butter and tightly capped, or you may can it according to standard canning instructions.

Pickled Peaches

I was a Johnny-come-lately to pickled peaches, yet they quickly became one of my favorite seasonal pickles. These are easier to make late in the season when the fruit is freestone, but your finished pickles will have a somewhat better flavor if made with earlier-ripening cling peaches. Eat them with bread (especially whole grain) and butter, serve with pork or game fowl dishes, or even use to give salsa a fruity kick. We'll also serve them pureed as a dipping sauce for fried plantains and oysters.

PREP TIME: 3 hours
EQUIPMENT NEEDED: 4-quart stock pot, long-handled slotted spoon or skimmer, 4-quart colander, 4-quart non-reactive braising pan with tight-fitting lid, wooden spoon, cheesecloth, digital clip-on thermometer, paring knife, ladle, four 1-quart canning jars with lids
MAKES: four 1-quart jars or eight 1-pint jars

6 pounds fresh peaches, peeled and halved, pits removed
    (weight before processing)
3 cups distilled white vinegar
5 cups granulated sugar
2 teaspoons kosher salt
3 bay leaves
2 tablespoons ginger, thinly sliced
1 stick cinnamon
1 tablespoon whole cloves
1 tablespoon whole allspice berries
2 stars anise
1 teaspoon crushed red pepper
Freshly squeezed orange juice, if needed

❦ Fill a 4-quart stock pot three-quarters of the way with water, and bring to a rolling boil. Plunge your peaches into the boiling water, two or three at a time, for 30 seconds per batch. Use a slotted spoon or skimmer to remove them, and place in a 4-quart colander to drain in a clean sink. You can peel and halve them right into the brine once the brine is at a low simmer.

❦ In a 4-quart non-reactive stock pot with a tight-fitting lid, heat the vinegar, sugar, and salt to simmer, stirring occasionally with a wooden spoon. Tie the spices into a cheesecloth sachet, and drop into the brine. Use a clip-on thermometer to set the temperature to 180°F, and you are ready to begin adding the peaches. Do not boil, or your finished pickles will be mush! Monitor the temperature with the clip-on thermometer—as you add peaches, the brine will drop a few degrees, so respond by turning the heat up just a notch. As the brine comes back up, turn the heat down. Try your best to maintain 170°F to 180°F, but as long as it's not boiling, they'll turn out all right.

❦ While the pot is steaming, begin slipping the softened skins off the peaches. Cut each peach in half by making a round slice around the pit, using the natural crease along one side of the peach as a guide. If your peaches are freestone, the two halves should pop right off; if they're cling, use a paring knife to dig the pit out and free each side. Carefully drop the peach halves into the hot brine. Repeat until all peaches are incorporated and begin to soften—if they don't all fit into the liquid at first, don't be too concerned, as they render they will shrink back into the syrup. If after a half hour they haven't, use enough orange juice to barely cover. Cover the pot and set to simmer for 30 minutes, until all pieces are just fork tender.

✤ Carefully ladle peaches into 1-quart or 1-pint canning jars and cover with brine. Refrigerates well for several months, or can according to standard canning instructions. Any excess brine that does not fit in the jars makes an excellent soda mixed with club soda over ice.

Preserved Quince

I love making this recipe because quinces are so delicious yet virtually forgotten today. A member of the rose family like apples and pears, quinces are apples' austere cousin, only giving up their secrets when properly coaxed to do so. They are mightily astringent and wholly undesirable to eat when raw, but cook them just right, and they reward you with a beguiling fragrance of apple, rose hips, vanilla, and that elusive yet seductive woody scent of an orchard the morning after a first frost.

My favorite pairing for preserved quince is duck, either roast or confit. It's also magnificent as a topping for French toast, with chocolate or a cheese plate, or toasted whole-grain bread and honey butter. The syrup makes a fantastic soda when mixed one part to five parts of club soda, or use it to spike an old-fashioned or any other bourbon cocktail.

PREP TIME: 3 hours
EQUIPMENT NEEDED: fine-mesh strainer, 4-quart non-reactive braising pan
    with tight-fitting lid, wooden spoon, digital clip-on thermometer, paring
    knife, ladle, seven 1-pint canning jars with lids
MAKES: seven 1-pint jars

    1 cup freshly squeezed lemon juice, measured after straining through a
        fine-mesh strainer
    1 cup freshly squeezed orange juice, measured after straining through
        a fine-mesh strainer
    1 cup apple cider vinegar
    ½ cup bourbon
    5 cups granulated sugar
    2 teaspoons kosher salt
    1 Tahitian vanilla bean, split lengthwise
    2 stars anise

3 bay leaves

1 tablespoon ginger, thinly sliced

1 stick cinnamon

1 teaspoon crushed red pepper

6 pounds fresh quince, peeled, cored and cut into ⅙ wedges (weight before processing)

꙳ In a 4-quart non-reactive braising pan with a tight-fitting lid, heat the lemon and orange juices, vinegar, bourbon, sugar, and salt to a simmer, stirring frequently with a wooden spoon until the sugar is dissolved into a heavy syrup. Add the vanilla and spices, and use a clip-on thermometer to set the temperature to 180°F, the temperature you will want to maintain through the process. ꙳ While the pot is steaming, peel and pare the quinces one by one, cutting out the cores and then cutting six wedges, lengthwise, out of each quince. Quickly drop the wedges into the pot before starting the next quince—they have a tendency to brown quickly. Do not boil or your finished product will be mushy! Repeat until all quinces are incorporated and begin to soften—if they don't all fit into the liquid at first, don't be too concerned, as they render they will shrink back into the syrup. Just gently toss them with a wooden spoon to ensure they are coated with the brine—the vitamin C in the lemon and orange juices will inhibit browning while they cook. If after a half hour they haven't fallen back into the brine, use enough orange juice to barely cover. Cover the pot and set to simmer for 1 hour, until all pieces are just fork tender.

꙳ Carefully ladle quinces into 1-pint canning jars and cover with the syrup. Refrigerates well for 2 months, or can according to standard canning instructions. Any excess brine that does not fit in the jars makes an excellent soda mixed with club soda over ice.

Kumquat Marmalade

I count kumquats among my many infatuations—I'll eat them like popcorn when they're in season and at their peak in midwinter. The in-your-face pungency of the peel and exquisite tartness of the juice are just too much—and by too much, I mean really awesome. A kumquat will take over your entire head in the same manner as, but by different means than, a fresh ripe chili pepper, a perfectly crispy crackling, or a shot of top-notch whiskey.

I developed a love for these as a youngster, when my mom would sometimes come home from the market with them during the winter. She was always tried to keep fresh produce around, and in January this was one of our few options. I loved them. I'm constantly fascinated when I meet people who have never tasted kumquats. On the one hand, it makes me realize that we have a long way to come to fully appreciate the diversity of foods we enjoyed historically; on the other hand, it makes me realize what a seriously nerdy food guy I am.

Kumquats have a little extra bitterness over oranges, and therefore in my opinion make better marmalade, as orange marmalade can often be too cloyingly sweet. This marmalade is great with biscuits, cornbread, and also as a glaze for poultry, pork, or with duck liver pâté.

PREP TIME: 90 minutes
EQUIPMENT NEEDED: 2-quart heavy-bottomed non-reactive saucepan, wooden spoon, candy thermometer, ladle, three 1-pint canning jars with lids
MAKES: three 1-pint jars

2½ pounds fresh kumquats, washed and cut into ¼-inch slices
½ cup water
2½ cups granulated white sugar
½ teaspoon kosher salt

⚜ Place the sliced kumquats and water in a 2-quart heavy-bottomed non-reactive saucepan. Bring to a boil over medium heat, stirring regularly with a wooden spoon; then reduce heat and maintain a low boil, stirring often, until fruit is tender, 30 to 45 minutes. Add the sugar and salt, and increase heat to medium high. Reduce liquid while checking the temperature frequently. When mixture registers 224°F on a candy thermometer, remove from heat at once. Carefully ladle into pint jars and cap tightly. Will refrigerate for several months, or can according to standard canning instructions.

Savory Benne Crackers

This is a recipe I picked up from one of Edna Lewis's cookbooks and adapted for our use at Big Jones. The historic importance of benne, also known as sesame, in Lowcountry cooking cannot be overestimated. When writing Big Jones's menus and recipes, I strongly prefer to use the name "benne" when referring to these seeds since we use a circa 1800 strain of benne seed grown by Anson Mills that is much closer to its original African crop than the modern, oily sesame seed we know today; the name "benne" comes from the African root *bene*. These heritage benne seeds are much higher in protein and lower in oil than modern industrial sesame. The flavor is also much stronger, nuttier, with bitter vegetal notes I just love.

We serve these benne crackers with charcuterie, pimiento cheese (page 107), and beer cheese, though you can serve them any time crackers are needed.

PREP TIME: 1 hour
EQUIPMENT NEEDED: sifter, stand mixer with flat beater attachment, rolling
    pin, 2-inch biscuit cutter, 2 cookie sheets, wire cooling racks
MAKES: 40 to 50 crackers

    2 cups all-purpose flour, sifted before measuring, plus extra for rolling
        out the crackers
    2 teaspoons baking powder
    1 teaspoon kosher salt
    ½ teaspoon cayenne pepper
    ⅔ cup Sea Island benne or sesame seeds
    ¼ cup plus 3 tablespoons freshly rendered lard or unsalted butter, well
        chilled and cut into tablespoon-size bits
    ¼ cup plus 3 tablespoons whole milk, divided
    Murray River or Maldon sea salt, for finishing

☗ Preheat oven to 350°F.
☗ Place the flour, baking powder, salt, and cayenne pepper in the bowl of a stand mixer with the flat beater attachment, and turn mixer on low speed. Staying on low speed, add benne and lard or butter. Work into the flour mix-

ture until integrated and the flour resembles a coarse, seed-studded meal, 4 to 5 minutes. Add the milk in thirds, giving the flour a chance to hydrate between each addition. With the third addition, the dough will start to come together. Continue on low speed until the dough forms a cohesive ball, 3 to 5 minutes.

♔ Transfer the dough to a well-floured work surface, and roll out to the thickness of two quarters stacked. Sprinkle evenly with the Murray River or Maldon sea salt, using your rolling pin to gently roll the salt into the dough while rolling it out to the thickness of a quarter. Score the rolled-out salted dough with the tines of a fork. Using a biscuit cutter, cut out 2-inch wafers and transfer to unoiled baking sheets. Scrap dough can be reworked and rolled out again until all is used up. Bake on the top rack of the oven until deep golden brown, 12 to 15 minutes.

♔ Cool on wire racks and store tightly sealed at room temperature. Will keep for weeks.

Worcestershire Sauce

There are many recipes about which I can say, "Your _____ is only as good as your Worcestershire sauce." You might insert gumbo, pimiento cheese, shrimp and grits, barbecue sauce, étouffée . . . You name it. A good Worcestershire sauce adds umami, the Japanese word for the fifth taste, savory. It also contributes a particular kind of acidity and pungency, and never fails to lift almost anything to which it's added out of the doldrums and into lip-smacking territory.

This recipe is even better if you make your own malt vinegar—take two quarts of malty brown ale (nothing too hoppy) and add ¼ cup of raw apple cider vinegar, such as Bragg. Put it in a gallon jug, preferably glass. Cover tightly with cheesecloth, and set in a dark place at room temperature for 6 to 8 weeks. It may develop a ribbon of "mother," the bacteria that converts alcohol to acid, which is normal. It should smell like vinegar and be sour to taste. Strain and use right away, or store in an airtight bottle in the refrigerator.

This recipe makes a lot of Worcestershire sauce, but it keeps indefinitely in the refrigerator or when canned according to standard canning instructions, so you might only have to make it once or twice a year. Make it an occasion.

PREP TIME: 6 hours

EQUIPMENT NEEDED: 4-gallon non-reactive stock pot, long-handled wooden spoon, 4-quart colander, 4-quart non-reactive stock pot, fine-mesh strainer, 5-quart or larger airtight container or canning jars with lids

MAKES: 5 cups

1 tablespoon vegetable oil

½ pound fresh horseradish, unpeeled, scrubbed, and sliced ¼ inch thick

6 cups yellow onion, peeled and coarsely chopped

1 teaspoon crushed red pepper

2 tablespoons fresh garlic, peeled and crushed

1 quart cold water

2 quarts malt vinegar

2 cups sorghum molasses

1 teaspoon freshly ground black pepper

2 ounces canned anchovies with oil, minced

2 teaspoons whole cloves

1 tablespoon whole allspice berries

3 bay leaves

¼ cup plus 2 tablespoons kosher salt

Zest and juice of 1 lemon

4 ounces whole tamarind, crumbled

1 cup shiitake or maitake mushrooms, thinly sliced

🌿 In a 4-gallon non-reactive stock pot, heat the vegetable oil over high heat until just beginning to smoke—stand by when heating the oil, as this will happen quickly! Add the horseradish, onion, red pepper, and garlic. Sauté over high heat, stirring constantly with a long-handled wooden spoon, until the vegetables are well sweated and just beginning to brown, about 6 to 8 minutes.

🌿 Once the onions are a rich tan color, quickly add the cold water, malt vinegar, and sorghum molasses, and maintain heat on high, stirring regularly, until the pot comes to a boil, 8 to 10 minutes. Reduce heat to a low boil, and add remaining ingredients. Simmer at a low boil for 2 to 3 hours, until vegetables are well rendered but not falling apart.

🌿 Strain through a 4-quart colander into a 4-quart non-reactive stock pot. Discard the rendered vegetables. Return to a boil over high heat, then reduce heat to maintain a low, gentle boil. Reduce by half until the sauce is slightly syrupy and coats a spoon lightly, 1 to 1½ hours. There should be about 5 cups. Strain again through a fine-mesh strainer into a jar or airtight container. Cover tightly and cool to room temperature before refrigerating, or can according to standard canning instructions. Will keep indefinitely in the refrigerator or in a sealed glass jar.

Basic Vinaigrette

This is the basic vinaigrette we serve on many of our salads or to dress vegetables that are to be roasted on the grill or next to the fire; it's a great way to add moisture, plus a little sweetness, acidity, and the creamy texture of cold-pressed oil. It's a fairly sweet vinaigrette, so feel free to cut down on the cane syrup or honey. Note that this dressing is not seasoned, so when you use it, you'll want to add salt and pepper to taste, but be careful—it's easy to over-salt a salad and then it just doesn't taste fresh at all. Julia Child was fond of calling for "a few grains of salt," and that's exactly right—not very much at all, but just a touch.

PREP TIME: 5 minutes
EQUIPMENT NEEDED: pint jar with tight-fitting lid
MAKES: 1½ cups

    ½ cup raw apple cider vinegar
    ½ cup cold-pressed raw untoasted sesame oil or extra-virgin olive oil
    ½ cup cane syrup or honey

♛ Pour all ingredients into a pint jar, cover tightly, and shake vigorously until emulsified. It will keep tightly covered in the refrigerator for months, but ingredients will settle. Shake vigorously until emulsified before each use.

Bourbon and Brown Sugar Mustard

When I wanted a house-made mustard that was a worthy foil for our head cheese, I knew I would need something pungent and maybe a bit sweet. It didn't take much experimentation to come up with this home run of a mustard, which is best with pork but can be used anywhere whole-grain mustard is appropriate. This recipe keeps really well, so it's great to make any time of year; just be sure to store it in an airtight container in the refrigerator.

PREP TIME: 1 hour

EQUIPMENT NEEDED: 1-quart non-reactive saucepan with tight-fitting lid, wooden spoon, blender, airtight container

MAKES: just over 1 pint

1 cup distilled white vinegar
½ cup cold water
1 cup dark brown sugar
½ cup whole yellow mustard seed
½ cup whole brown mustard seed
1 tablespoon kosher salt
¼ cup best bourbon

❧ Place the vinegar, water, sugar, mustards, and salt in a 1-quart non-reactive saucepan with a tight-fitting lid. Bring to a boil over medium heat, stirring occasionally with a wooden spoon until sugar and salt have dissolved into a thick syrup with the vinegar; cover and reduce heat to a low simmer, not a boil. Simmer for 30 minutes, then remove from heat. Let stand to steep and bloom, covered, for another 30 minutes.

❧ Transfer to a blender, and puree on low speed while adding the bourbon through the opening in the lid in a thin, steady stream. Once all bourbon is in, increase to high speed and puree for 2 to 3 minutes, when the mustard will look like a coarse whole-grain mustard. Transfer to an airtight storage container, and refrigerate for up to 6 months.

The
Whole Hog

One warm summer evening, my dad and a few of my brothers and I were sitting out on the porch talking about the old arts—we were curious to hear once again about wild cherry wine and homemade beer before the days of retail DIY kits, and about butchering deer and hogs. Inevitably this conversation led to a broader discussion of getting things done in the days before you could just pay other people to do anything you wanted done for you.

The latest, biggest change in this regard is cooking. It's true for many families that TV dinners and eventually fast food became commonplace during the 1950s, 1960s, and 1970s; but at that time, for most folks those deviations from home-cooked meals were seen as a treat, even as a vacation, from the family's regular duties of getting food on the table. Over time, this "vacation" from daily duties has become more and more common. For many folks today, it's a daily convenience rather than an occasional treat.

The unintended consequence is that we have become ever more separated from the source of our food. My grandparents—who grew, hunted, or foraged nearly everything they ate on their farm—always knew where their food came from. The same was true of many families back then, especially in the rural parts of the country, where until recent generations a majority of Americans lived. This is all part of the trend of our move away from the land. Unfortunately, this severed that generations-old bond of the land and the eater.

Much has been written about the rise of obesity and other maladies in this country, with everyone from professional nutritionists to armchair politicians to militant vegans casting blame in the direction of fast food or high-fructose corn syrup or starchy convenience foods, and, yes, even high-meat diets. But let me tell you something—we're not eating appreciably more meat today than we were a generation ago, and we're much fatter. I'm not interested in casting blame at anyone for the state of the American diet, but I am interested in re-creating something that worked and kept folks healthy: the old farmstead way, as my grandparents practiced, where everyone knew everyone else in their food chain, and everything was made by hand from real ingredients. Central to this way of life was a most wonderful animal, the hog.

While Big Jones has access to any ingredient that we want the world over, and our presentations are decidedly contemporary—a reflection of my own personal tastes and a reflection of our location in a gentrified Chicago neighborhood—the spirit of our cooking is the homestead. Not just home cooking, but home processing. It's true I can't grow the hogs myself, kill them, process them, and then turn them into your brunch or dinner—but I can come close. The Gunthorps, Slagels, Sparrows, LaPryors, Travises, and Carrs will raise animals as well as my grandparents did, have them slaughtered, and deliver them to Big Jones whole, where we take over.

There's little doubt that the decline of whole hog cookery is due to the incredible dedication and hard work it takes to cook this way—before the days of industrial slaughterhouses and processors, hog killings were big events that took place at the onset of winter, and many families were involved to make sure all the work got done, from scalding and scraping the hairs, cleaning the intestines for sausage casings, rendering lard, and processing every other cut in one way or another to be salted, pickled, or smoked. These events would often turn into parties, with great feasts prepared along the way as a reward for a hard day's work. But it was difficult work, and eventually families were happy to let it be done by professionals in industrial operations.

In our restaurant kitchen, while the slaughter and initial cleaning are done in USDA-inspected operations, to take over where we do requires its own obsessive dedication. A cook who starts working at Big Jones will often work for more than a year before being trusted with the precise and critical tasks of breaking down a carcass and processing the many products we make from it. Even then, it takes months for a talented cook to learn the entire process: it is as much an art as a science because every carcass is different and a great deal of feeling is required in addition to the requisite knife and cooking skills. Even so, we have no shortage of ambitious young cooks who want to learn this process, which encourages me to believe that these arts are in fact undergoing a great revival.

From start to finish, it takes us about 24 hours to get the initial processing of a carcass done, and then curing takes longer—2 days for andouille and up to 2 weeks for hams. Given the amount of planning that goes into this undertaking, it's easy to see why most restaurants choose to order finished processed cuts from a distributor. In my opinion, however, doing so is a lost opportunity to retain a connection to the land, as well as to create something truly unique and therefore special.

I made the decision to go exclusively whole hog in early 2010, and these recipes represent the means by which we have done so. Andouille has always been important for obvious reasons, as has tasso, and no one ever has trouble selling pork loin or pork shoulder. Brunch is a challenge, sometimes putting pressure on the amount of belly or ham we have since it's a very busy meal every weekend. In all, serving thousands of guests a week, we also don't have trouble selling the head, blood, liver, and using the fat to make lard for our biscuits and the cracklins to garnish all sorts of dishes. Waste not, want not is the best way to eat, and a community is how it happens.

Andouille

Andouille is definitely one of the core cured meats of our kitchen at 30 to 40 pounds a week, more than we can even get off of a single hog. I'm often asked what makes our andouille so good, and that's a humbling question. As is the case so many times in our restaurant and in good restaurants across the country, it has more to do with our selection of ingredients than it does some fancy secret recipe. Use good pork—make sure it's pasture or, ideally, woodland raised. Use the best spices you can get your hands on—notice how much of this recipe is actually dried spices, and you'll get a clue as to how important that component is. See "Notes on Sources" if you have any questions about where to get good spices. And, of course, pay very close attention to the smoking process. In my opinion, the smokier the andouille, the better, so learn to maximize smoke while maintaining your cooking temperature fairly low, and you'll come out with a sausage better than you can buy anywhere.

Louisiana's andouille bears little resemblance to the French andouille, which is often attributed as its forebear. The French andouille is ancient in origins and utilizes the entire gastrointestinal system of the pig, while the Cajun andouille originated around the turn of the twentieth century on the German coast of Louisiana—the area upriver encompassing St. Charles, St. John the Baptist, and St. James Parishes, where German immigrants settled to farm in the eighteenth and nineteenth centuries. Thus it is commonly thought that Cajun andouille draws heavily upon German influence. Proper Cajun andouille is coarsely ground pork, typically highly seasoned with garlic and red pepper, and stuffed into beef casings before being heavily smoked over pecan wood and sugarcane. When made accurately according to these guidelines, Cajun andouille combines the succulence of fatty pork with the pungency of garlic, pepper, and chilies; the grassy barnyard funk of beef intestine; and the intense smoke reminiscent of a campfire at dusk. Heady stuff.

We use a lot of trim in our andouille, but you're totally within reason to use pork shoulder for this one, as it has the optimal fat ratio, plus nice thick veins of fat that will result in a nicely marbled sausage.

PREP TIME: 90 minutes for grinding and stuffing, overnight for curing, 6 hours for smoking

EQUIPMENT NEEDED: sausage grinder with ½-inch grinding plate, 4-gallon plastic or metal tub, large mixer with paddle attachment, ¾-inch stuffing tube, 4 to 5 feet butcher twine cut into 4-inch lengths, large drip-proof pan with fitted perforated drain pan (restaurant hotel pans work perfectly and are inexpensive at restaurant and kitchen supply stores), smoker, digital food thermometer

MAKES: 10 to 11 pounds

¼ cup granulated garlic
¼ cup granulated onion
2 tablespoons ground cayenne pepper
¼ cup Spanish paprika
¼ cup freshly ground black pepper.
¼ cup plus 2 tablespoons kosher salt
2 tablespoons dried thyme
1 tablespoon crushed red pepper
1 tablespoon pink curing salt
1½ cups ice water
10 pounds 60% to 70% lean pork
Approximately 12 feet natural beef middle casings, soaked and flushed

🐖 Use a ½-inch grinder plate for your grinder. Chill all grinder parts thoroughly before beginning. Combine all spices and salts with the ice water, mix well, and refrigerate while you grind the meat. Pass the meat through the grinder only once, letting the meat fall into a large plastic or metal tub, making a very coarse grind. Combine with the spice mixture, cover, and refrigerate overnight.

❦ The following day, soak and flush the beef casings, then place the force-meat in a large mixer with paddle attachment. Mix on low speed until sticky and beginning to emulsify, 3 to 4 minutes. Stuff into the beef casings, tying off with butcher twine into 12-inch chubs. Place sausages in a perforated drain pan set inside a larger drip-proof pan to catch the juices that fall during curing. Refrigerate, uncovered, in a spot where nothing will drip on them, overnight to cure further and to dry the casings.

❦ The following day, place in a smoker with pecan or hickory wood for smoke. Smoke for 4 hours at 155°F, then raise the temperature to 180°F and continue smoking until the sausage registers 165°F in the center on a meat thermometer, 5 to 6 hours total smoking time. Rinse thoroughly in very cold water to arrest the cooking, and refrigerate at once. Will keep for up to a month in the refrigerator if tightly wrapped.

Boudin

Boudin is one of those foods that is so intimately associated with a particular region, in this case south Louisiana especially concentrated around the default Cajun capital of Lafayette, that it really commanded me for a spot on our menu at Big Jones. Some have called our menu "revivalist," insinuating that we are driven to revive lost and forgotten foods of the South, and that's not entirely inaccurate. However, I'm more driven to seek out and find those foods that are peculiar because they bear their fruit in a particular time and place in Southern history (which by nature includes the present) and therefore give us another vantage point through which to see and appreciate our history and celebrate our heritage.

There is certainly one aspect of this boudin recipe that might be considered revivalist—many butcher shops in Cajun country no longer even put liver in their boudin, arguing that their younger consumers don't like the taste of liver. I hope this practice comes back around, and all indications are that it will eventually, as offal and organ meats have been white hot in the trendy big-city restaurants for some time. Hopefully this trend has legs, and we can see this traditional regional food once again made according to its historic specifications.

Boudin dates to medieval France and made it to south Louisiana and, like other cooking traditions, was adapted to local conditions. Only in the

twentieth century did rice become the primary binder used in boudin—
before the rice industry moved west from the Carolinas after the Civil War,
the binder was most likely cornmeal, yielding a mixture that might have
resembled the livermush that's still celebrated in parts of North Carolina.
Both versions are a far cry from the boudin of France, where the typical
binder is leftover bread made from wheat flour.

My first recipe for boudin was gifted by a Cajun family that visited from
Louisiana a few times, as they had relatives who had moved to Chicago
after Hurricane Katrina. It's a great recipe that underwent one modifica-
tion after I toured the Boudin Trail of the Southern Foodways Alliance.
I was particularly blown away by the highly seasoned sausage to be had
at Poche's Market outside Breaux Bridge, and dramatically increased the
black pepper and cayenne in the recipe. I think this is one of the very best
ways to eat liver. Even people who don't like the strong mineral taste of
organ meats can appreciate boudin—it tastes more of pork than it does
liver specifically. If you like pork, you'll love boudin.

PREP TIME: 30 minutes to cook the rice, 5 hours for cooking, 1 hour for
  grinding and stuffing
EQUIPMENT NEEDED: 4- to 5-gallon stock pot, large colander, large shallow pan
  for cooling cooked meat, sausage grinder with ¼-inch grinding plate
  and ½-inch stuffing tube, 4- to 5-gallon plastic or metal tub
MAKES: 20 pounds

    10 pounds pork shoulder or fatty trimmings, cut into 1-inch strips
    3 pounds pork liver, or 1 whole liver, cut into 1-inch strips
    6 cups coarsely chopped yellow onion
    4 ribs celery, coarsely chopped
    2 cups coarsely chopped green bell pepper
    6 bay leaves
    2 quarts rice cooked in 3 quarts water, then thoroughly chilled
    6 bunches green onion, finely chopped
    ½ cup Cajun seasoning (page 67)
    ½ cup kosher salt
    ½ cup freshly ground black pepper
    2 tablespoons crushed red pepper
    16 to 20 feet natural pork casings, soaked and flushed

꙰ Place the pork meat or trimmings, liver, onions, celery, bell peppers, and bay leaves in a large 4- or 5-gallon stock pot, and cover with cold water by 1 inch. Place over medium-high heat, and bring to a boil. Reduce heat to maintain a low boil, and cook until the meat is falling apart, about 4 hours. Add water periodically as needed to make sure all ingredients remain covered. Once meat is falling-apart tender, carefully strain through a large colander and retain the boiling liquid for later use. Spread meat and vegetables on a shallow pan to cool to room temperature for 1 hour, after which they will be cool enough to handle. If you don't have time to finish the sausage after 1 hour cooling time, refrigerate for up to 3 days before proceeding.

꙰ Grind the meat and vegetables, discarding the bay leaves, through a ¼-inch sausage-grinding plate. Add the cooked chilled rice, green onion, Cajun seasoning, salt, and peppers. Mix well and add enough leftover cooking liquid to soften the mixture to the consistency of creamy pâté. Pass half of the mixture once more through the grinder, and combine again with the whole. Cover and refrigerate thoroughly before stuffing into pork casings or breading into boudin balls.

Boudin Rouge

I don't remember where I first read about boudin rouge, but it made sense—every pork-eating culture in history has had some preparation made with the blood, as no part of the animal was ever left to waste in agrarian cultures that ate pork. I do remember that when I decided to make boudin rouge (actually I didn't decide to make it—I *had* to make it), recipes were virtually impossible to come by. In fact, it would seem that blood sausage was very effectively being erased from our foodways, something that made me even more determined.

My research led me back to France, where, like the standard liver boudin, the blood version finds its roots. The French boudin noir recipes I was able to find served as a footprint over which I could juxtapose what I did know about Cajun boudin. I came up with a blood sausage bound with rice and a few flourishes that are surely more French than Cajun— the chopped fatback for an indulgent presentation and the addition of traditional game spices, apple brandy, and wine. It's mighty delicious.

If you wish to make this sausage, your greatest challenge will be securing the blood. Contrary to widespread rumors, it is perfectly legal to save and sell pig's blood; you just have to fill out a slew of paperwork and file a HACCP Plan with the USDA. Consequently, only larger processors typically have it for sale. At retail, your best bets for finding it are at Southeast Asian (including Filipino) markets and some Latin American markets. You'll most likely find it in the freezer section, or ask at the meat counter, they'll often be willing to order it for you if they don't have it on hand. Just be sure to look for the USDA Inspected stamp before you pay for it and take it home.

PREP TIME: 30 minutes to cook the rice, 90 minutes for grinding and stuffing, 3 hours for cooking

EQUIPMENT NEEDED: Blender, 5-gallon braising pan, sausage grinder with ¼-inch grinding plate, 4-gallon plastic or metal tub, stand mixer with flat beater attachment, ¾-inch stuffing tube, 4 to 5 feet butcher twine cut into 4-inch lengths, large drip-proof pan with fitted perforated drain pan (restaurant hotel pans work perfectly and are inexpensive at restaurant and kitchen supply stores), digital food thermometer, wire cooling rack

MAKES: 12 pounds

¼ cup plus 1 tablespoon kosher salt

1 tablespoon pink curing salt

1 tablespoon cayenne pepper

2 teaspoons ground cloves

2 teaspoons ground allspice

2 teaspoons ground coriander

¼ cup freshly ground black pepper

¼ cup applejack or Calvados

1 cup ruby port wine

3 pounds (1½ quarts) pig's blood, chilled as close to freezing as possible

3 pounds lean pork, partially frozen

2 pounds fatty pork, partially frozen

1½ pounds fresh fatback, diced into ½-inch pieces and partially frozen
1 quart long-grain rice cooked in 1½ quarts water, then thoroughly
    chilled
12 to 15 feet beef middle casings, soaked and flushed

❦ Use a ¼-inch grinding plate for the lean and fatty pork. Chill all grinder parts thoroughly, plus the bowl and paddle attachment for a stand mixer. Make sure all meat, fatback, and blood are thoroughly chilled—partially frozen is even ideal for the meat and fatback. Mix the salts and spices into the wine and brandy. If the blood has coagulated, as is most often the case, puree it in batches in your blender, being careful that the blender bowl is tightly capped.

❦ Fill a 5-gallon braising pan (or two or three smaller ones) two-thirds full with cold water and heat to 175°F to cook the sausages as soon as they are stuffed.

❦ Grind the lean and fatty pork together, giving them two passes through the grinder blade into a large plastic or metal tub. Transfer the ground meat and fat and chopped fatback together with the rice into the bowl of a stand mixer with the flat beater attachment. (If you have a standard-size home mixer such as a KitchenAid with 4-quart mixing bowl, you will need to divide ingredients into three batches and combine after mixing but before stuffing.) Turn on low speed until the mixture becomes a little sticky, 4 to 5 minutes, then increase speed to medium and continue mixing until the mass is sticky and holds together well when you form a patty, another 3 to 4 minutes. Reduce speed to low, and add the wine and spices a little at a time, incorporating between each addition, then repeat with the pig's blood, being careful of splatter. Once all the wine and blood are in, increase speed to medium again, and mix until evenly combined and emulsified—the mixture will be loose for a sausage, about the consistency of a lumpy milk shake.

❦ Stuff into the beef casings, tying off with butcher twine into 12-inch chubs. Transfer stuffed links to a large drip-proof pan lined with a perforated drain pan and keep refrigerated while you finish stuffing all the sausages. Once all sausage are stuffed, drop into the simmering water, carefully maintaining the temperature over 165°F but below 185°F. Cook to an internal temperature of 165°F, and carefully remove to a wire rack to cool. Allow to cool for 30 minutes at room temperature, then wrap tightly in plastic wrap or butcher paper and refrigerate for up to 1 week or freeze for up to 3 months.

Chaurice

Chaurice is one of my favorite sausages. You might guess by the name that it's closely associated with chorizo, the Mexican/Spanish sausage that's ubiquitous in the cocidos of Spain and countless Mexican dishes, and you'd be right.

When folks inevitably ask what chaurice is, my short explanation is that it's a Creole knockoff of chorizo. The unanswered question is whether, as some hypothesize, its origins date to the Spanish period in Louisiana (1762–1802) or later. What is undisputed is that it's ubiquitous in Creole cookery, appearing in a wide variety of presentations. The most famous, of course, is as a side with red beans and rice.

I love this sausage because, first of all, it's as delicious as Mexican chorizo, an obsession I developed from a very early age as my step-grandfather on my mom's side of the family was Mexican. Grandpa Fernando was fond of fixing us eggs with chorizo for breakfast, and chorizo with onions and tortillas for lunch when we would visit. It's home cooking to me, as much as fried chicken and even more so than macaroni and cheese. The other reason I love it is that it's spot-on representative of the global influence in New Orleans' cooking. Like Mexican or Spanish chorizo, it works well as a main event or used more sparingly to season everything from poultry to fish and even vegetable dishes.

PREP TIME: 90 minutes

EQUIPMENT NEEDED: sausage grinder with ¼-inch grinding plate and ½-inch stuffing tube, 4- to 5-gallon plastic or metal tub, large drip-proof pan with fitting perforated drain pan (restaurant hotel pans work perfectly and are inexpensive at restaurant and kitchen supply stores)

MAKES: 12 pounds

7 pounds lean pork
3 pounds pork fatback or belly trimmings
1 pound yellow onion, minced
¼ cup fresh garlic, smashed and minced
½ cup celery, minced
½ cup red bell pepper, minced

6 tablespoons kosher salt

2 teaspoons pink curing salt

¼ cup ground pepper

3 tablespoons freshly ground black pepper

1 tablespoon crushed red pepper

¼ cup Spanish paprika

1 tablespoon ground allspice

2 tablespoons dried thyme leaves

1 tablespoon dried oregano

1¼ cups ice water

¼ cup red wine vinegar

25 feet of natural hog casings, soaked and flushed

🌱 Make sure your meat, vegetables, seasonings, and grinding equipment are all thoroughly chilled, and your hands are washed and scrubbed well. Grind the pork and vegetables through a ¼-inch grinding plate into a large, clean plastic or metal tub. Add seasonings, ice water, and vinegar, and mix well. Pass the entire mixture through the ¼-inch grinding plate once more. Stuff into hog casings, and tie into links of your desired size, 6 to 8 inches recommended. Place in a drip-proof pan with fitting perforated drain pan, in the refrigerator where nothing will drip on it, uncovered, overnight to cure the casings. The following day, you can cut into smaller batches and freeze in airtight freezer bags or refrigerate up to 1 week.

🌱 To cook chaurice in whole links, I recommend poaching it in simmering water to cook it through to 165°F before either grilling or pan-frying. Alternatively, you can remove it from casings (or not stuff it in the first place) to cook the sausage as ground meat, either in patties or as a hash or in chili.

Head Cheese

Word once came back to me through a friend in the industry that Big Jones is known amongst the charcuterie crowd for our head cheese. It was at once flattering and puzzling. I mean, I am proud of our head cheese—I think it's great—but everyone these days makes head cheese, while tasso, andouille, boudin, and boudin rouge are much harder to come by, at least when your standard is house-made small-batch production from pastured hogs.

Why our head cheese? I've tried many around town and around the country, and I'll say I think the big difference is that this recipe is soaked in vinegar, something I learned from one of our African American cooks, Phyllis Thomas, the very first time I made head cheese at Big Jones. I sought her input because I thought she'd have some insight since she came from a Southern family that cooked at home, and she did. The vinegar makes all the difference—the acid at once denatures some of the collagen proteins so that the colloid is tender and melts readily on your tongue, making for a luscious mouth feel—and a heavy hand with red pepper prickles the tongue so your taste buds stand at attention. We don't use so much red pepper to make the head cheese *hot* spicy, just enough to keep the tongue standing at attention for the parade of rich, otherwise cloying flavors.

Head cheese is a colloid, actually in the same chemistry class as mayonnaise—an even suspension of protein, fat, and water—it's rich. Really rich. Vinegar and red pepper cut the richness yet at the same time amplify it, making the flavor more intense; but since they also make your mouth water, the flavor is cleaner and less cloying. A neat little trick.

PREP TIME: 6 to 7 hours, plus overnight for setting

EQUIPMENT NEEDED: 3 or 4 terrines or loaf pans, 5-gallon stock pot, 4- or 5-gallon heat-proof tub, 4-quart saucepan or stock pot, small ladle, large colander

MAKES: approximately four 2-pound terrines or three 3-pound terrines, depending on the size of the hog's head. This recipe assumes one 12-pound head. Scale accordingly.

1 hog's head, about 12 pounds, scalded and scraped (have your butcher do this)
6 large yellow onions, peeled and coarsely chopped
6 cloves garlic, smashed
1 tablespoon whole cloves
2 tablespoons allspice berries
2 tablespoons crushed red pepper
2 whole anise stars
8 large bay leaves
2 ounces Calvados or applejack
1 cup ruby port

½ cup red wine vinegar

¼ cup or more kosher salt, to taste

3 tablespoons whole black peppercorns

❦ Prepare terrines by lining with vegetable oil then plastic wrap. Keep cold until ready to use.

❦ Place the hog's head in a 5-gallon stock pot and cover with cold water. Set over medium-high heat, and bring to a boil, skimming off any foam or scum that rises to the top with a small ladle. Maintain the low boil until the fleshy parts of the head are falling apart, like a dreamy pot roast, about 5 hours. Drain off stock into a 4- or 5-gallon heat-proof tub, then return to the stock pot and add the onion, garlic, clove, allspice, red pepper, anise, and bay leaves. Bring to a boil and start reducing gently. Once reduced to about 1 gallon, another 30 minutes, strain through a large colander, returning the stock to the stove in a 4-quart saucepan or stock pot to continue reducing. Discard the strained vegetables and spices. Add the Calvados, port, and vinegar to the stock, and continue reducing to 4 to 6 cups.

❦ In the meantime, cool the hog's head in a large drip-proof tray. After an hour, it will be cool enough to handle. Pick all of the meat, fat, skin, and gristle clean, remove the tongue, and peel with a knife. Chop everything—the pulled meat, fat, skin, and gristle—coarsely.

❦ Once the stock has reduced to 6 cups, add the pulled and chopped meat, salt, and the whole peppercorns; check seasoning and re-season as needed. Turn into prepared terrine molds, cover tightly with plastic wrap, and refrigerate immediately. Will keep in the refrigerator for 2 to 3 weeks. Do not freeze.

Tasso

Tasso is up there with andouille and smoked ham in terms of pure volume within our whole hog program. It was actually our first charcuterie product: we've made our own tasso since day one because we couldn't buy real tasso from anyone who would cite the source of their pork—and the one area we will never, ever compromise is the conditions in which our animals are raised. So, we made our own tasso. Once we went whole hog at the beginning of 2010, we only needed to fit it into the steady and even utilization of an entire animal.

In my own admittedly limited experience checking out tassos around south Louisiana, I'd say this might be the most disparate pork product in almost every aspect. Historically, tassos were made with lean trim, hence their enduring description as ham—ham being one of a pig's leaner primal cuts. If you can find tasso at a market today, it is likely made with the dreaded pork shoulder, the catch-all cut for anyone looking to make charcuterie because of its optimal fat ratio, even as it's too fatty for traditional tasso. I wanted to do better at a minimum by ensuring our tasso is from a lean cut, therefore much of our tasso comes from the ham, which is pulled apart by individual muscles and cut into rough planks 4 to 6 inches long and 2 to 3 inches high and wide. Some sirloin cut from the tail end of the loin always finds itself in the mix as well.

You can make this with boneless pork loin if you want an easier cut to work with; you will at least get a lean finished ham according to tradition. Use pork shoulder if you must; it will be delicious.

PREP TIME: 1 hour for butchering and salting, 5 days for curing, 6 hours for rubbing and smoking

EQUIPMENT NEEDED: 4-quart mixing bowl, large drip-proof pan with fitting perforated drain pan (restaurant hotel pans work perfectly and are inexpensive at restaurant and kitchen supply stores), 8-quart mixing bowl, smoker with wire racks or pans, pecan or fruit wood for smoking, digital food thermometer, wire cooling racks

MAKES: 12 to 15 pounds

STAGE ONE, THE CURE

3 cups kosher salt
¼ cup pink curing salt
1 pound dark brown sugar
¼ cup whole black pepper
¼ cup whole cloves
¼ cup whole allspice berries
¼ cup crushed red pepper
¼ cup whole coriander
2 dozen bay leaves
1 fresh ham, pulled apart at the muscles and cut into 2-by-2-by-4-inch pieces, yielding about 12 pounds lean meat trimmings

❧ Combine dry ingredients in a 4-quart mixing bowl and rub well into ham pieces, layering bay leaves and extra cure in between layers of ham. Place in a perforated pan for drainage and place over a drip-proof pan to catch the liquid that will render during curing. Cover loosely with plastic wrap and refrigerate to cure for 5 days.

STAGE TWO, DRY RUB AND SMOKING
2 cups honey
6 tablespoons freshly ground black pepper
6 tablespoons dried thyme
6 tablespoons dried oregano
6 tablespoons dried sage
3 tablespoons ground cloves
1 cup ground cumin
½ cup Spanish paprika

❧ Scrape and discard all cure from the cured meat, and rinse well with very cold running water, then pad dry with paper towels. Discard the rendered liquid in the drain pan. Place all washed and dried meat in an 8-quart mixing bowl, and pour the honey over the pork. Toss well until the honey is evenly distributed and coats all pieces heavily.

❧ Place the dry ingredients in a 4-quart mixing bowl, and toss until evenly combined. Put on some clean latex or rubber gloves for this next step. One by one, dip each piece of honey-coated meat in the spices and toss to evenly coat, padding the spices into each before placing on perforated pans or grills for your smoker.

❧ Smoke at 165°F for 4 hours, then check the temperature of your larger pieces. If they haven't yet registered 165°F internally, raise heat in the smoker to 180°F and continue smoking until the meat registers 165°F internally. Cool on wire racks for an hour, then wrap tightly in plastic wrap and refrigerate. Will keep for 3 to 4 weeks, or freeze for months.

Bacon

When I decided we would only use whole hogs at Big Jones, bacon was easily the most intimidating project, in part because our brunches have always been high volume while each pig only has one belly with two sides, presenting the very real possibility that there would not be enough pork belly relative to the other parts of the hog. Cooking any day part of almost any world cuisine, we would have many options to use the pork belly, but in the current state of brunch in America, people want bacon, and they want it with texture. I love bacon that's crispy around the edges yet chewy and even creamy as you chew through it, unleashing waves of salt, creamy pork fat and sweet brown sugar from the cure, all the while filling your head with clean smoke. Now that's a standard to which I really wanted to meet, and I did.

Beginning with my favorite reference of old cookbooks, I quickly learned that most of the old recipes I came up with yielded bacon so salty it could kill a horse, a quality that was surely useful in the days before refrigeration but not all that palatable by today's standards. It ultimately came down to months of trial and error, but we eventually nailed it. You can make it at home pretty easily, just follow these instructions, especially the curing time. Too little time and your bacon will be on the bland side and too wet to crisp well; too much curing time and it will be too salty. I'm a big fan of fruit woods for bacon but an even bigger fan of pecan wood. Of course, you can use your favorite wood to get a bacon you can call your own. Whatever wood you decide to use for smoking, if you make this recipe, no other bacon will ever be good enough again.

PREP TIME: 30 minutes for salting, 5 days for curing, 3 to 4 hours for smoking
EQUIPMENT NEEDED: large drip-proof pan with fitting perforated drain pan (restaurant hotel pans work perfectly and are inexpensive at restaurant and kitchen supply stores), smoker, pecan or apple wood for smoking, digital food thermometer
MAKES: 1 side bacon, 8 to 12 pounds

1 side pork belly, squared
1 pound dark brown sugar

10 ounces kosher salt

2 tablespoons pink curing salt

2 tablespoons crushed red pepper

18 bay leaves

2 tablespoons whole coriander seed

3 tablespoons whole cloves

3 tablespoons whole allspice berries

꙳ Have your butcher square the pork belly so it will cut into nice strips when finished—your butcher will know what this means. Also have your butcher peel the belly for you—you don't want the skin on the bacon.

꙳ Place the sugar, salts, and red pepper in an 8-quart mixing bowl and toss well. Working on a large, clean surface, rub the cure well into both sides and all ends of the meat. Then place in a perforated pan over a drip-proof pan to catch the juices that will render during curing. Evenly distribute remaining spices over the belly, then cover with any cure left over from rubbing. Cover with a clean dry towel, and refrigerate for 5 days, placing in a spot where nothing will drip on it.

꙳ Wash all cure from the bacon under very cold running water, and pat dry with paper towels. Smoke at 155°F for 2 hours, retaining a fairly thin smoke—you don't want bacon to be too smoky. After 2 hours, cease smoking but continue cooking until bacon registers 140°F internally, about another hour. Rinse under cold water to stop the cooking, pad dry, wrap tightly in plastic wrap, and refrigerate at once. Will keep for 3 to 4 weeks.

Ham

The hams we made when we first started working with whole hogs were traditional dry-cured hams done in the style of old German mountain hams from the same part of Germany that my dad's side of the family came from: Swabia, in the far southwestern Black Forest. Why look there for inspiration? Well, I had my grandpa's formula as told by my dad to work with, and many Appalachian folks also came from that part of Germany and probably brought their pork-curing formulas with them, as my family did. It fit my own family's story and the South's story, a sweet spot that's hard to ignore.

As we got busier and busier, it was rather untenable to maintain a 5-week cure time on two hams a week; we just didn't have room to store that many hams in process. I once again began working on a formula to duplicate that taste and texture with a shorter process: the brine injection. This yields a delicious ham in about 10 days—the texture is less dense than dry-cured, but in nearly every recipe calling for ham, this will fit the bill. The key is to use good pork and pay attention during every step of the smoking and cooking process. If your ham is larger or smaller than 25 pounds, scale your brine recipe accordingly, although a couple of pounds lighter or heavier isn't of much concern.

PREP TIME: 1 hour for making the brine and injecting, 10 days for curing, 8 to
12 hours for smoking and cooking
EQUIPMENT NEEDED: 2-quart saucepan, fine-mesh strainer, large drip-
proof pan with fitting wire draining rack (hotel pans are perfect
and inexpensive at restaurant and kitchen supply stores), butcher's
injecting needle, smoker, pecan or apple wood for smoking, digital food
thermometer
MAKES: one 25-pound ham

¾ cup kosher salt
¾ cup granulated white sugar
2 tablespoons pink curing salt
1 tablespoon crushed red pepper
1 tablespoon whole coriander
2 tablespoons whole cloves
2 tablespoons whole allspice berries
2 whole stars anise
4 bay leaves
3 cups cold water
1 uncured "green" fresh ham

Place all salts, sugar, and spices in a 2-quart saucepan, and add the water. Bring to a boil over medium heat, stirring occasionally. Boil 15 seconds,
remove from heat, and cool to room temperature, uncovered. Cover and refrigerate overnight.
Pad the ham dry, and place on a drainage rack in a drip-proof pan large
enough to hold the ham. Look for the vein that will be found near the bone

on the open end, in the direction of the kneecap about 3 to 4 inches. A good way to look for the vein is to press and squeeze around the exposed flesh near the bone, and eventually you may see a small amount of blood drain from the vein.

❧ Strain the cold brine. *I cannot overemphasize that the brine must be ice-cold before proceeding, as close to freezing as possible.* Using a butcher's injecting needle, inject all of the brine into the vein, resting a few minutes between each injection so the ham has time to absorb. Once all brine has been injected, cover with plastic wrap and refrigerate for at least 1 week (10 days is best) before smoking.

❧ Smoke at 225°F for 6 hours, then increase temperature to 325°F until the ham reaches 155°F internally, checking especially near the joints. This will take anywhere from 8 to 12 hours total smoking time, depending on the size of your ham, so it's best to begin checking as soon as you raise the temperature to 325°F at the 6-hour mark.

❧ Allow to cool in a breezy spot for an hour before wrapping in butcher paper and refrigerating. Will keep for at least 1 month, or freeze up to 1 year.

Pickled Pig's Feet

Pig's feet were a bit of a conundrum in the beginning of our whole hog commitment. Sure, there are plenty of examples of high-end fine dining pig's feet recipes that are far too labor intensive for a mid-priced restaurant to produce, given only 4 to 8 feet a week and therefore a lack of scale to make the labor worthwhile.

It's true that many Southern cooks over generations have used pig's feet in souse, but head cheese had already fit the bill for congealed hog parts. Finally, I put two and two together, starting with the classic Creole red beans recipe's call for pickled pork, and crossing it with my mom's occasional mention that she really didn't like pickled pig's feet. I have to concur with her on the point of eating pickled pig's feet straightaway, but their rich flavor and high gelatin content, tempered by the lightness of acidity, could surely contribute mightily to a rich, sticky bean recipe. And because they are pickled, we also get that exciting, refreshing acid tingle in every bite. This recipe has the added bonus of making one of the pig's most perishable cuts keep indefinitely.

PREP TIME: 20 minutes for preparing brine, overnight for brining, 1 hour for cooking

EQUIPMENT NEEDED: 2-gallon non-reactive container with tight-fitting lid, wooden spoon, 2-gallon non-reactive stock pot, digital food thermometer, non-reactive container or jar with tight-fitting lid, large fine-mesh strainer

MAKES: pickles 4 feet

4 quarts distilled white vinegar
2 quarts cold water
6 tablespoons kosher salt
1 tablespoon pink curing salt
1 tablespoon whole cloves
1 tablespoon whole allspice
8 bay leaves
1 tablespoon brown mustard seed
½ cup white sugar
2 teaspoons crushed red pepper
4 fresh pig's feet, scrubbed and any excess hairs burned off

❦ Be sure the pig's feet are scalded and scraped of all hair before purchasing. Place vinegar, water, and all salts and seasonings in a non-reactive 2-gallon or larger container, and stir with a wooden spoon to dissolve salts and sugar. Add the feet, which should be fully submerged—if not, try to rearrange them, or add enough vinegar and water in a 2:1 ratio to cover. Cover the container tightly and refrigerate for 24 hours.

❦ Place feet and brine in a 2-gallon or larger non-reactive stock pot, and bring to a simmer. Cook at a simmer—try to maintain 180°F with a clip-on thermometer—until the feet register 155°F internally, about 1 hour. Transfer feet to a clean non-reactive container or jar, and strain the brine through a large fine-mesh strainer to cover, discarding the spices. Cover tightly and cool in an ice bath until the brine is cool to the touch, about two hours, then refrigerate. Allow pickle to set one week before using, or store up to two months under refrigeration.

Lard

If you're a fan of fried chicken or big into baking, you need lard to be at the top of your game. Most butcher shops will stock pure hog lard, but it's easy to make yourself and you'll be rewarded with crackling to boot. In my family there was never an equal to lard for pie crust, a conviction I still hold close to my heart; and for many breads, it's as good or better than butter, especially when you want a snow-white crumb in your finished bread, or if you're pairing it with porky flavors, such as in BLTs or ham sandwiches. As far as frying goes, nothing is better for chicken, vegetables, or fish, and only beef tallow equals it for frying potatoes.

Don't let the nutrition police scare you away from lard—it is wholesome and nutritious when used occasionally and eaten in reasonable portions. You may also find that when you eat something made with lard, your hunger is sated faster and after eating less—it's rich and calorie-dense, for sure. It also has a broad range of useful fats your body will be able to put to good use. I say it often, our family was raised on lard and we never had weight problems, so I trust it more than the food police.

If you plan to make cracklings or gratons with your leftover rendered bits, it's best to use all, or a high ratio, of fatback diced with the skin still attached. The skin will cook and render along with the lard, and when fried, will puff up like a chicharrón. Great stuff!

PREP TIME: 5 to 7 hours
EQUIPMENT NEEDED: 2-gallon cast-iron or enamel Dutch oven or stock pot, wooden spoon, 4-quart or larger colander, heat-proof container with tight-fitting lid
MAKES: about 3 quarts

8 pounds pork leaf fat or fatback, diced into ½-inch pieces
3 quarts cold water, plus more as needed

☗ Use a 2-gallon or larger cast-iron or enamel Dutch oven or stock pot. Place the pork fat in the pot, and cover with the water. Stir gently with a wooden spoon to separate all the bits of fat, and set over medium heat. As the temperature rises to a boil, gradually reduce heat to maintain a low boil. Be very wary of high heat in order to avoid scorching. The process of rendering will take several hours—at first the fat will begin rendering into the liquid to produce a milky soup. If, during this stage, the water level drops below the top of the fat, cover with additional cold water. Eventually, after 5 to 6 hours, the fat will begin clarifying, and the fat pieces will turn translucent and shrink dramatically as they give up their oils. Reduce heat to low and continue cooking until all water is cooked out and the remaining bits of translucent fat are simply frying in their own oil. Cook until the chunks just barely begin to brown—you're not looking to get any real color on them, just verifying that rendering is completed. Before the chunks even turn a light tan color, remove from heat and set in a cool spot. It will continue cooking for another 15 to 20 minutes due to residual heat. After 30 minutes, when the fat is still clear and hot but not boiling hot, strain through a colander into a heat-proof container. Retain the leftover "cracklings," or rendered chunks, for use in making crackling, cornbread, or to add to your bean pot. Allow the lard to cool to room temperature for several hours before covering with a tight-fitting lid and refrigerating. Will keep for several months in the refrigerator, but best used within a few weeks.

Crackling, aka Gratons

If pure indulgence had a name, it would be crackling, aka gratons in the Cajun parlance. Made from the leftover bits after lard rendering, they are pure essence of pork-fried crisp, while their composition of cellulite and fat gives them a sticky and juicy character unlike anything else.

In Cajun country these crackly bits of goodness are often sold in gas stations and markets alongside boudin, which is usually in a steaming crockpot behind the counter. In many other parts of the South, they're most often used to enrich cornbread. We also like to use them to garnish gumbo and all manner of pork and bean dishes.

PREP TIME: 30 minutes
EQUIPMENT NEEDED: cookie sheet pan, 2-gallon or larger cast-iron or enamel stock pot, slotted spoon, splatter screen, wire-mesh skimmer, stainless-steel bowl, serving bowl lined with paper towels
MAKES: a few cups

A few handfuls leftover rendered fatback pieces
Hot lard, for deep frying
Cajun seasoning, to taste (page 67; optional)
Kosher salt and freshly ground black pepper, to taste

✤ Do not attempt this recipe without a deep pot for frying and a splatter screen (available at most kitchenware stores). A recommended additional safety measure is to wear safety goggles. Yes, they are so good, they are worth the trouble.

✤ To make the best cracklings, look for the leftover bits of fatback with skin attached—these will offer both the unctuous fried cellulite of the fat, but additionally the attached skin will puff like a chicharrón. Working while they are still very cold, separate them into individual bits (they will be somewhat congealed after refrigeration) and lay them out on a cookie sheet to have ready.

✤ In the bottom of a deep 2-gallon or more cast-iron or enamel stock pot, heat 4 inches of lard to 425°F over medium-high heat. Carefully add the rendered fatback, being careful of splatter, stir briefly with a slotted spoon to be sure they are not sticking, cover the pot with a splatter screen, and stand back.

✤ Now it's time to learn why these are called cracklings. They will spit, pop, and veritably explode while they fry. Stay out of the way and let the splatter screen do its work. Eventually, the popping and crackling will stop, which is an indication that they are done cooking.

✤ Turn the heat off, and use two hands to remove the cracklings—in one hand, hold the splatter screen between you and the cracklings, as a shield, just in case there are any late poppers. With the other hand, use a skimmer to remove the cracklings from the hot oil and transfer to a stainless-steel bowl. Toss with Cajun seasoning if desired, and season to taste with salt and pepper. Transfer to a serving bowl lined with paper towels.

✤ These are best served right away while still hot, with a beer as a snack, or with boudin, beans, gumbo, or rice dishes. Will keep in a tightly sealed container at room temperature for a few days.

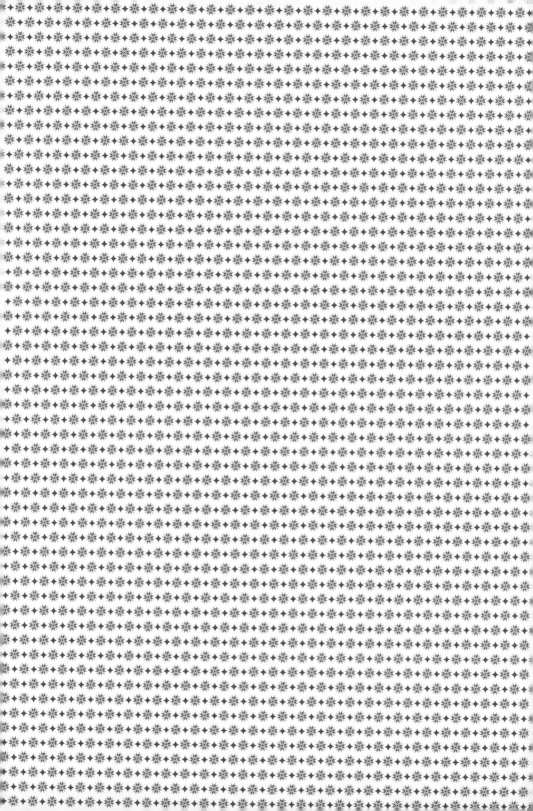

Notes on Sources

Our ingredients at Big Jones are carefully sourced, often painstakingly so. There are a few key suppliers here we will list because you can also order from them mail order. For heirloom vegetables, poultry, and most meats, you should shop at your local farmers' market or natural foods store to find products of comparable quality. Small-scale, local butcher shops featuring humanely raised local meats are popping up all over the country as well, and these folks are your best source for odd animal parts or custom cuts. Whenever possible, the individual recipes will list logical substitutions if any are appropriate.

Kitchen Equipment and Smallwares

CAST-IRON AND ENAMEL COOKWARE: My favorite sources are Lodge Manufacturing (www.lodgemfg.com) and Bayou Classic Cookware (www .bayouclassicshop.com), both of which have an excellent range of cast-iron options. Lodge is also an excellent source for enameled cast-iron Dutch ovens and casseroles, essential equipment when you want a non-reactive piece of cookware when working with high-acid foods or items that tend to discolor, such as custards. Bayou Classic has plenty of options for over-size stock pots as well for larger projects.

DIGITAL FOOD THERMOMETERS, CLIP-ON THERMOMETERS, AND OTHER ODD SMALLWARES: If you have a local restaurant supply store, try them first. Many restaurant supply stores are cash-and-carry and more than happy to sell to the general public; call first to make sure they sell directly to the public. For items like sheet pans with edges, stock pots, saucepans, cutlery, wire-mesh skimmers, thermometers, and the like, you are likely to find far better prices at a restaurant supply store than at a specialty retailer. If none are located locally, Sur La Table is the best-stocked specialty retailer for these items.

HOME MEAT-PROCESSING SUPPLIES: Butcher & Packer (www.butcher-packer.com) has everything you need, from sausage casings and curing salt to meat grinders, smokers, and heavier equipment.

Grains and Milled Goods

Anson Mills (www.ansonmills.com) is one of our most significant suppliers, and the company behind our beloved grits. We buy all manner of heritage milled goods from them throughout the year. You can buy directly from them. At retail, you may find some reasonable substitutes by Bob's Red Mill (http://www.bobsredmill.com), but we will warn you of the Big One: Anson Mills's antebellum coarse-ground grits are nonpareil, and some of the most interesting and delicious goods we buy from them, such as bennecake flour, have no substitutes. Some farmers' markets have growers that sell cornmeal or various flours, and I always advise to buy as close to home as you can if you are confident of their growing practices.

Spices, Extracts, and Pantry Items

Terra Spice Company (www.terraspice.com) is our go-to for spices and hard-to-find kitchen ingredients. They cater to culinary professionals worldwide, but are happy to sell to ambitious home cooks. Want a choice of three different vanilla beans and a dozen artisan salts? Call Terra Spice. Some of the hydrocolloids we use—such as xanthan gum, guar gum, or gellan—can also be purchased on Amazon.com. Terra Spice's spices are of truly exceptional quality; however, at retail stores I suggest you look for Frontier spices at natural food stores, while Whole Foods's organic line is also excellent. McCormick spices are the most widely available spices of good quality, though your results will not be as satisfactory as with other labels previously mentioned. Most gourmet food stores will have a selection of artisan salts available, as well as our favorite black pepper variety, tellicherry.

The Spice House (www.thespicehouse.com), the best retail mail-order firm for spices, happens to be located in our sweet home, Chicago. They are not cheap, but what they say is true—you pay for quality, especially when we're talking about the Spice House. Their spices are nonpareil, easily worth the price charged; and when you think about what goes into growing, curing, and milling of spices, then calculate the cost per teaspoon, their exquisite quality is actually a bargain.

Seafood

Big Jones is a Right Bite partner with the John G. Shedd Aquarium to help promote sustainable seafood, and it is our firm commitment to serve only seafood that comes from sustainable sources. We believe sustainable seafood is not only better for fish populations and a healthy marine ecosystem, but that it also tastes better. Some of these ingredients might not be specifically used in this book, but I want to point out some very important examples of fish we serve at Big Jones over the course of the year, and to give you the information you need to be a more informed seafood shopper. For further reading, visit www.sheddaquarium.org or www.montereybayaquarium.org.

SHRIMP: The only shrimp we serve regularly at Big Jones are Laughing Bird, Key West pink, and U.S. fishery wild-caught Gulf of Mexico shrimp. Occasionally we bring in Markea blue prawns from New Caledonia. Laughing Bird and Markea are two of the only farm-raised shrimp operations to be certified sustainable by independent agencies, and both operate inland in retaining ponds so as not to affect the natural environment offshore. Both take measures to treat the water, similar to an urban water-treatment facility, with gravity and sunlight, before returning the water to sea as pure as possible. In general, when you see "farm-raised" on a shrimp package or display, pass them over and consider other options for dinner. Key West pink shrimp are a highly sustainable wild-caught fishery, and, boy, are they delicious. U.S. Gulf of Mexico wild-caught shrimp are considered to be a good alternative to more sustainable sources (such as Laughing Bird and Key West pinks), but overall the fishery is healthy and you can buy with confidence. Ask your fishmonger about these options when looking for shrimp.

CRAB: We use Pontchartrain Blue Crab Inc. (http://www.pontchartrain-bluecrab.com) in Slidell, Louisiana. As of this writing they are the only Marine Stewardship Council–certified sustainable crab. As an alternative,

I recommend domestic American crab. Avoid imported crab at all costs, and be careful—it's everywhere.

CRAWFISH: We only serve Louisiana crawfish and recommend you do the same. Besides concerns over environmental pollution, antibiotics, and sanitary conditions, the imported crawfish taste terrible when compared to their Louisiana counterparts. Louisiana crawfish just taste better—way better. There is of course a huge price difference due to the labor involved in crawfish processing, and this has led to a cottage industry of unscrupulous importers of inferior products giving their crawfish Cajun-sounding names complete with fleurs-de-lys and other trademarks of south Louisiana, so read the label carefully. Talk to your local fishmonger or the seafood department at your favorite store. Tell them you want American crawfish and refuse to buy the imported stuff. Give them time and stay on their case, and they'll come around. That's exactly how I got Louisiana crawfish back into the Chicago market, and it will work for you, too. Cajuncrawfish.com and Louisiana Crawfish Co. (lacrawfish.com) are two reliable online sources if you wish to go that route. And it's OK to buy the frozen tail meat—believe me, the professionals in Louisiana will do a much better job than you will of cleaning the crawfish and keeping the meat and head fat intact.

Meats, Poultry, and Dairy

Our gold standard for these products is that the animals must be raised outdoors with access to indoor shelter. In the end, most animals are a lot like people: they'll spend most of their time indoors, but healthy animals will get out for a walk, run, or frolic periodically throughout the day—this gets them sunshine (great for vitamin D) and green matter to eat (great for vitamins A and E and healthy fats) and improves their muscle tone, circulation, and fat profiles. We like an animal with fat—it makes them more succulent—but the quality of the fat is important. During spring when the pastures are at their most lush, Kilgus Farmstead's cream is yellow from all of the vitamin A in the milk, and the eggs we receive from our three egg farmers have the darkest yolks they'll have all year long. Pork from Gunthorp Farms in the fall smells of freshly fallen acorns, as Guinea hogs from Spence Farm smell of fresh green pastures in early summer. I'm going to share a dirty little secret of the commercial protein factory complex: commercial chicken eggs would have gray yolks were it not for the dye that's added to their feed. It's a reflection of the animals' lack of sunlight and green food. We believe that healthy animals make healthy food.

Most of us don't think about these things at all, but in dairy herds, farmers keep a large group of heifers and only a very few bulls. The heifers need to give birth in order to give milk, and it doesn't take that many bulls to keep a large group of heifers productive. However, nearly half of all calves born into a dairy herd are male. Nearly all of them become veal.

To that end, I recommend cultivating relationships with your local farmers either at farm stores or at your farmers' market. Many groceries nowadays carry healthier options for meat, poultry, and dairy, and in the absence of a personal relationship with a farm you can visit and trust, look for the USDA Organic label. It's not the be-all and end-all. Many of the most splendid small farms that give their animals the best care can't afford the certification. Many, many of these farms far exceed the standards set by the USDA Organic Standards Board, but when you don't know the farm personally, the organic label is a good reassurance that certain minimum standards are being met.

For fresh produce, always look first at your local farmers' market and try to buy in season. For those of us in northern climes, however, many months of the year we do find ourselves sourcing from outside our local area. In this case, talk to your produce market or grocery store about ordering more challenging items, and always look for the certified organic label when you don't know the farmer directly.

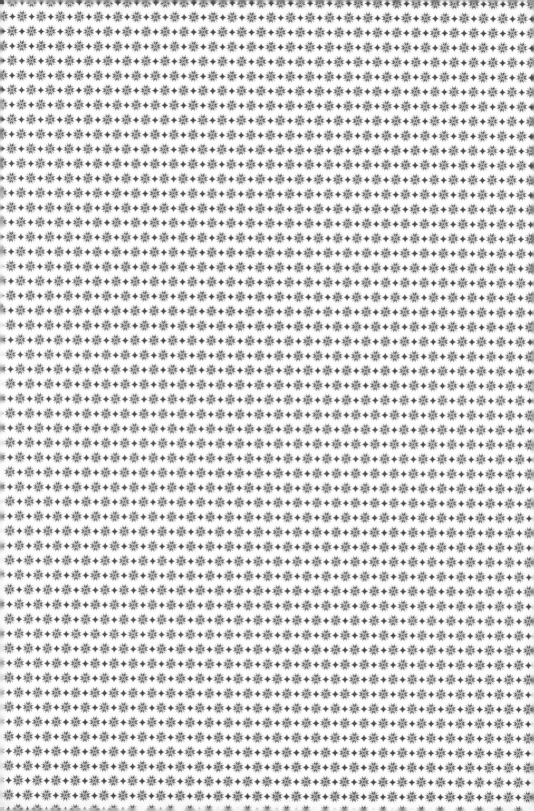

Index